CREATED BY **JOSS WHEDON**

GREG **PAK**   DAN **McDAID**   MARCELO **COSTA**

firefly™

THE UNIFICATION WAR PART THREE

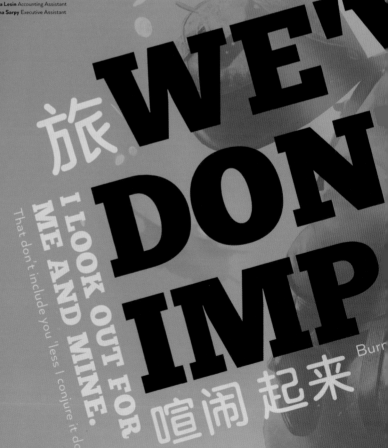

Designer
Scott Newman with **Marie Krupina**

Assistant Editor
Gavin Gronenthal

Editor
Chris Rosa

Executive Editor
Jeanine Schaefer

Special Thanks to **Sierra Hahn**,
Becca J. Sadowsky, and **Nicole Spiegel**
& **Carol Roeder** at Twentieth Century Fox.

Ross Richie CEO & Founder
Joy Huffman CFO
Matt Gagnon Editor-in-Chief
Filip Sablik President, Publishing & Marketing
Stephen Christy President, Development
Lance Kreiter Vice President, Licensing & Merchandising
Arune Singh Vice President, Marketing
Bryce Carlson Vice President, Editorial & Creative Strategy
Scott Newman Manager, Production Design
Kate Henning Manager, Operations
Spencer Simpson Manager, Sales
Elyse Strandberg Manager, Finance
Sierra Hahn Executive Editor
Jeanine Schaefer Executive Editor
Dafna Pleban Senior Editor
Shannon Watters Senior Editor
Eric Harburn Senior Editor
Matthew Levine Editor
Sophie Philips-Roberts Associate Editor
Amanda LaFranco Associate Editor
Jonathan Manning Associate Editor

Gavin Gronenthal Assistant Editor
Gwen Waller Assistant Editor
Allyson Gronowitz Assistant Editor
Jillian Crab Design Coordinator
Michelle Ankley Design Coordinator
Marie Krupina Production Designer
Grace Park Production Designer
Chelsea Roberts Production Design Assistant
Samantha Knapp Production Design Assistant
José Meza Live Events Lead
Stephanie Hocutt Digital Marketing Lead
Esther Kim Marketing Coordinator
Cat O'Grady Digital Marketing Coordinator
Amanda Lawson Marketing Assistant
Holly Aitchison Digital Sales Coordinator
Morgan Perry Retail Sales Coordinator
Megan Christopher Operations Coordinator
Rodrigo Hernandez Mailroom Assistant
Zipporah Smith Operations Assistant
Sabrina Lesin Accounting Assistant
Breanna Sarpy Executive Assistant

FIREFLY: THE UNIFICATION WAR **Volume Three**,
April 2020. Published by BOOM! Studios, a division of
Boom Entertainment, Inc. Firefly ™ & © 2020 Twentieth
Century Fox Film Corporation. All rights reserved. Originally
published in single magazine form as FIREFLY No. 9-12.
™ & © 2019 Twentieth Century Fox Film Corporation. All
rights reserved. BOOM! Studios™ and the BOOM! Studios
logo are trademarks of Boom Entertainment, Inc., registered
in various countries and categories. All characters, events,
and institutions depicted herein are fictional. Any similarity
between any of the names, characters, persons, events, and/
or institutions in this publication to actual names, characters,
and persons, whether living or dead, events, and/or institutions
is unintended and purely coincidental. BOOM! Studios does
not read or accept unsolicited submissions of ideas, stories,
or artwork.

BOOM! Studios, 5670 Wilshire Boulevard,
Suite 400, Los Angeles, CA 90036-5679.
Printed in China. First Printing.

ISBN: 978-1-68415-500-2
eISBN: 978-1-64144-658-7

SHINY, LE
BAD
旅
WE'V
I LOOK OUT FOR
ME AND MINE.
That don't include you 'less I conjure it does.
DON
IMP
喧闹 起来
Burr

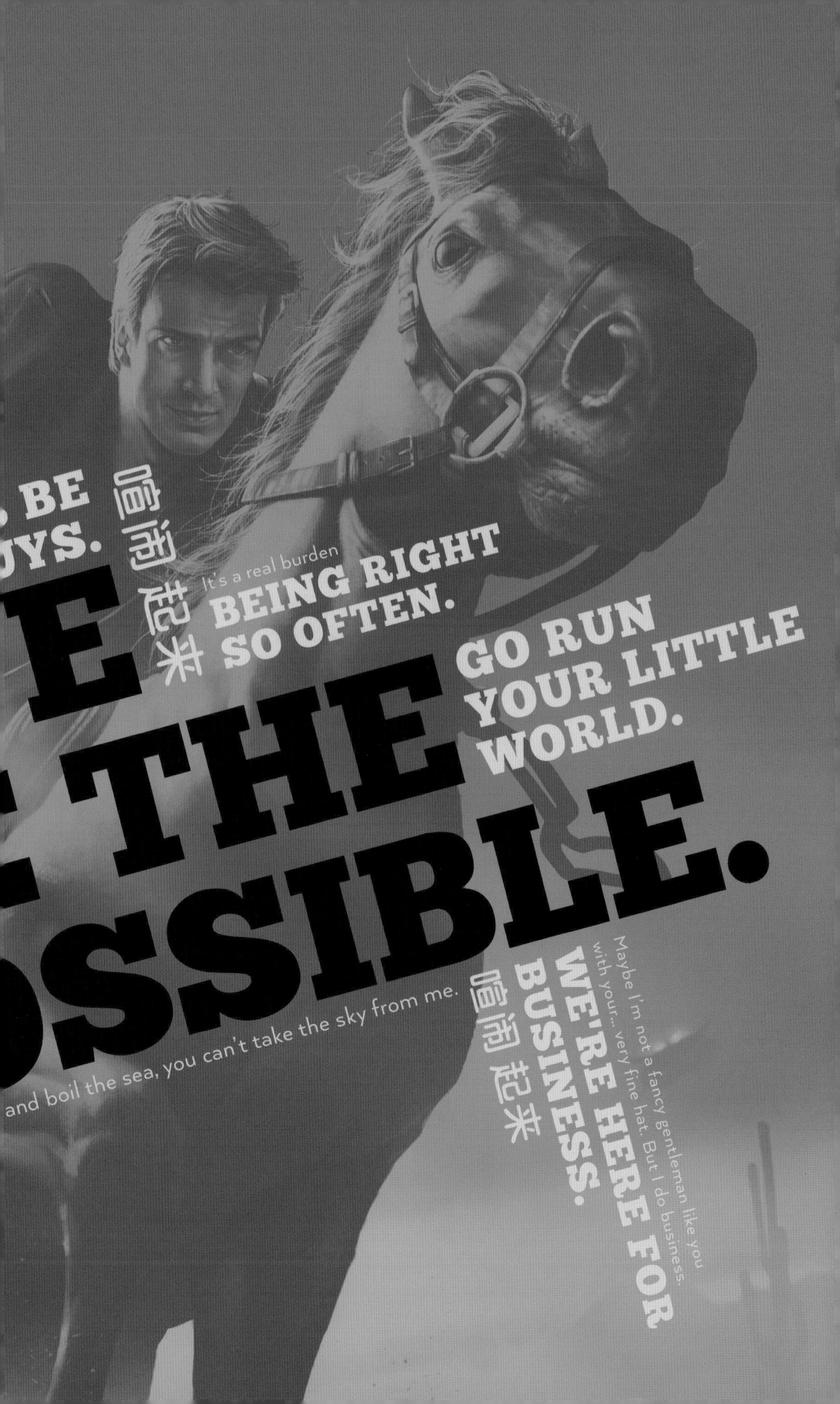

BE
UYS.
喧闹起来
It's a real burden
BEING RIGHT
SO OFTEN.
E
THE
GO RUN
YOUR LITTLE
WORLD.
SSIBLE.
and boil the sea, you can't take the sky from me.
喧闹起来
Maybe I'm not a fancy gentleman like you
with your... very fine hat. But I do business.
WE'RE HERE FOR
BUSINESS.

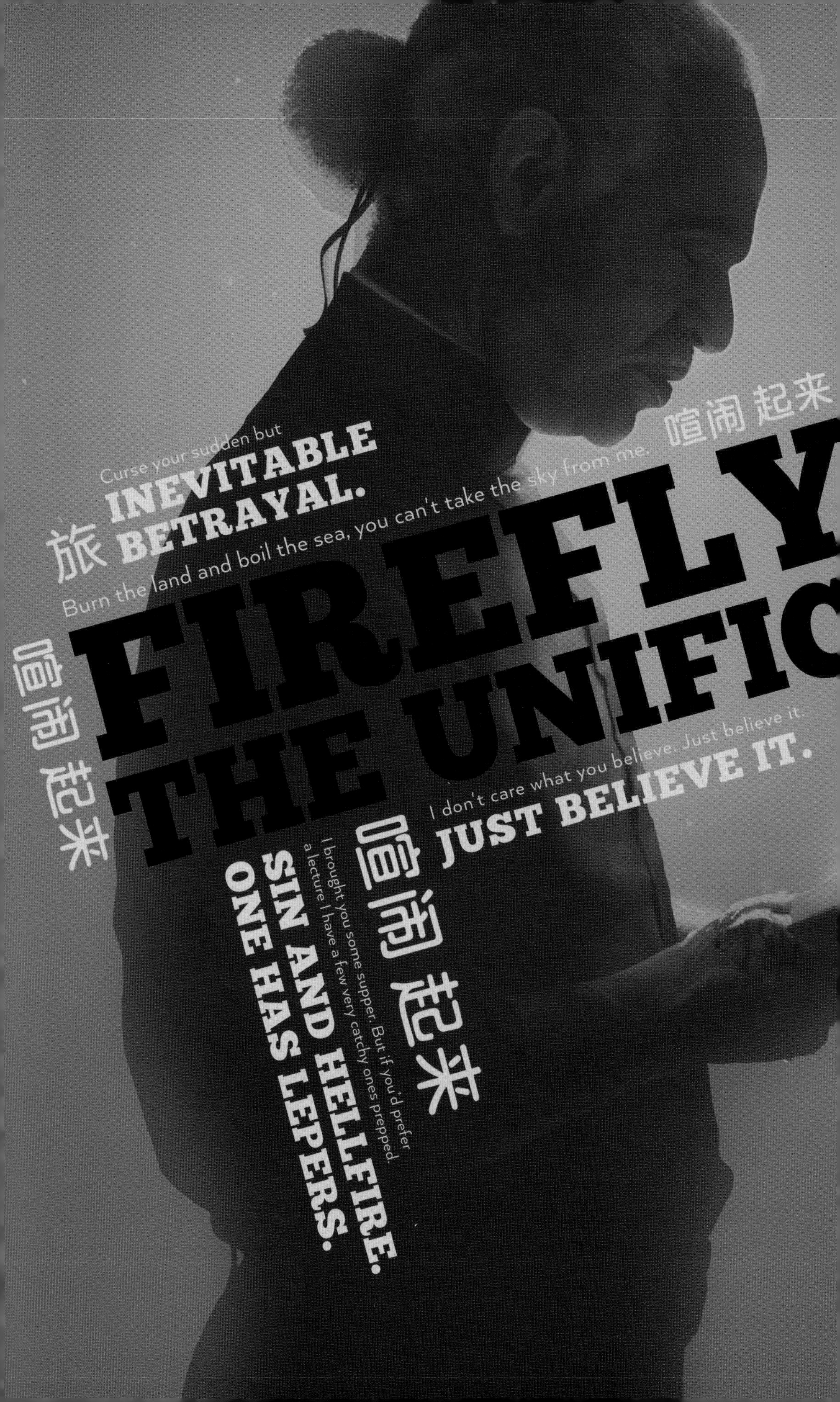

Curse your sudden but
INEVITABLE
BETRAYAL.
旅
Burn the land and boil the sea, you can't take the sky from me.
喧闹 起来
喧闹 起来
FIREFLY
THE UNIFIC
I don't care what you believe. Just believe it.
JUST BELIEVE IT.
喧闹 起来
I brought you some supper. But if you'd prefer
a lecture I have a few very catchy ones prepped.
SIN AND HELLFIRE.
ONE HAS LEPERS.

OH, I GOT HEATHENS
APLENTY RIGHT HERE.

ATION WAR

喧闹 起来

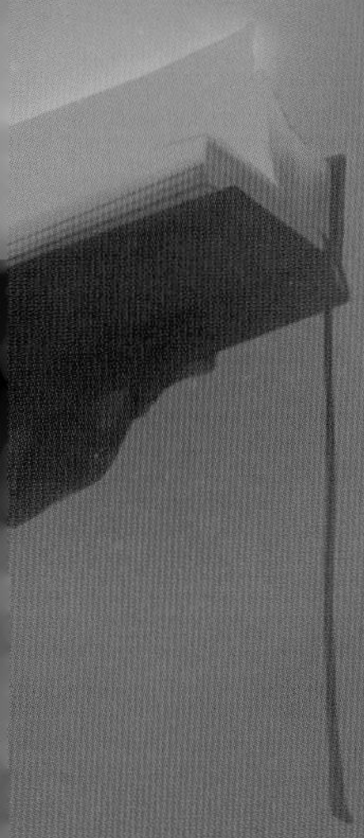

Created by
Joss Whedon

Written by
Greg Pak

Illustrated by
Dan McDaid
with Inks by **Vincenzo Federici**, Chapters Ten through Twelve

Colored by
Marcelo Costa
and **Joana LaFuente**, Chapter Ten

Lettered by
Jim Campbell

Cover by
Lee Garbett

CHAPTER NINE

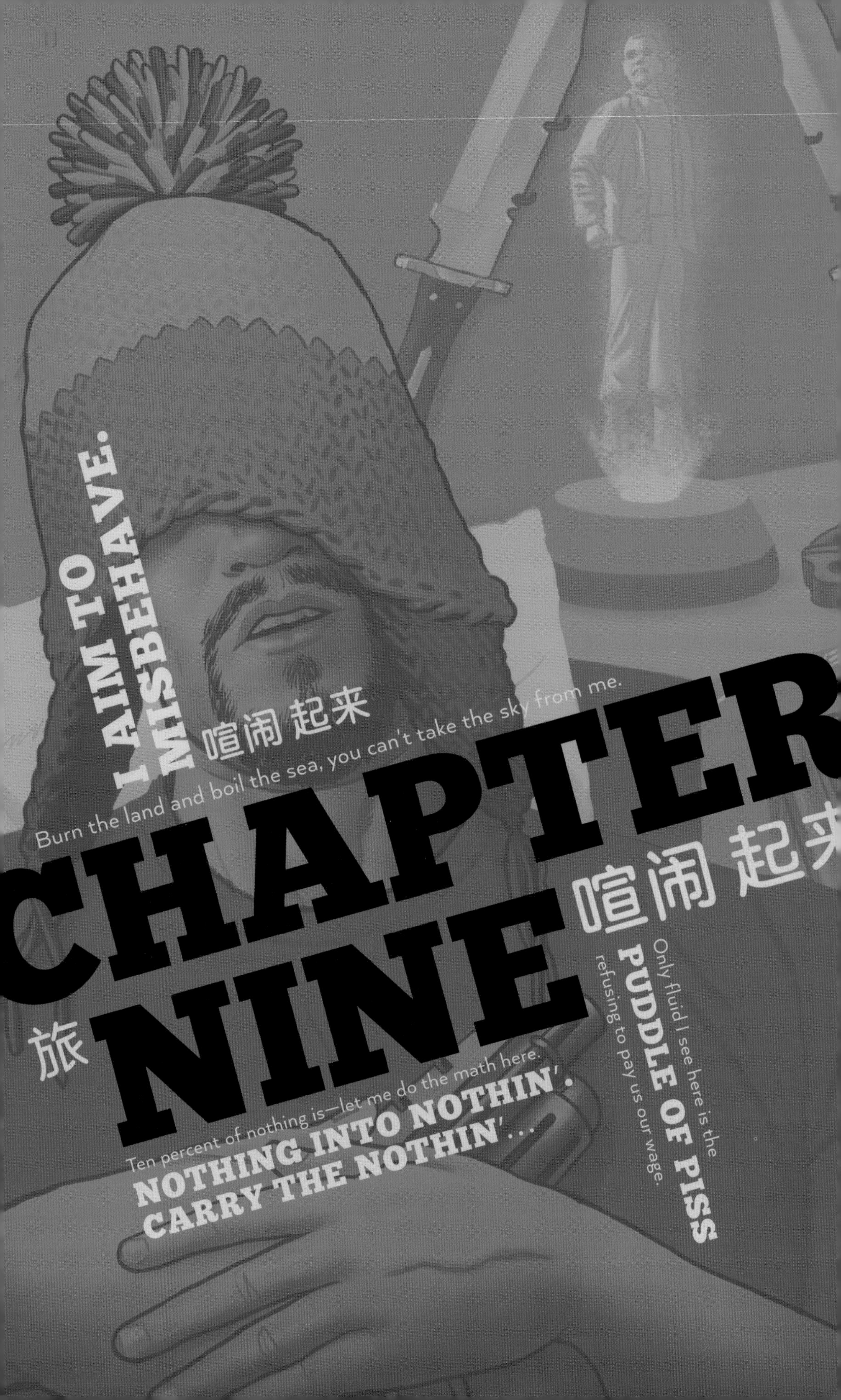
I AIM TO MISBEHAVE.
喧闹 起来
Burn the land and boil the sea, you can't take the sky from me.
喧闹 起来
旅
Ten percent of nothing is—let me do the math here.
NOTHING INTO NOTHIN'.
CARRY THE NOTHIN'...
Only fluid I see here is the
PUDDLE OF PISS
refusing to pay us our wage.

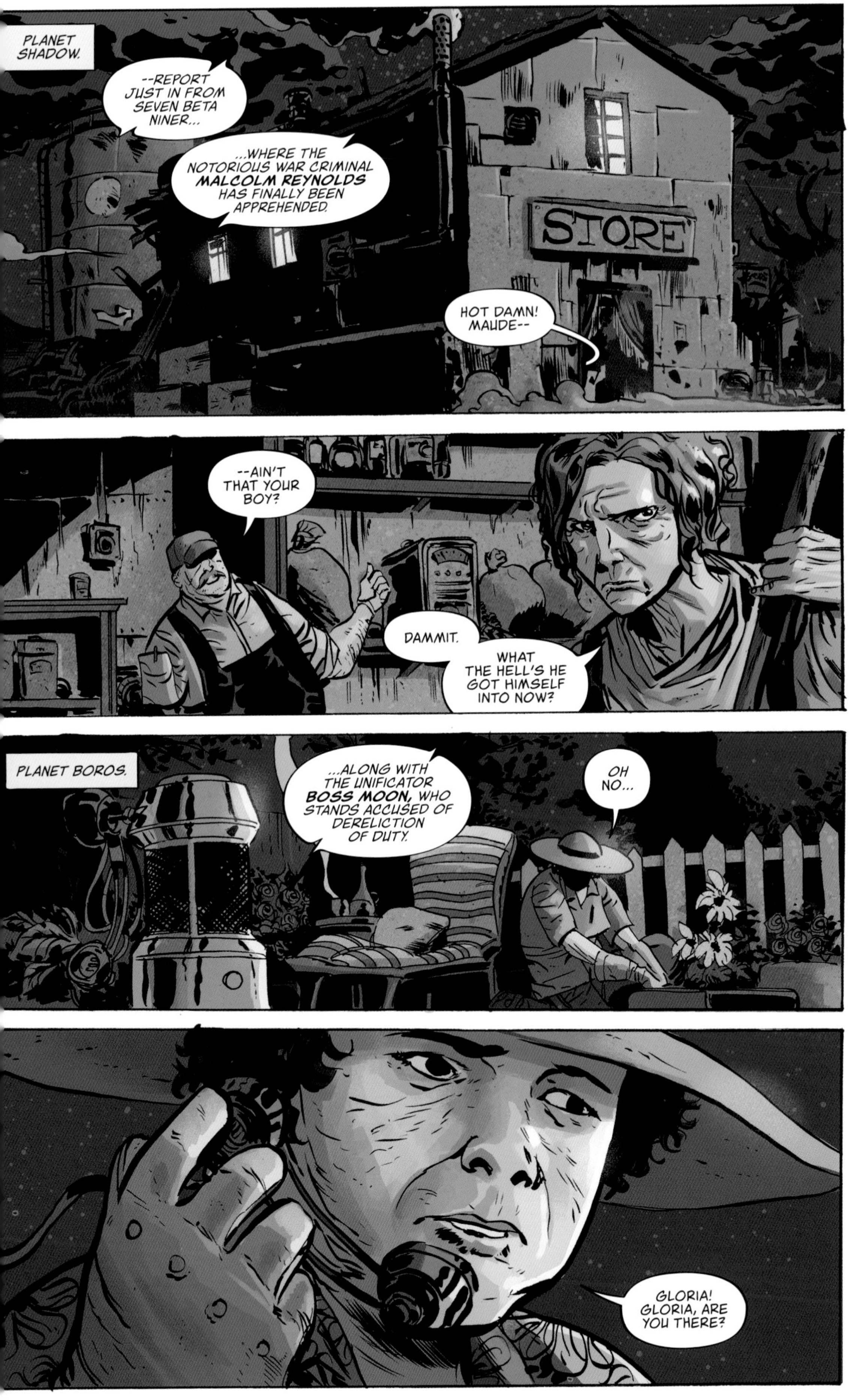
PLANET SHADOW.
--REPORT JUST IN FROM SEVEN BETA NINER...
...WHERE THE NOTORIOUS WAR CRIMINAL **MALCOLM REYNOLDS** HAS FINALLY BEEN APPREHENDED.
STORE
HOT DAMN! MAUDE--
--AIN'T THAT YOUR BOY?
DAMMIT.
WHAT THE HELL'S HE GOT HIMSELF INTO NOW?
PLANET BOROS.
...ALONG WITH THE UNIFICATOR **BOSS MOON,** WHO STANDS ACCUSED OF DERELICTION OF DUTY.
OH NO...
GLORIA! GLORIA, ARE YOU THERE?

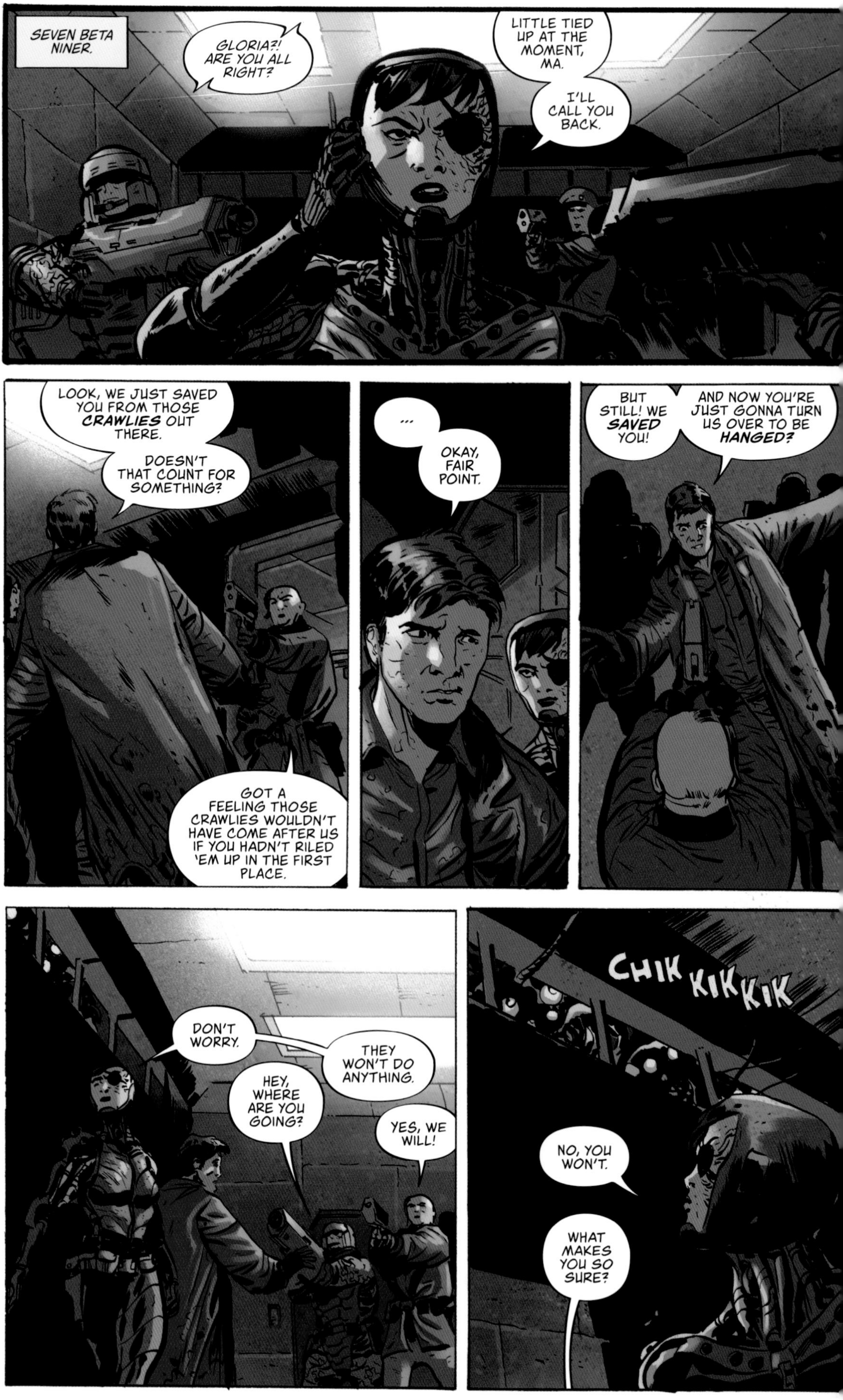

SEVEN BETA NINER.
GLORIA?! ARE YOU ALL RIGHT?
LITTLE TIED UP AT THE MOMENT, MA.
I'LL CALL YOU BACK.
LOOK, WE JUST SAVED YOU FROM THOSE CRAWLIES OUT THERE.
DOESN'T THAT COUNT FOR SOMETHING?
GOT A FEELING THOSE CRAWLIES WOULDN'T HAVE COME AFTER US IF YOU HADN'T RILED 'EM UP IN THE FIRST PLACE.
...
OKAY, FAIR POINT.
BUT STILL! WE SAVED YOU!
AND NOW YOU'RE JUST GONNA TURN US OVER TO BE HANGED?
DON'T WORRY.
THEY WON'T DO ANYTHING.
HEY, WHERE ARE YOU GOING?
YES, WE WILL!
CHIK KIK KIK
NO, YOU WON'T.
WHAT MAKES YOU SO SURE?

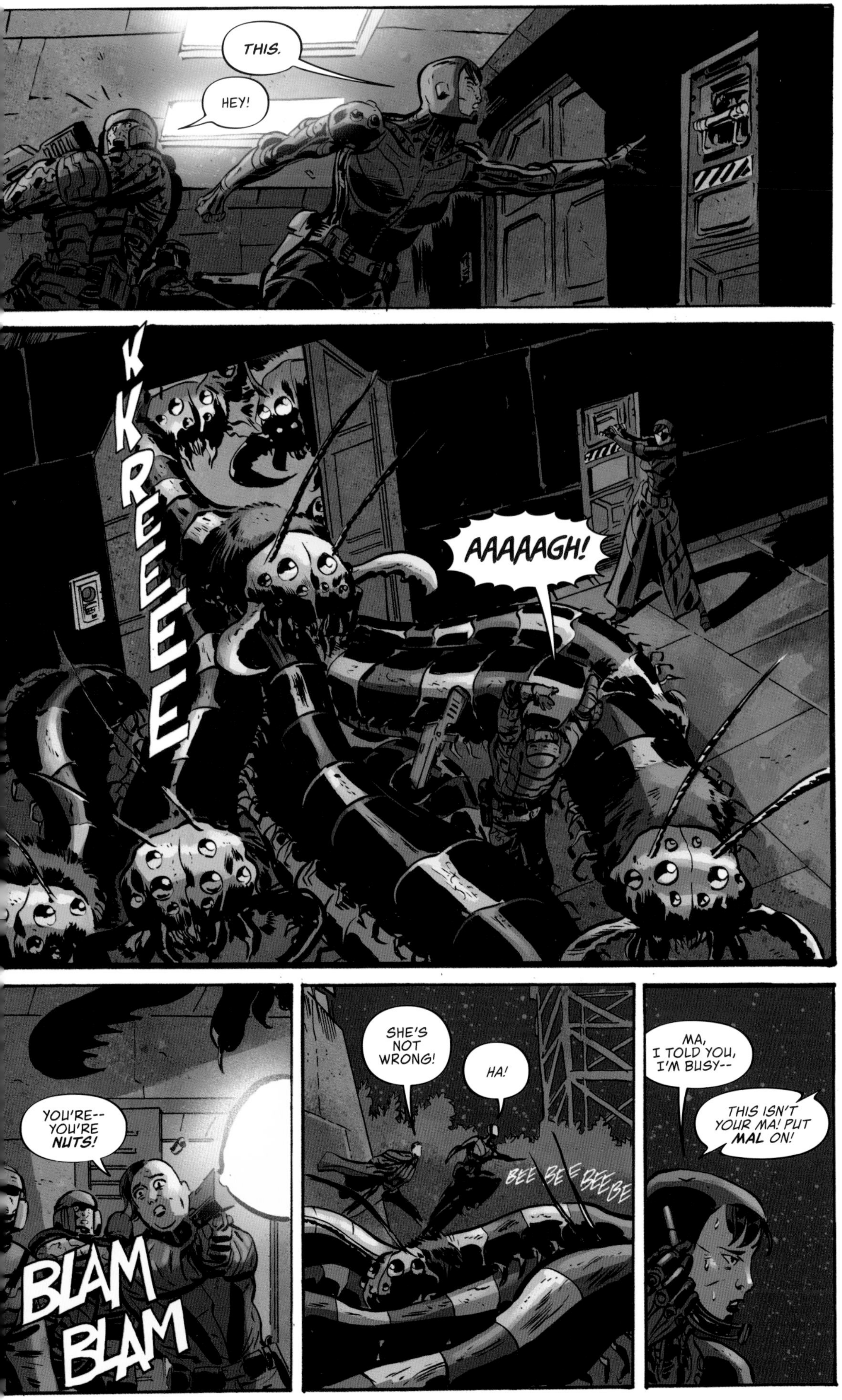
THIS.
HEY!
KKREEEEEE
AAAAAGH!
YOU'RE-- YOU'RE NUTS!
BLAM BLAM
SHE'S NOT WRONG!
HA!
BEE BEE BEE BE
MA, I TOLD YOU, I'M BUSY--
THIS ISN'T YOUR MA! PUT MAL ON!

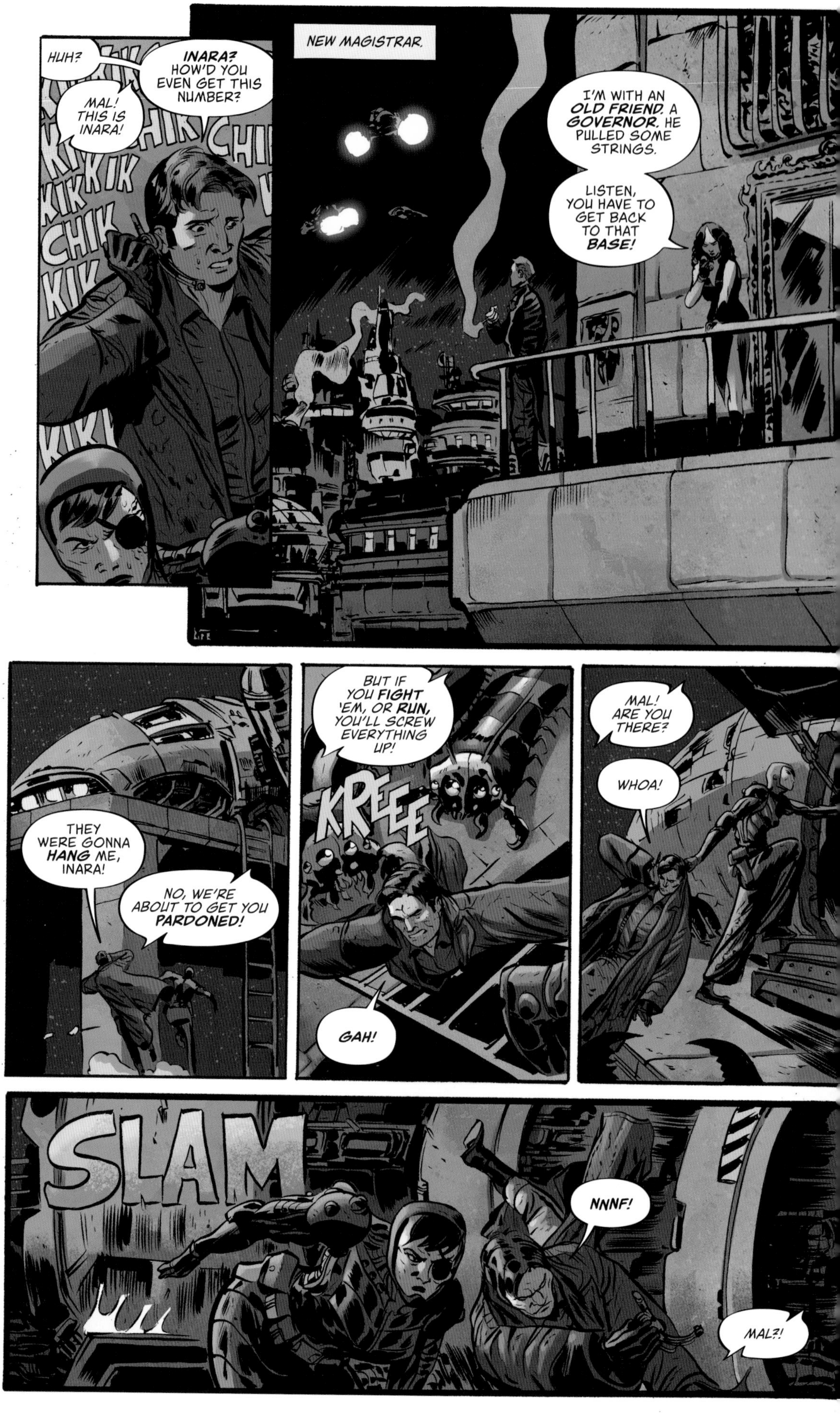
KIK CHIK KIK KIK CHIK KIK CHIK
HUH?
MAL! THIS IS INARA!
INARA? HOW'D YOU EVEN GET THIS NUMBER?
NEW MAGISTRAR.
I'M WITH AN OLD FRIEND. A GOVERNOR. HE PULLED SOME STRINGS.
LISTEN, YOU HAVE TO GET BACK TO THAT BASE!
THEY WERE GONNA HANG ME, INARA!
NO, WE'RE ABOUT TO GET YOU PARDONED!
BUT IF YOU FIGHT 'EM, OR RUN, YOU'LL SCREW EVERYTHING UP!
KREEE
GAH!
MAL! ARE YOU THERE?
WHOA!
SLAM
NNNF!
MAL?!

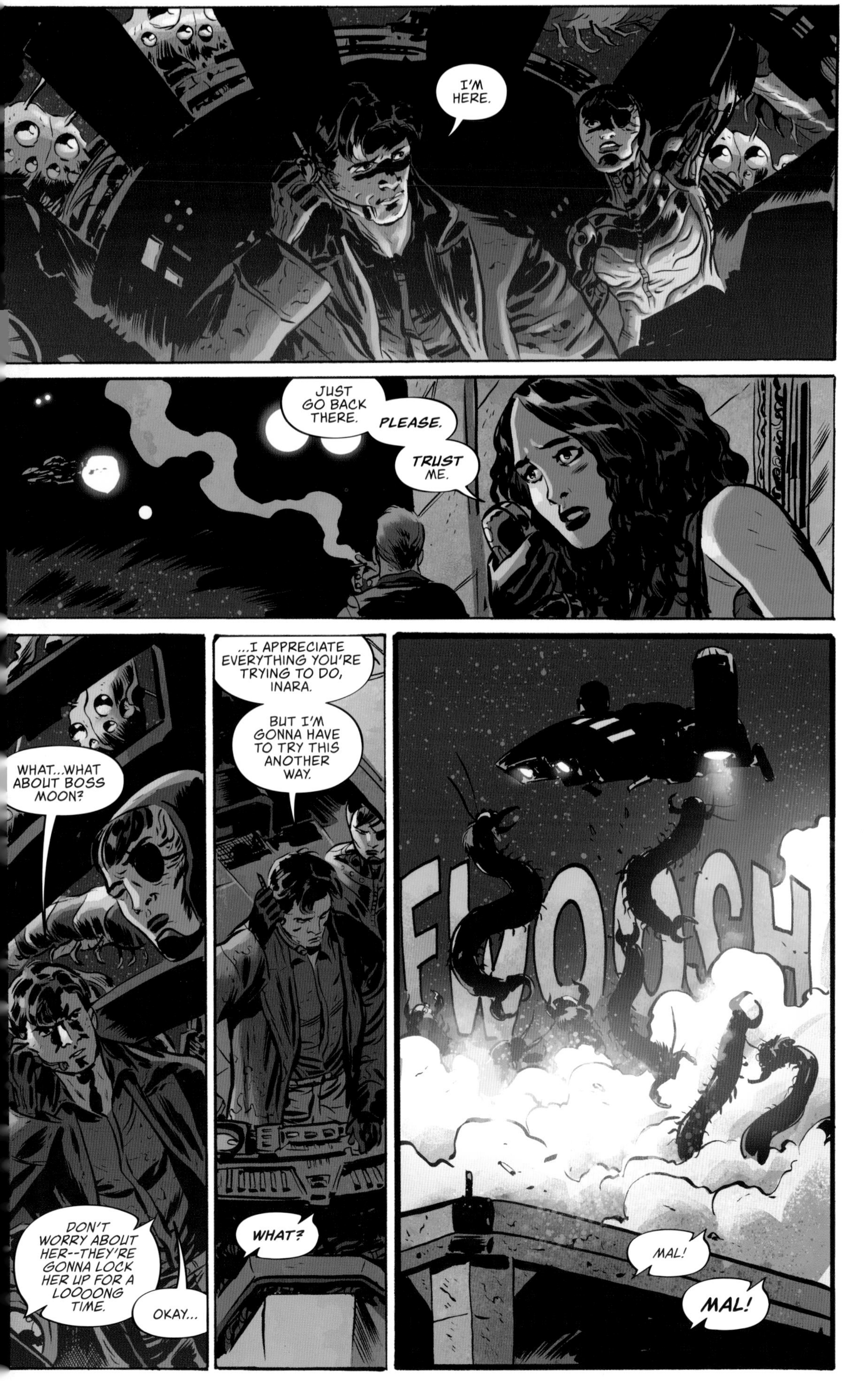
I'M HERE.
JUST GO BACK THERE.
PLEASE.
TRUST ME.
WHAT...WHAT ABOUT BOSS MOON?
DON'T WORRY ABOUT HER--THEY'RE GONNA LOCK HER UP FOR A LOOOONG TIME.
OKAY...
...I APPRECIATE EVERYTHING YOU'RE TRYING TO DO, INARA.
BUT I'M GONNA HAVE TO TRY THIS ANOTHER WAY.
WHAT?
FWOOSH
MAL!
MAL!

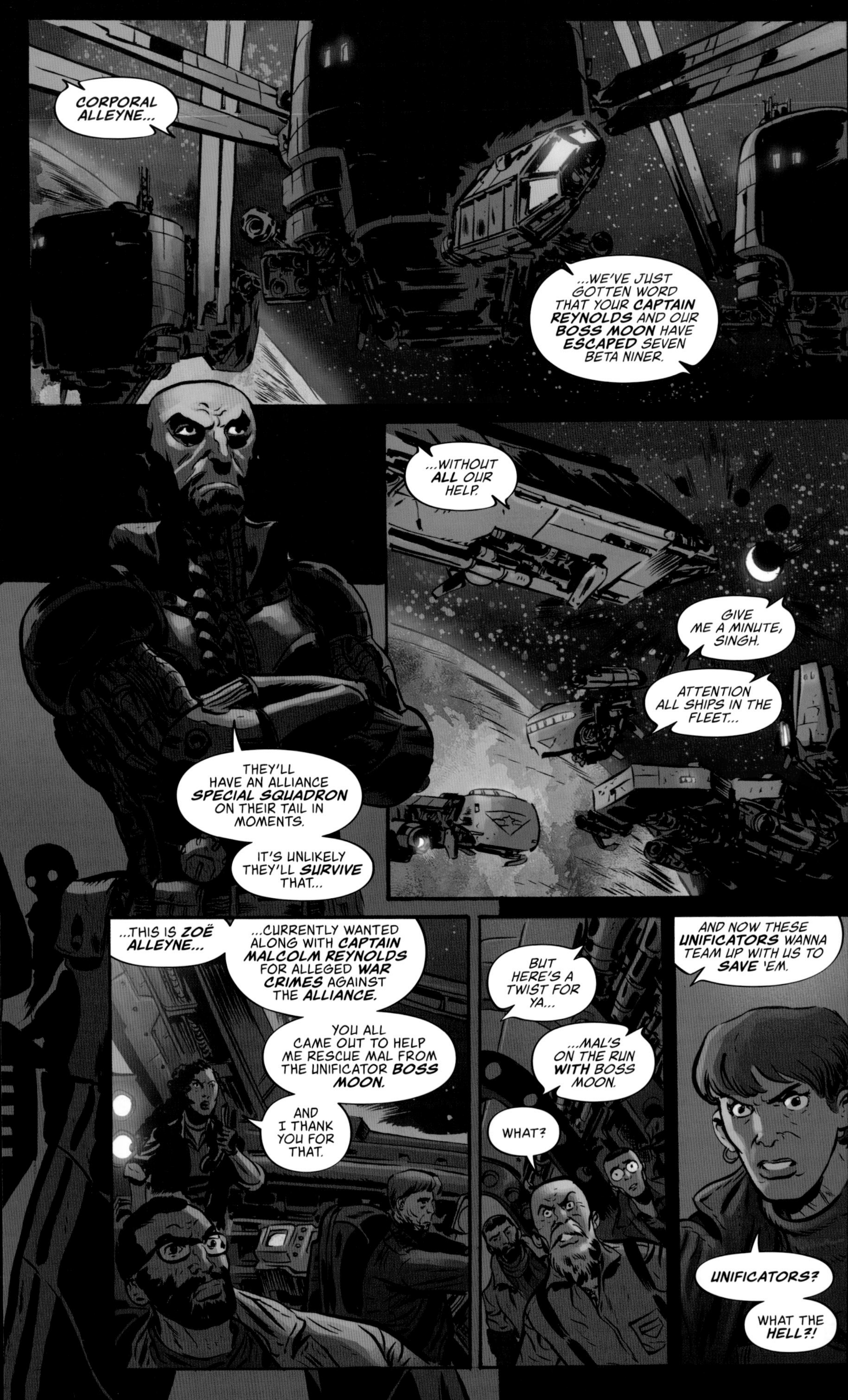

CORPORAL ALLEYNE...
...WE'VE JUST GOTTEN WORD THAT YOUR CAPTAIN REYNOLDS AND OUR BOSS MOON HAVE ESCAPED SEVEN BETA NINER.
...WITHOUT ALL OUR HELP.
THEY'LL HAVE AN ALLIANCE SPECIAL SQUADRON ON THEIR TAIL IN MOMENTS.
IT'S UNLIKELY THEY'LL SURVIVE THAT...
GIVE ME A MINUTE, SINGH.
ATTENTION ALL SHIPS IN THE FLEET...
...THIS IS ZOË ALLEYNE...
...CURRENTLY WANTED ALONG WITH CAPTAIN MALCOLM REYNOLDS FOR ALLEGED WAR CRIMES AGAINST THE ALLIANCE.
YOU ALL CAME OUT TO HELP ME RESCUE MAL FROM THE UNIFICATOR BOSS MOON.
AND I THANK YOU FOR THAT.
BUT HERE'S A TWIST FOR YA...
...MAL'S ON THE RUN WITH BOSS MOON.
WHAT?
AND NOW THESE UNIFICATORS WANNA TEAM UP WITH US TO SAVE 'EM.
UNIFICATORS?
WHAT THE HELL?!

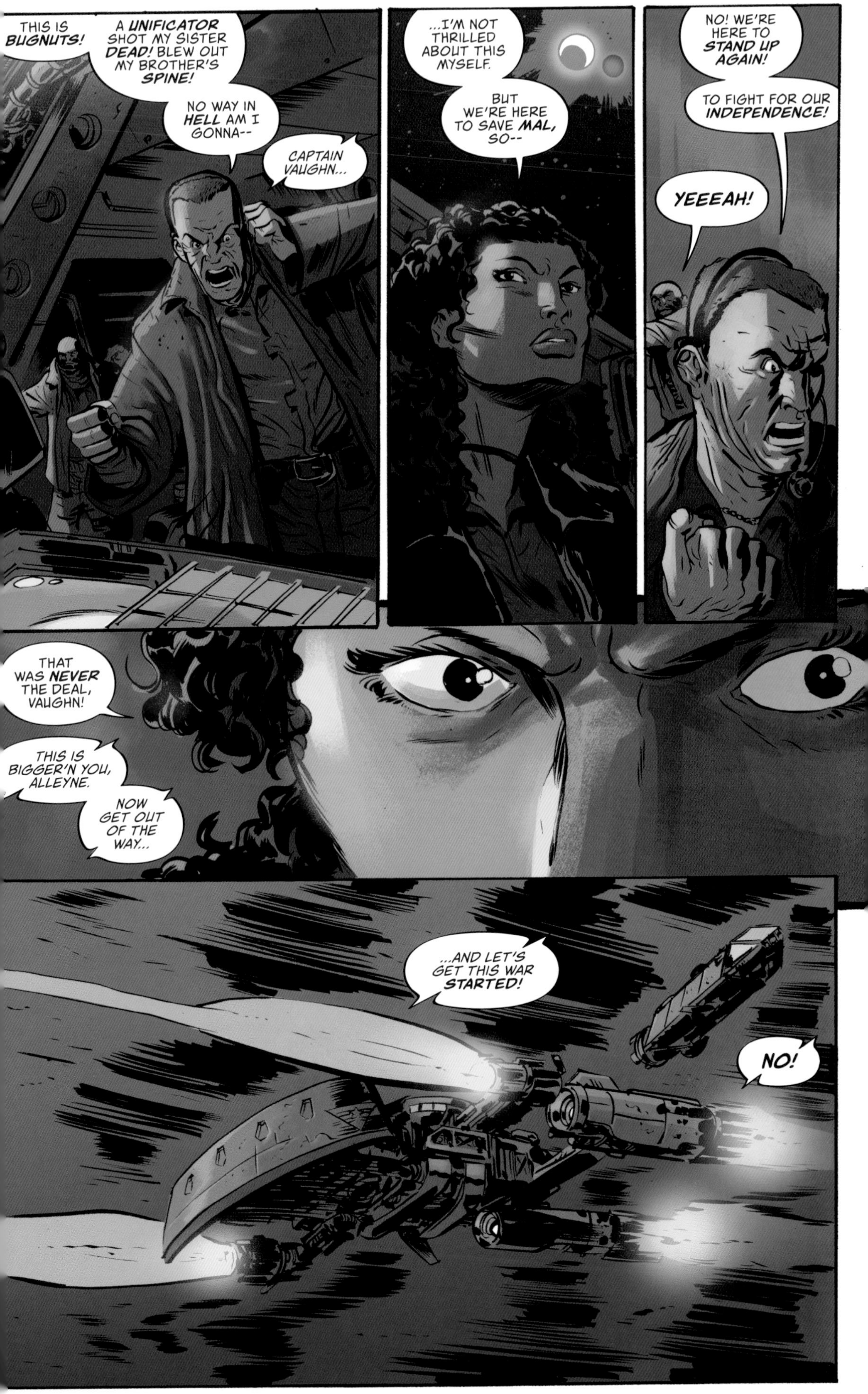
THIS IS BUGNUTS!
A UNIFICATOR SHOT MY SISTER DEAD! BLEW OUT MY BROTHER'S SPINE!
NO WAY IN HELL AM I GONNA--
CAPTAIN VAUGHN...
...I'M NOT THRILLED ABOUT THIS MYSELF.
BUT WE'RE HERE TO SAVE MAL, SO--
NO! WE'RE HERE TO STAND UP AGAIN!
TO FIGHT FOR OUR INDEPENDENCE!
YEEEAH!
THAT WAS NEVER THE DEAL, VAUGHN!
THIS IS BIGGER'N YOU, ALLEYNE.
NOW GET OUT OF THE WAY...
...AND LET'S GET THIS WAR STARTED!
NO!

BOSS SINGH, SHOULD WE...

ABSOLUTELY.

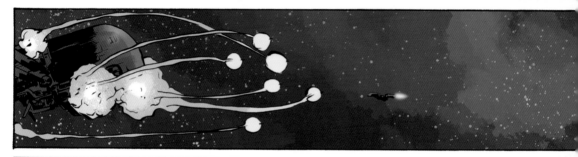

OH, NO...

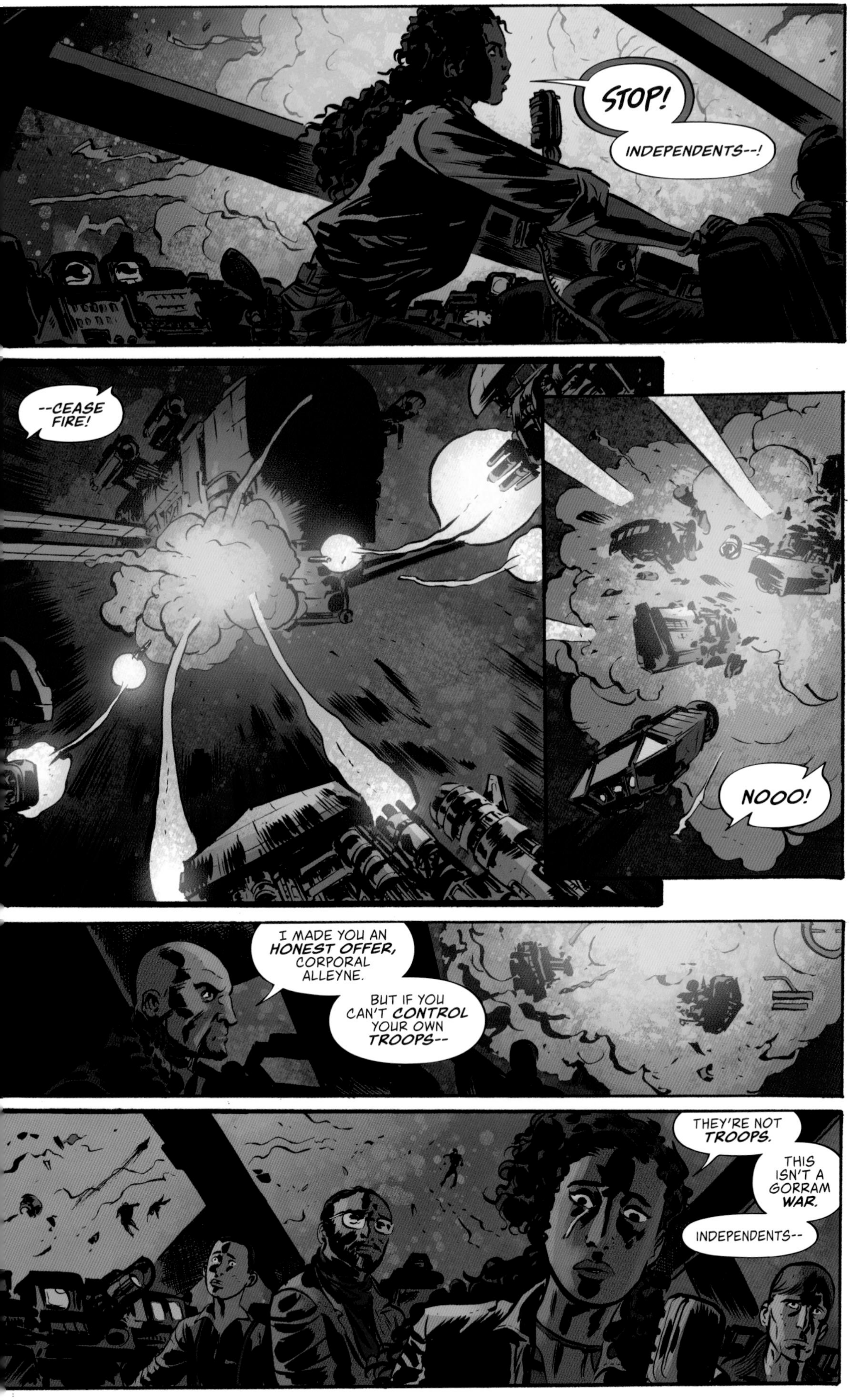
STOP!
INDEPENDENTS--!
--CEASE FIRE!
NOOO!
I MADE YOU AN HONEST OFFER, CORPORAL ALLEYNE.
BUT IF YOU CAN'T CONTROL YOUR OWN TROOPS--
THEY'RE NOT TROOPS.
THIS ISN'T A GORRAM WAR.
INDEPENDENTS--

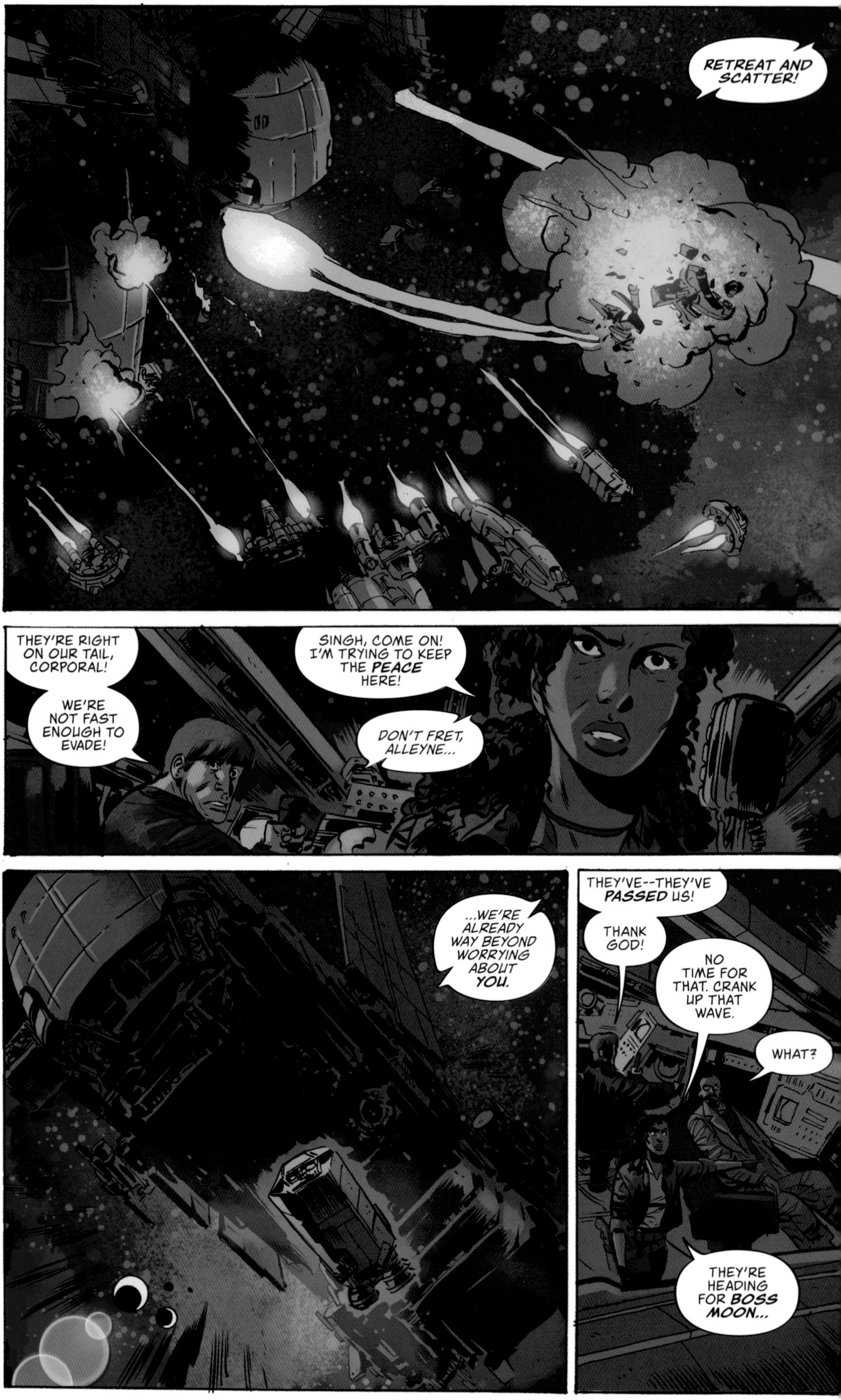
RETREAT AND SCATTER!
THEY'RE RIGHT ON OUR TAIL, CORPORAL!
WE'RE NOT FAST ENOUGH TO EVADE!
SINGH, COME ON! I'M TRYING TO KEEP THE PEACE HERE!
DON'T FRET, ALLEYNE...
...WE'RE ALREADY WAY BEYOND WORRYING ABOUT YOU.
THEY'VE--THEY'VE PASSED US!
THANK GOD!
NO TIME FOR THAT. CRANK UP THAT WAVE.
WHAT?
THEY'RE HEADING FOR BOSS MOON...

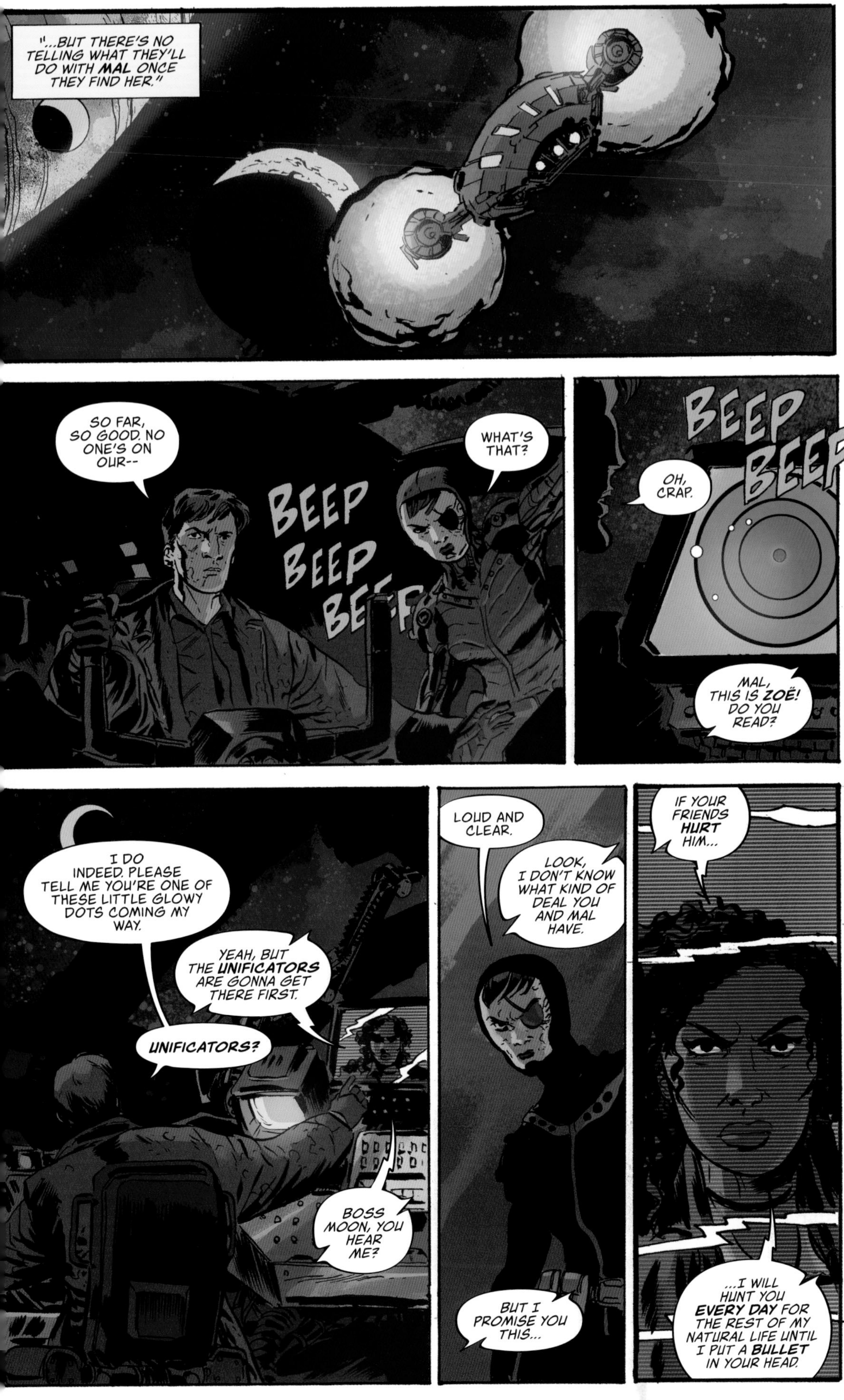
"...BUT THERE'S NO TELLING WHAT THEY'LL DO WITH MAL ONCE THEY FIND HER."
SO FAR, SO GOOD. NO ONE'S ON OUR--
BEEP BEEP BEEP
WHAT'S THAT?
BEEP BEEP
OH, CRAP.
MAL, THIS IS ZOË! DO YOU READ?
I DO INDEED. PLEASE TELL ME YOU'RE ONE OF THESE LITTLE GLOWY DOTS COMING MY WAY.
YEAH, BUT THE UNIFICATORS ARE GONNA GET THERE FIRST.
UNIFICATORS?
BOSS MOON, YOU HEAR ME?
LOUD AND CLEAR.
LOOK, I DON'T KNOW WHAT KIND OF DEAL YOU AND MAL HAVE.
BUT I PROMISE YOU THIS...
IF YOUR FRIENDS HURT HIM...
...I WILL HUNT YOU EVERY DAY FOR THE REST OF MY NATURAL LIFE UNTIL I PUT A BULLET IN YOUR HEAD.

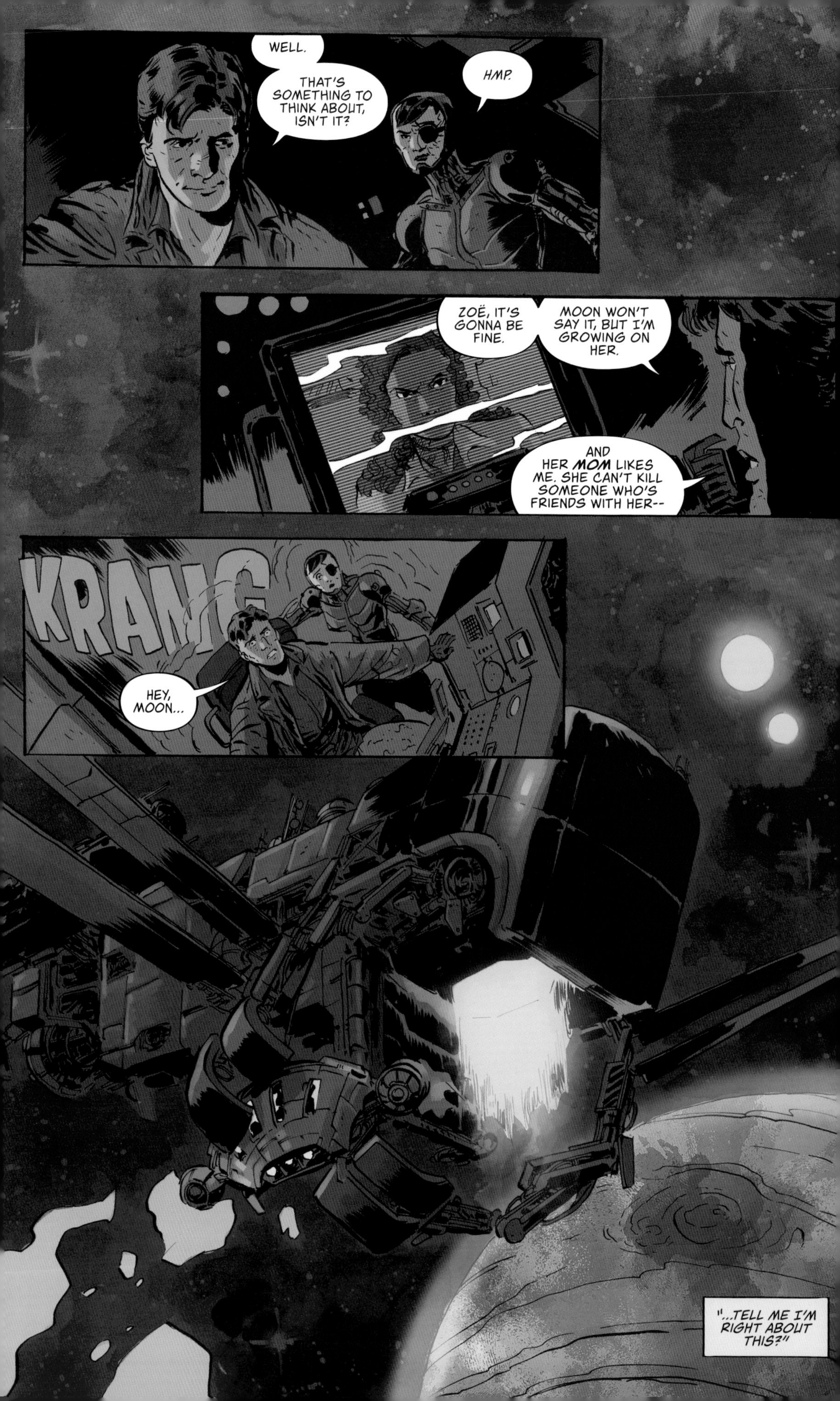
WELL.
THAT'S SOMETHING TO THINK ABOUT, ISN'T IT?
HMP.
ZOË, IT'S GONNA BE FINE.
MOON WON'T SAY IT, BUT I'M GROWING ON HER.
AND HER MOM LIKES ME. SHE CAN'T KILL SOMEONE WHO'S FRIENDS WITH HER--
KRANG
HEY, MOON...
"...TELL ME I'M RIGHT ABOUT THIS?"

IT'S GONNA BE FINE.
TRUST ME.
DON'T TRUST HER!
AAAAH...
...I'M GONNA TRUST HER, ZOË.
WE KEEP SAYING THE WAR'S OVER.
MAL! DAMMIT!
WHIRRRR
MAYBE IT'S TIME FOR US ALL TO START ACTING LIKE IT.
GRRRAAAAA!
SSSLAM!
HEY!
DAMMIT!
UKK!

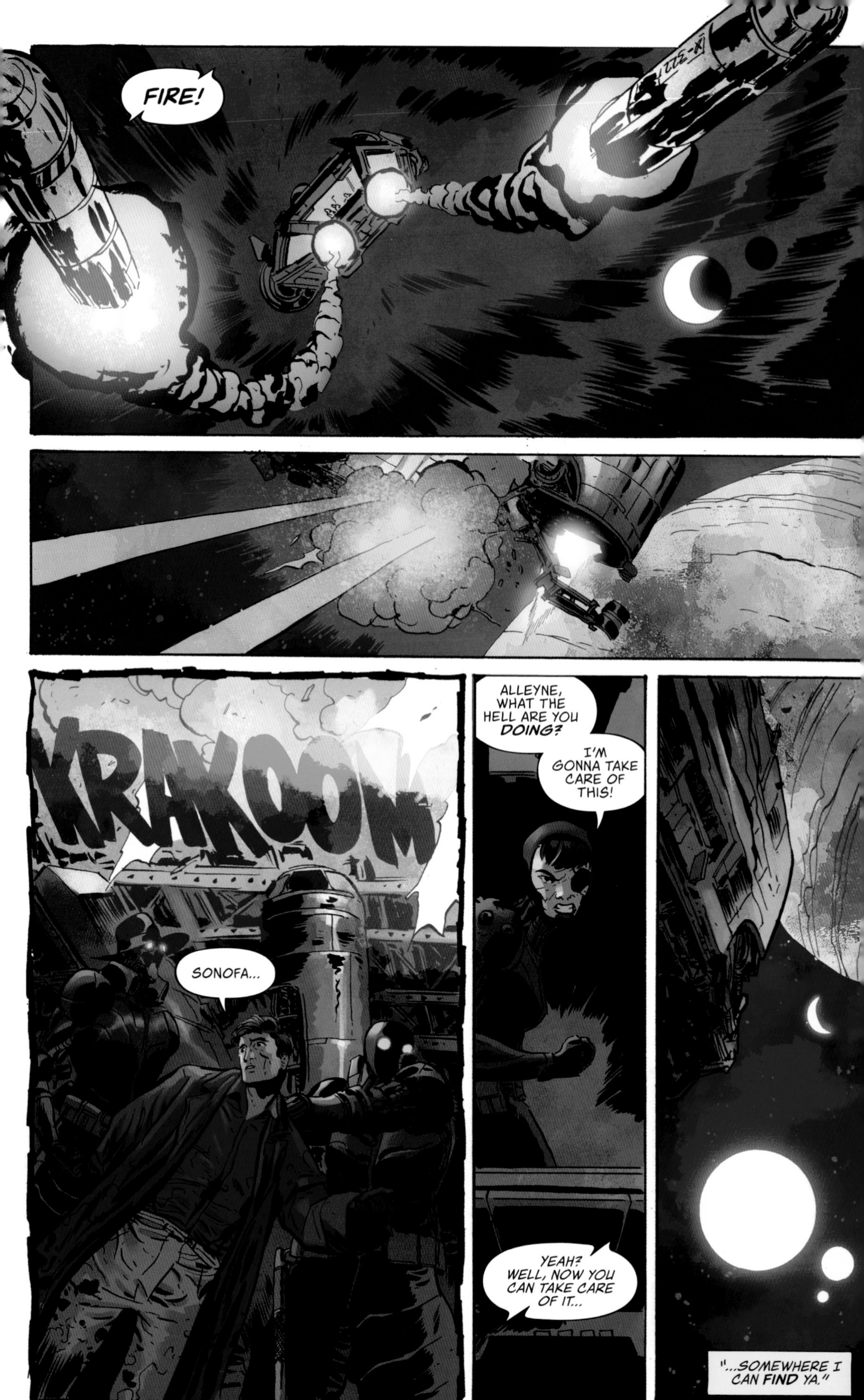
FIRE!
KRAKOOM
SONOFA...
ALLEYNE, WHAT THE HELL ARE YOU DOING?
I'M GONNA TAKE CARE OF THIS!
YEAH? WELL, NOW YOU CAN TAKE CARE OF IT...
"...SOMEWHERE I CAN FIND YA."

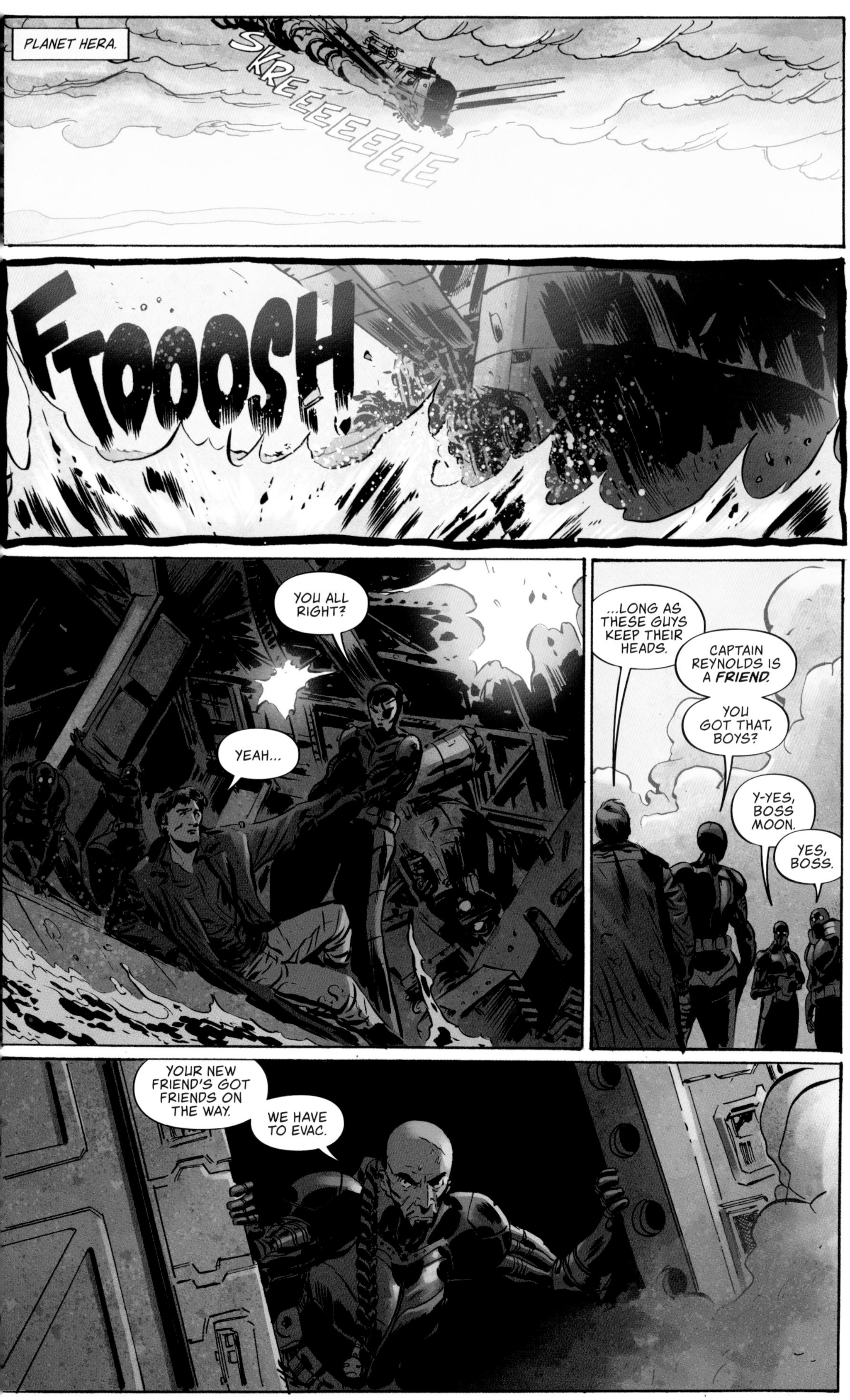
PLANET HERA.
SKREEEEEEEE
FTOOOSH!
YOU ALL RIGHT?
YEAH...
...LONG AS THESE GUYS KEEP THEIR HEADS.
CAPTAIN REYNOLDS IS A **FRIEND.**
YOU GOT THAT, BOYS?
Y-YES, BOSS MOON.
YES, BOSS.
YOUR NEW FRIEND'S GOT FRIENDS ON THE WAY.
WE HAVE TO EVAC.

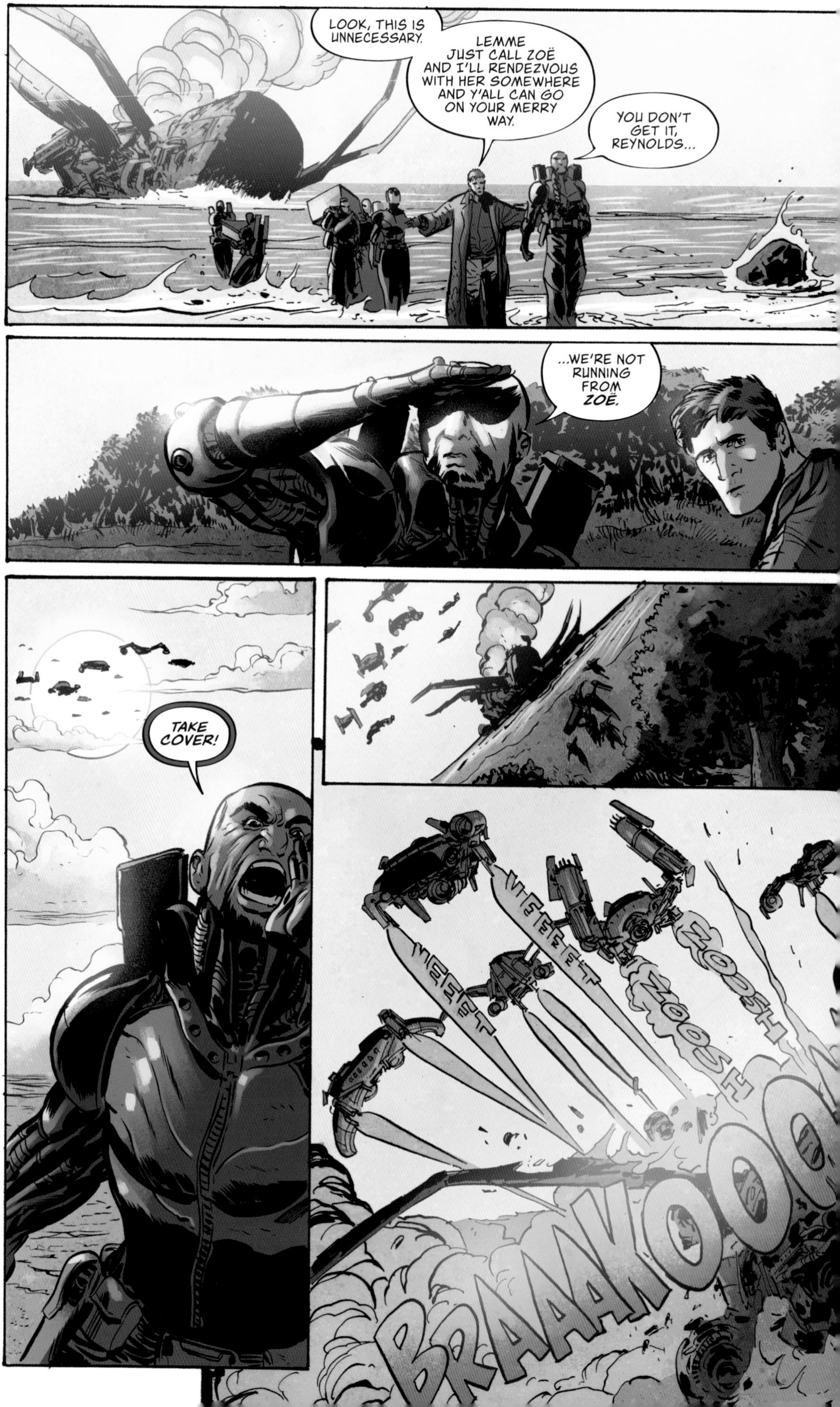
LOOK, THIS IS UNNECESSARY.
LEMME JUST CALL ZOË AND I'LL RENDEZVOUS WITH HER SOMEWHERE AND Y'ALL CAN GO ON YOUR MERRY WAY.
YOU DON'T GET IT, REYNOLDS...
...WE'RE NOT RUNNING FROM ZOË.
TAKE COVER!
ZOOOSH
BRAAAWOOO

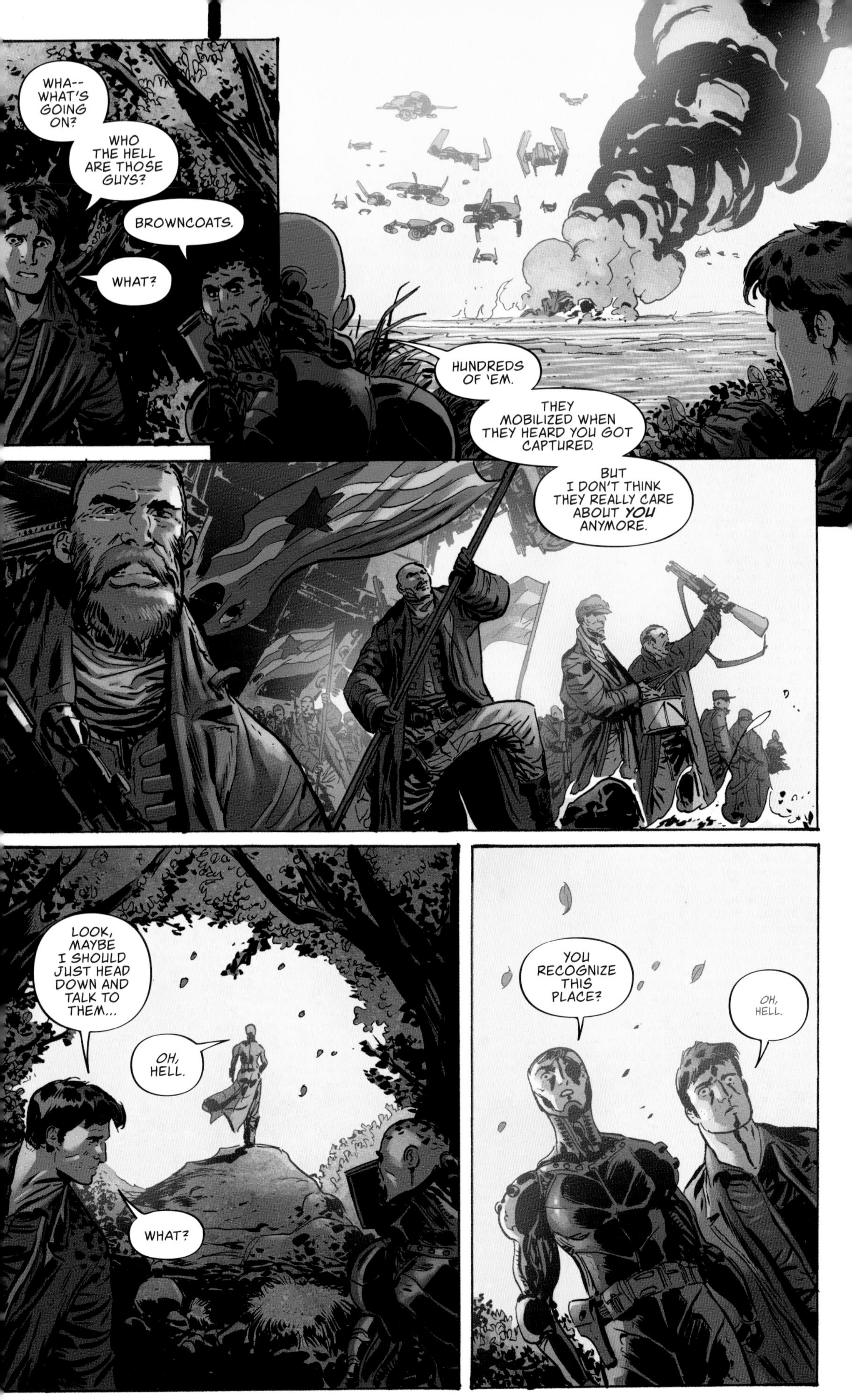
WHA-- WHAT'S GOING ON?
WHO THE HELL ARE THOSE GUYS?
BROWNCOATS.
WHAT?
HUNDREDS OF 'EM.
THEY MOBILIZED WHEN THEY HEARD YOU GOT CAPTURED.
BUT I DON'T THINK THEY REALLY CARE ABOUT YOU ANYMORE.
LOOK, MAYBE I SHOULD JUST HEAD DOWN AND TALK TO THEM...
OH, HELL.
WHAT?
YOU RECOGNIZE THIS PLACE?
OH, HELL.

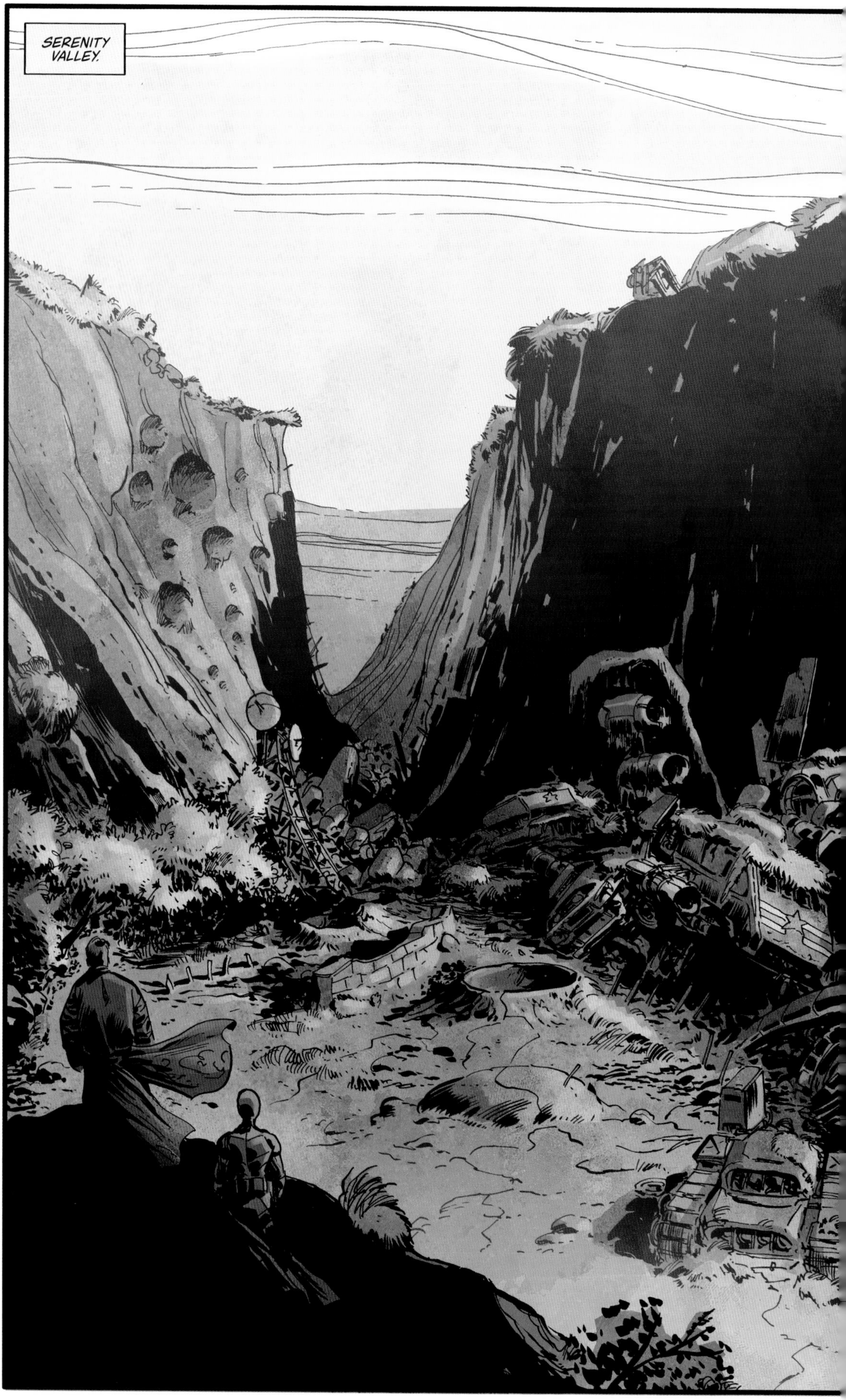
SERENITY VALLEY.

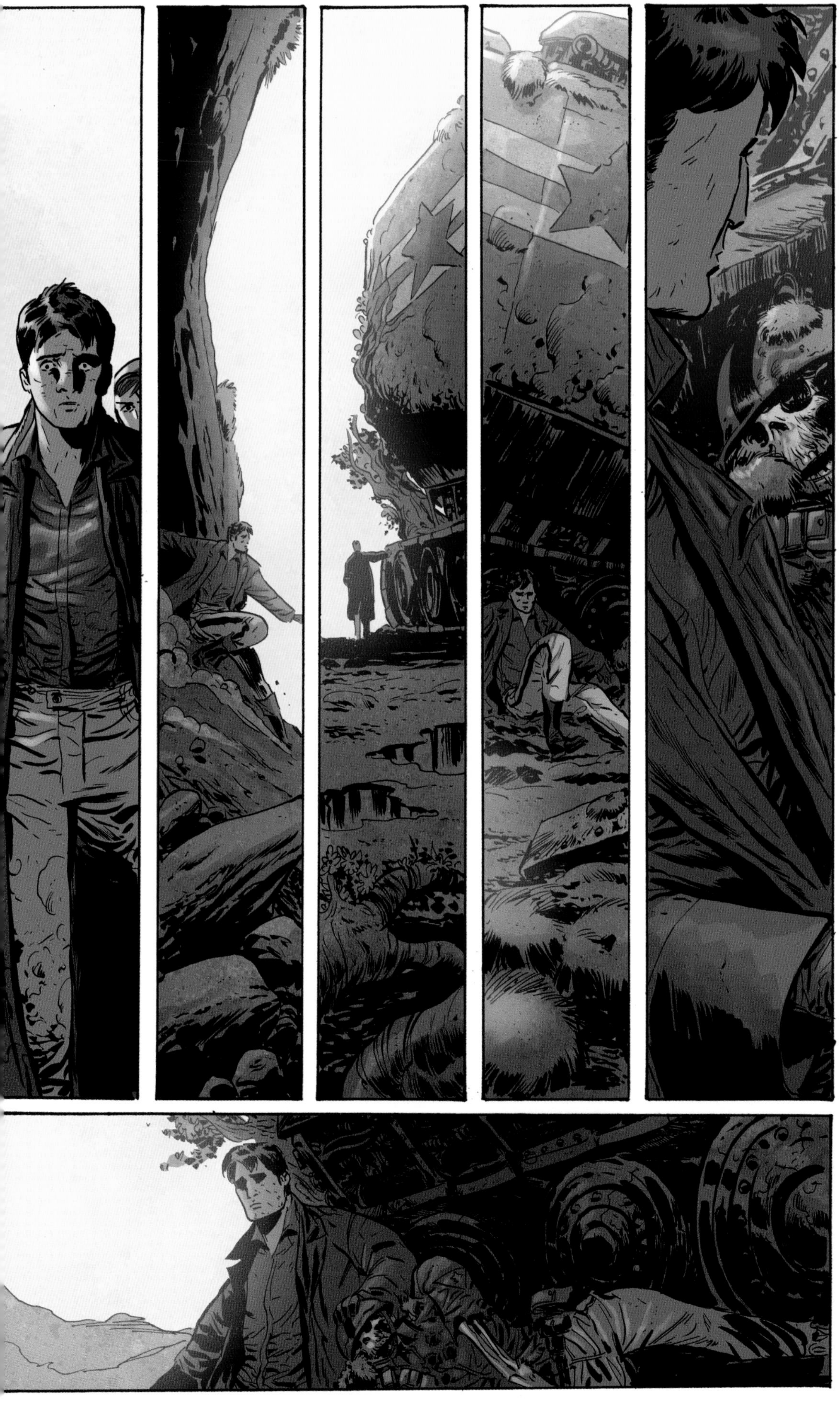

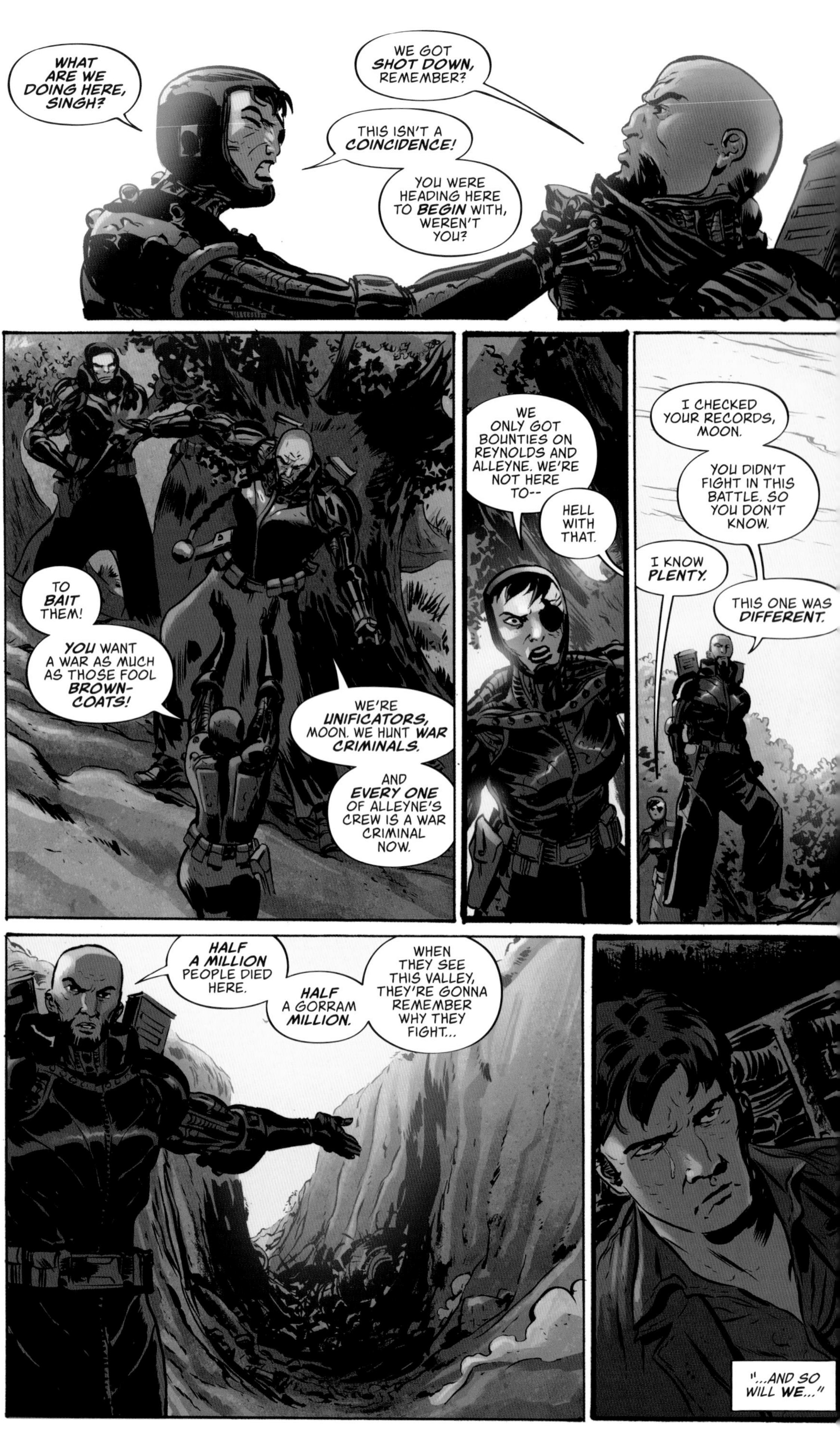
WHAT ARE WE DOING HERE, SINGH?
WE GOT SHOT DOWN, REMEMBER?
THIS ISN'T A COINCIDENCE!
YOU WERE HEADING HERE TO BEGIN WITH, WEREN'T YOU?
TO BAIT THEM!
YOU WANT A WAR AS MUCH AS THOSE FOOL BROWN-COATS!
WE'RE UNIFICATORS, MOON. WE HUNT WAR CRIMINALS.
AND EVERY ONE OF ALLEYNE'S CREW IS A WAR CRIMINAL NOW.
WE ONLY GOT BOUNTIES ON REYNOLDS AND ALLEYNE. WE'RE NOT HERE TO--
HELL WITH THAT.
I CHECKED YOUR RECORDS, MOON.
YOU DIDN'T FIGHT IN THIS BATTLE. SO YOU DON'T KNOW.
I KNOW PLENTY.
THIS ONE WAS DIFFERENT.
HALF A MILLION PEOPLE DIED HERE.
HALF A GORRAM MILLION.
WHEN THEY SEE THIS VALLEY, THEY'RE GONNA REMEMBER WHY THEY FIGHT...
"...AND SO WILL WE..."

"...AND WE'RE GONNA **END** THIS ONCE AND FOR ALL."

NEW MAGISTRAR.

WASH, YOU'RE BREAKING UP! CAN YOU REPEAT?

~~ BZZZTTT HEADING TO **SERENITY VALLEY**! I'M TELLING YOU, THIS IS **TOTALLY INSANE**--

SERENITY VALLEY?

~~BRRZZZZZTTT~~

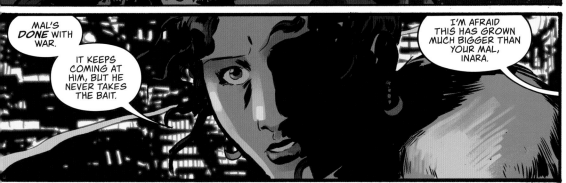

THAT'S ONE OF MY **FRIENDS**. HE'S WITH A GROUP OF **BROWNCOATS** WHO SAY MAL'S CRASHED ONTO--

YES. I'M GETTING THE SAME MESSAGE FROM OUR SCOUTS.

THIS-- THIS DOESN'T MAKE ANY **SENSE**.

MAL'S **DONE** WITH WAR.

IT KEEPS COMING AT HIM, BUT HE NEVER TAKES THE BAIT.

I'M AFRAID THIS HAS GROWN MUCH BIGGER THAN YOUR MAL, INARA.

EVEN AS WE SPEAK, AT LEAST THIRTY-THREE DIFFERENT SHIPS ARE CONVERGING ON SERENITY VALLEY.

UNIFICATORS AND BROWNCOATS. ALL ITCHING FOR A **FIGHT**.

YOU'VE GOT **RESOURCES**, PAUL. YOU DON'T HAVE TO BE **INVOLVED**--I JUST NEED A **SHUTTLE**, AND A LITTLE **INTELLIGENCE**--

I'M SORRY, INARA...

...THIS IS NO LONGER A **PRIVATE AFFAIR** THAT I CAN ASSIST YOU WITH.

I'M THE **GOVERNOR** OF THIS REGION...

...AND WITH **WAR** LOOMING...

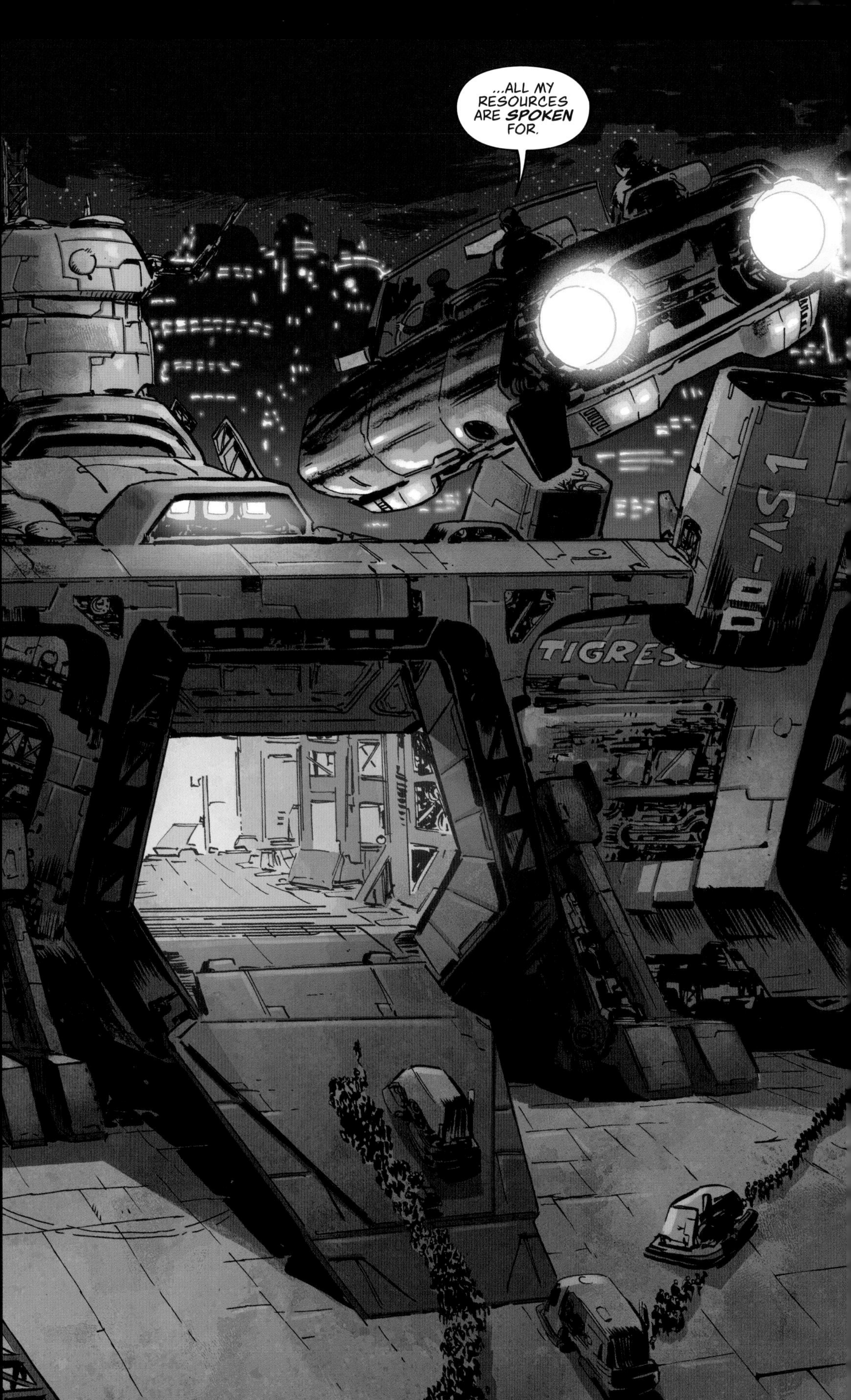
...ALL MY RESOURCES ARE **SPOKEN** FOR.

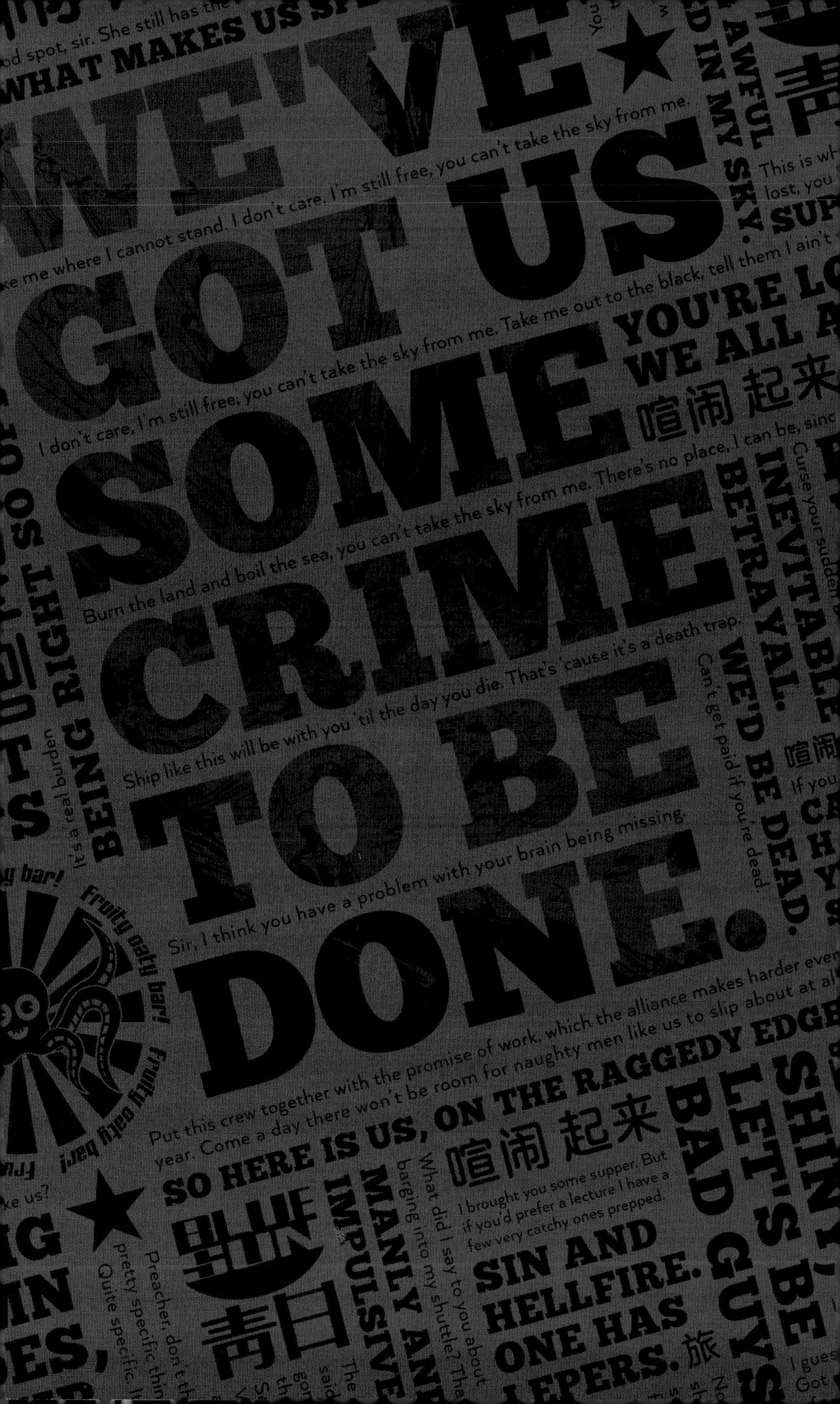

WHAT MAKES US

WE'VE GOT US SOME CRIME TO BE DONE.

ood spot, sir. She still has the...

ke me where I cannot stand. I don't care, I'm still free, you can't take the sky from me.

I don't care, I'm still free, you can't take the sky from me. Take me out to the black, tell them I ain't...

Burn the land and boil the sea, you can't take the sky from me. There's no place, I can be, since...

Ship like this will be with you 'til the day you die. That's 'cause it's a death trap.

Sir, I think you have a problem with your brain being missing.

YOU'RE LO

WE ALL A

AWFUL

D IN MY SKY.

This is wh

lost, you

SUP

喧闹 起来

INEVITABLE BETRAYAL. WE'D BE DEAD.

Curse your sudden

Can't get paid if you're dead.

If you

CA

喧闹

BEING RIGHT SO

It's a real burden

y bar!

Fruity oaty bar!

Fruity oaty bar!

Fruity oaty bar!

ke us?

Put this crew together with the promise of work, which the alliance makes harder every year. Come a day there won't be room for naughty men like us to slip about at all.

SO HERE IS US, ON THE RAGGEDY EDGE.

喧闹 起来

BLUE SUN

MANLY AND IMPULSIVE.

What did I say to you about barging into my shuttle? Tha...

I brought you some supper. But if you'd prefer a lecture I have a few very catchy ones prepped.

SIN AND HELLFIRE. ONE HAS LEPERS.

LET'S BE BAD GUYS

SHINY BE

喧闹 起来

旅

Preacher, don't th... pretty specific thin... Quite specific...

青日

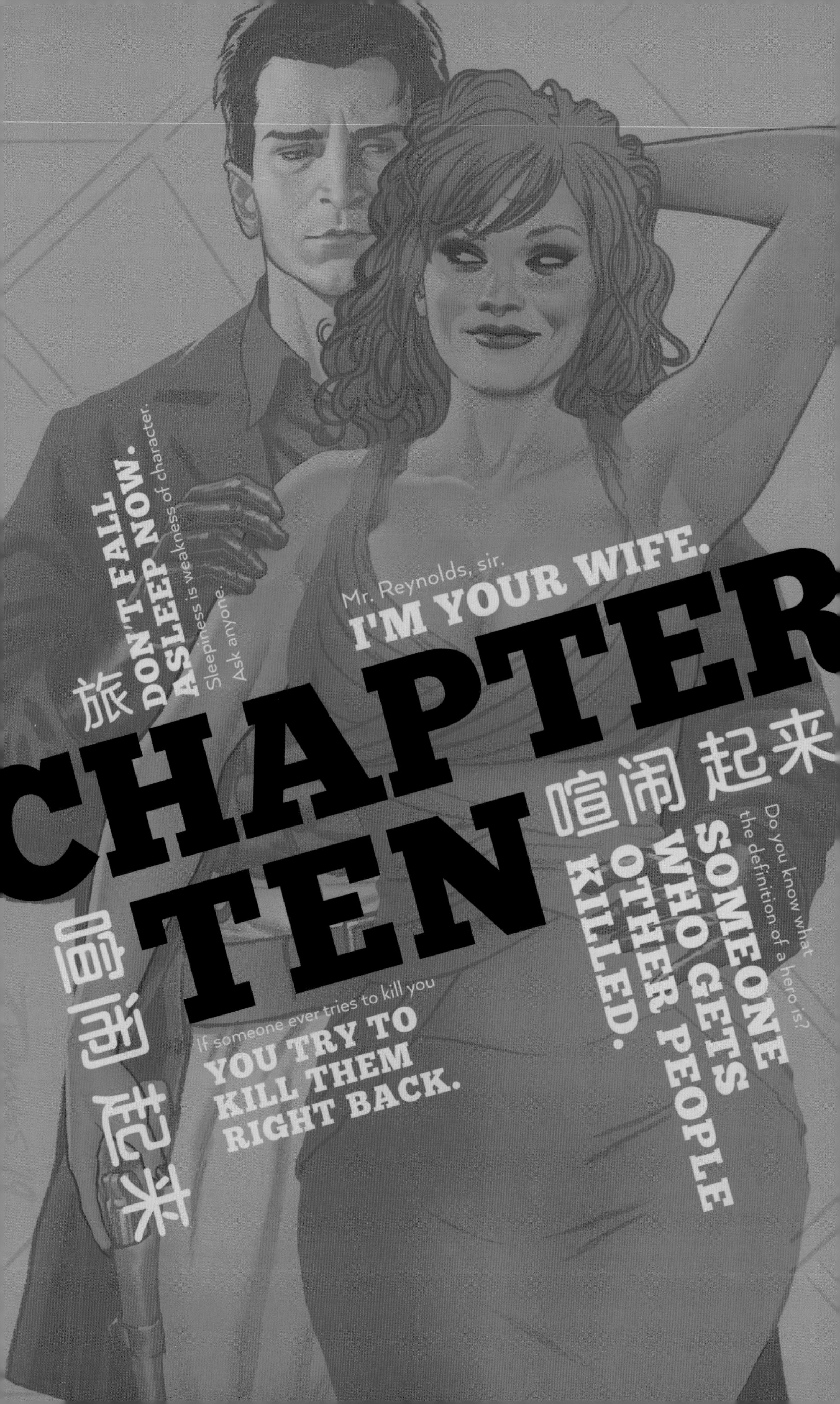
CHAPTER
TEN
旅
DON'T FALL
ASLEEP NOW.
Sleepiness is weakness of character.
Ask anyone.
Mr. Reynolds, sir.
I'M YOUR WIFE.
喧闹起来
Do you know what
the definition of a hero is?
SOMEONE
WHO GETS
OTHER PEOPLE
KILLED.
If someone ever tries to kill you
YOU TRY TO
KILL THEM
RIGHT BACK.
喧闹起来

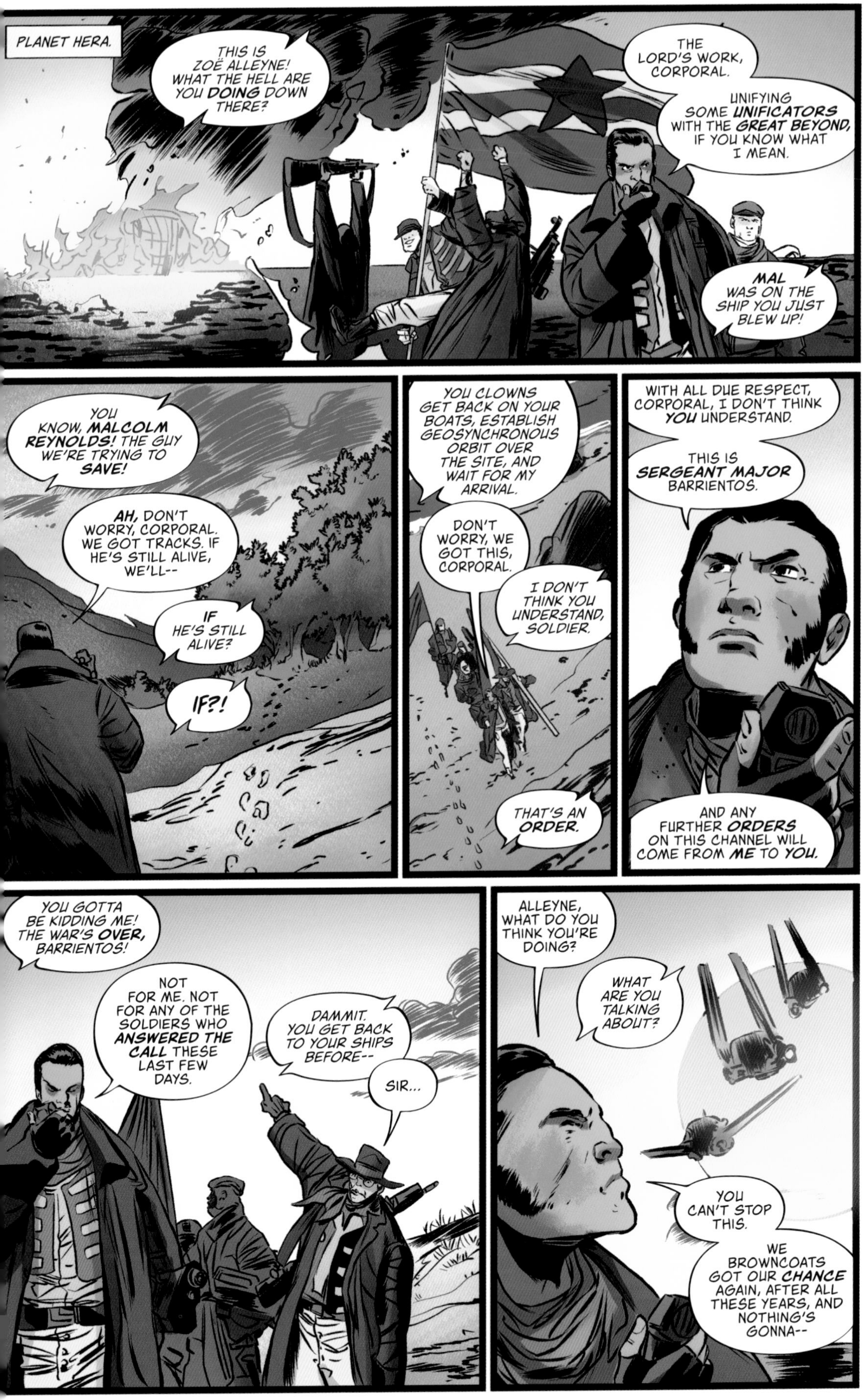

PLANET HERA.
THIS IS ZOË ALLEYNE! WHAT THE HELL ARE YOU DOING DOWN THERE?
THE LORD'S WORK, CORPORAL.
UNIFYING SOME UNIFICATORS WITH THE GREAT BEYOND, IF YOU KNOW WHAT I MEAN.
MAL WAS ON THE SHIP YOU JUST BLEW UP!
YOU KNOW, MALCOLM REYNOLDS! THE GUY WE'RE TRYING TO SAVE!
AH, DON'T WORRY, CORPORAL. WE GOT TRACKS. IF HE'S STILL ALIVE, WE'LL--
IF HE'S STILL ALIVE?
IF?!
YOU CLOWNS GET BACK ON YOUR BOATS, ESTABLISH GEOSYNCHRONOUS ORBIT OVER THE SITE, AND WAIT FOR MY ARRIVAL.
DON'T WORRY, WE GOT THIS, CORPORAL.
I DON'T THINK YOU UNDERSTAND, SOLDIER.
THAT'S AN ORDER.
WITH ALL DUE RESPECT, CORPORAL, I DON'T THINK YOU UNDERSTAND.
THIS IS SERGEANT MAJOR BARRIENTOS.
AND ANY FURTHER ORDERS ON THIS CHANNEL WILL COME FROM ME TO YOU.
YOU GOTTA BE KIDDING ME! THE WAR'S OVER, BARRIENTOS!
NOT FOR ME. NOT FOR ANY OF THE SOLDIERS WHO ANSWERED THE CALL THESE LAST FEW DAYS.
DAMMIT. YOU GET BACK TO YOUR SHIPS BEFORE--
SIR...
ALLEYNE, WHAT DO YOU THINK YOU'RE DOING?
WHAT ARE YOU TALKING ABOUT?
YOU CAN'T STOP THIS.
WE BROWNCOATS GOT OUR CHANCE AGAIN, AFTER ALL THESE YEARS, AND NOTHING'S GONNA--

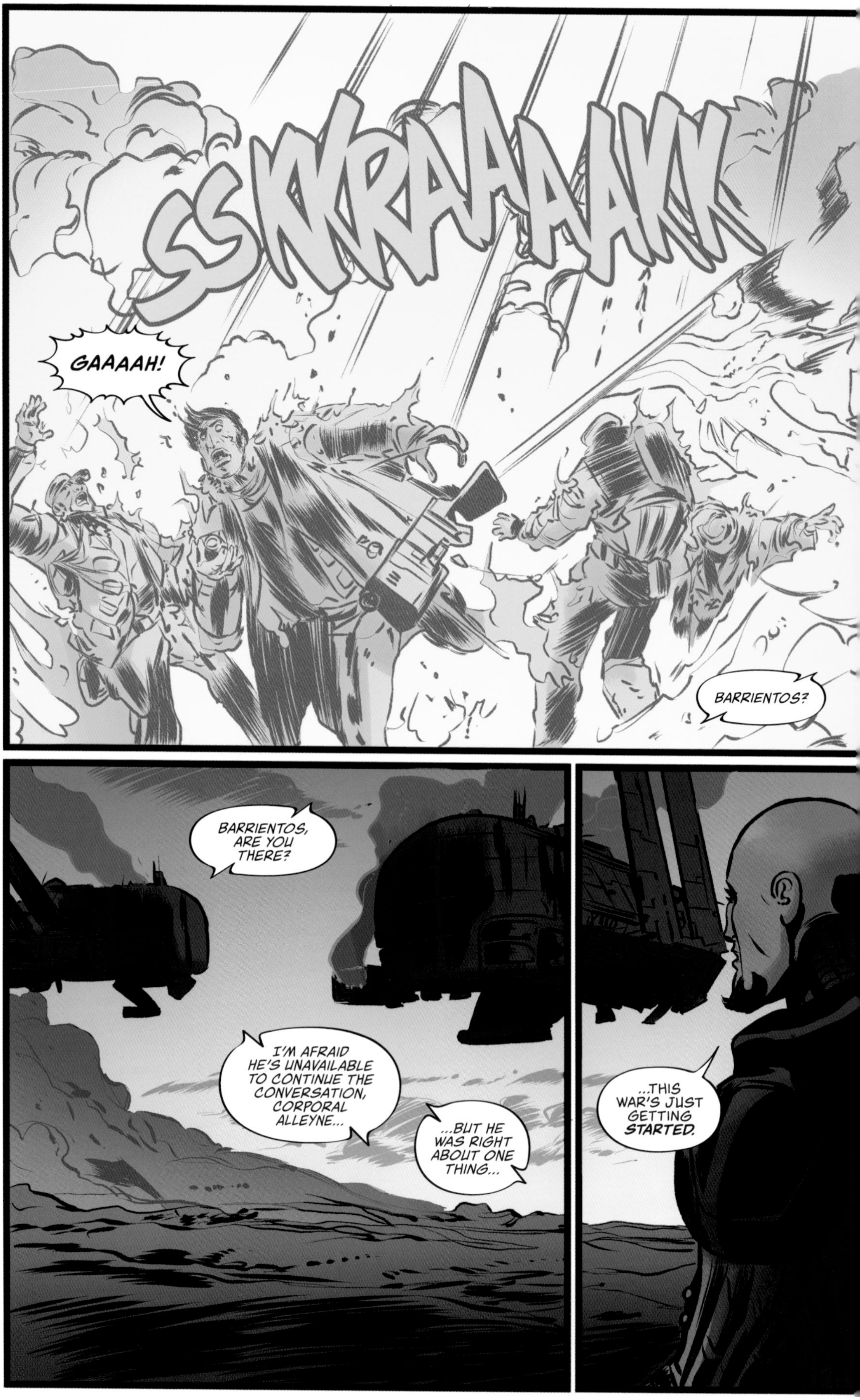

SSKKRAAAAKK
GAAAAH!
BARRIENTOS?
BARRIENTOS, ARE YOU THERE?
I'M AFRAID HE'S UNAVAILABLE TO CONTINUE THE CONVERSATION, CORPORAL ALLEYNE...
...BUT HE WAS RIGHT ABOUT ONE THING...
...THIS WAR'S JUST GETTING STARTED.

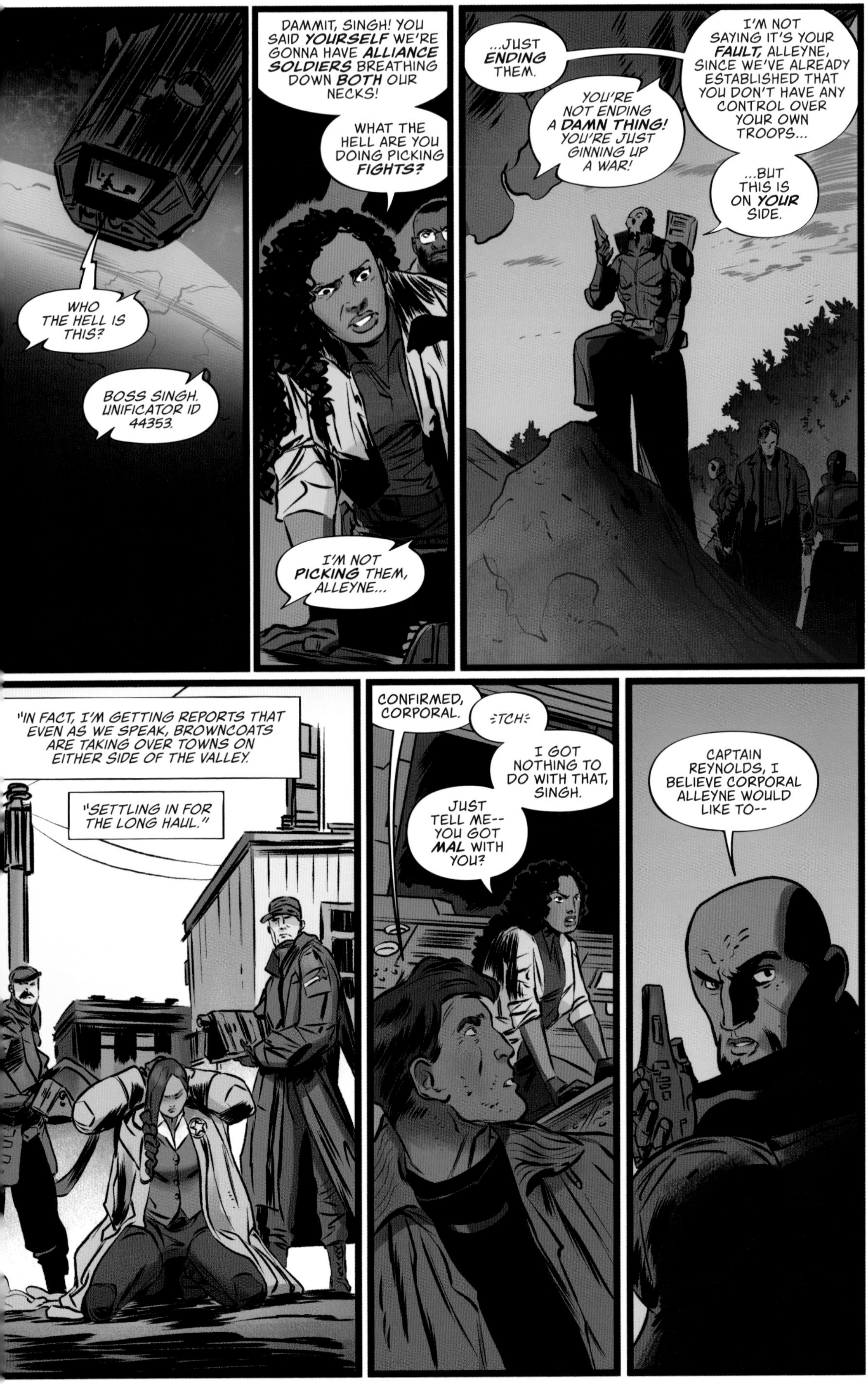
WHO THE HELL IS THIS?
BOSS SINGH. UNIFICATOR ID 44353.
DAMMIT, SINGH! YOU SAID YOURSELF WE'RE GONNA HAVE ALLIANCE SOLDIERS BREATHING DOWN BOTH OUR NECKS!
WHAT THE HELL ARE YOU DOING PICKING FIGHTS?
I'M NOT PICKING THEM, ALLEYNE...
...JUST ENDING THEM.
YOU'RE NOT ENDING A DAMN THING! YOU'RE JUST GINNING UP A WAR!
I'M NOT SAYING IT'S YOUR FAULT, ALLEYNE, SINCE WE'VE ALREADY ESTABLISHED THAT YOU DON'T HAVE ANY CONTROL OVER YOUR OWN TROOPS...
...BUT THIS IS ON YOUR SIDE.
"IN FACT, I'M GETTING REPORTS THAT EVEN AS WE SPEAK, BROWNCOATS ARE TAKING OVER TOWNS ON EITHER SIDE OF THE VALLEY.
"SETTLING IN FOR THE LONG HAUL."
CONFIRMED, CORPORAL.
=TCH=
I GOT NOTHING TO DO WITH THAT, SINGH.
JUST TELL ME-- YOU GOT MAL WITH YOU?
CAPTAIN REYNOLDS, I BELIEVE CORPORAL ALLEYNE WOULD LIKE TO--

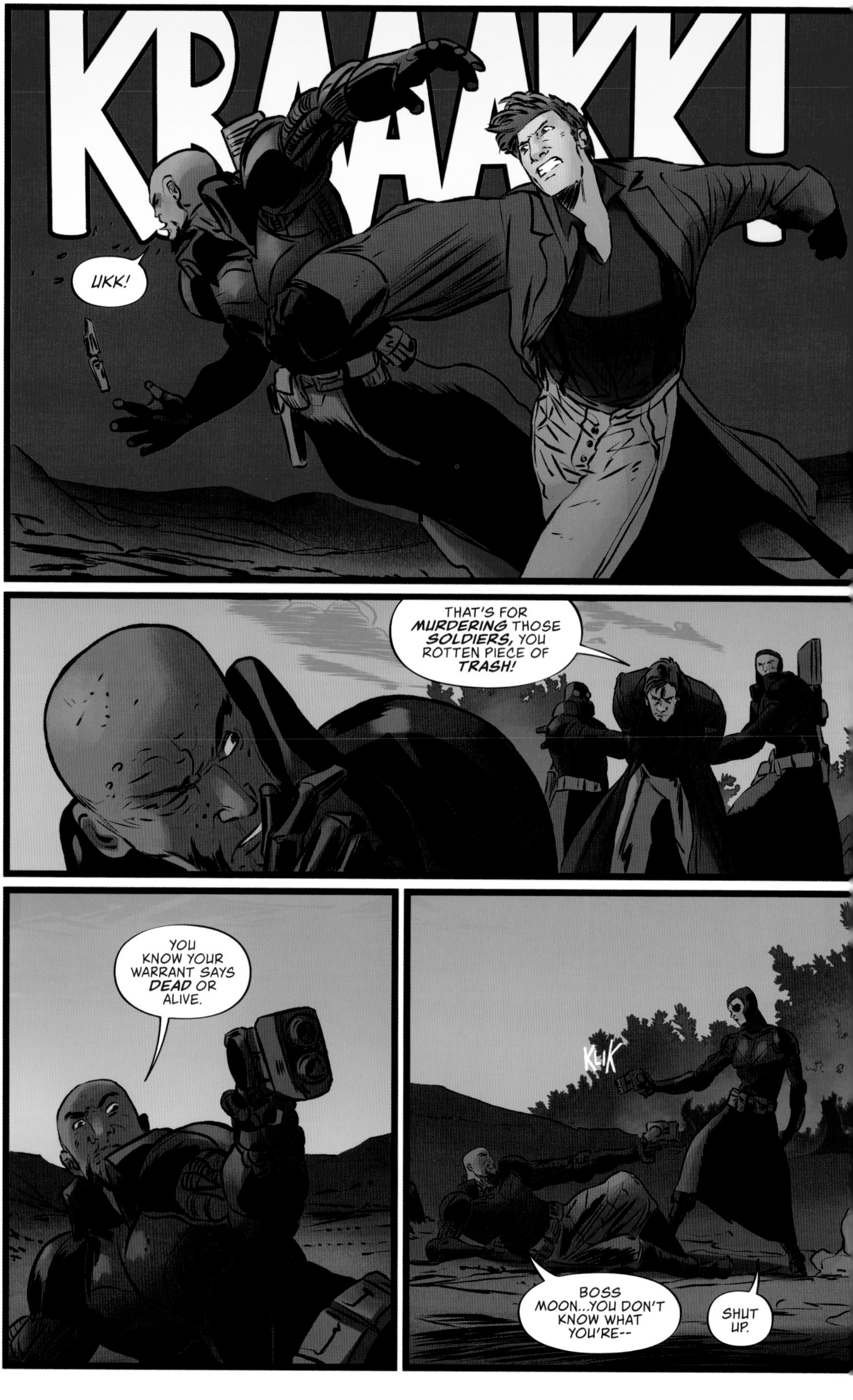
KRAAKK!
UKK!
THAT'S FOR MURDERING THOSE SOLDIERS, YOU ROTTEN PIECE OF TRASH!
YOU KNOW YOUR WARRANT SAYS DEAD OR ALIVE.
KLIK
BOSS MOON...YOU DON'T KNOW WHAT YOU'RE--
SHUT UP.

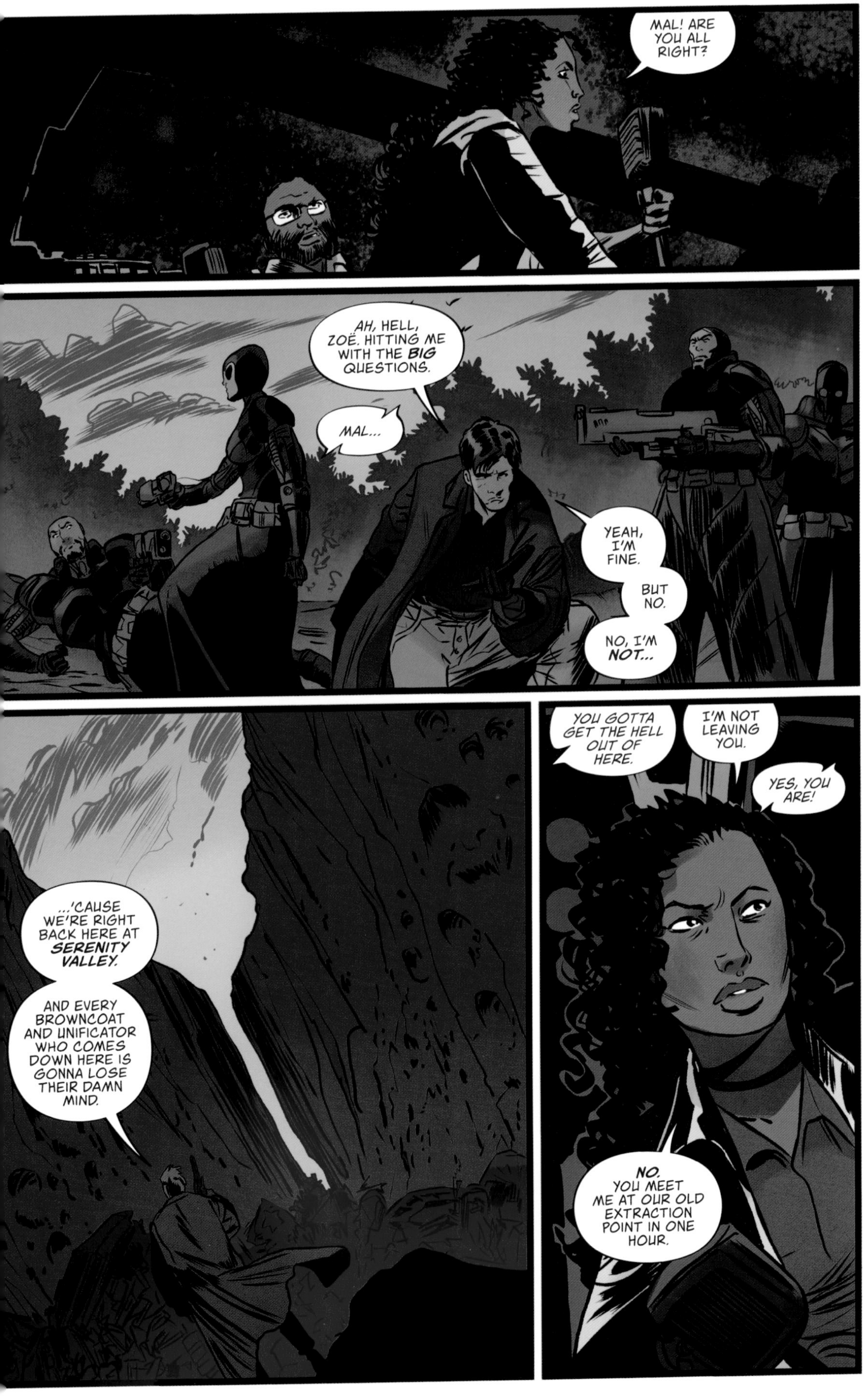
MAL! ARE YOU ALL RIGHT?
AH, HELL, ZOË. HITTING ME WITH THE BIG QUESTIONS.
MAL...
YEAH, I'M FINE.
BUT NO.
NO, I'M NOT...
...'CAUSE WE'RE RIGHT BACK HERE AT SERENITY VALLEY.
AND EVERY BROWNCOAT AND UNIFICATOR WHO COMES DOWN HERE IS GONNA LOSE THEIR DAMN MIND.
YOU GOTTA GET THE HELL OUT OF HERE.
I'M NOT LEAVING YOU.
YES, YOU ARE!
NO. YOU MEET ME AT OUR OLD EXTRACTION POINT IN ONE HOUR.

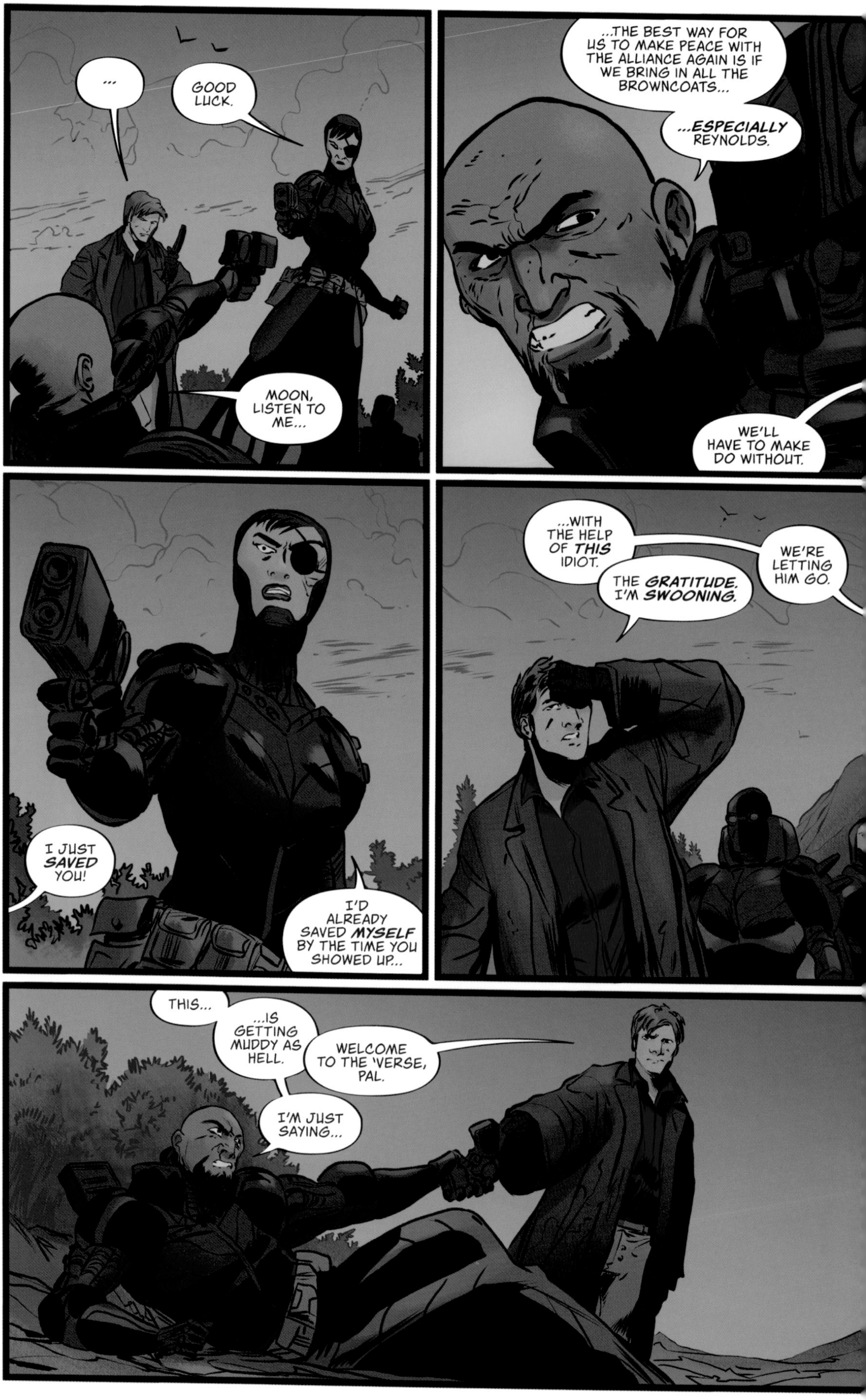
...
GOOD LUCK.
MOON, LISTEN TO ME...
...THE BEST WAY FOR US TO MAKE PEACE WITH THE ALLIANCE AGAIN IS IF WE BRING IN ALL THE BROWNCOATS...
...ESPECIALLY REYNOLDS.
WE'LL HAVE TO MAKE DO WITHOUT.
I JUST SAVED YOU!
I'D ALREADY SAVED MYSELF BY THE TIME YOU SHOWED UP...
...WITH THE HELP OF THIS IDIOT.
THE GRATITUDE. I'M SWOONING.
WE'RE LETTING HIM GO.
THIS...
...IS GETTING MUDDY AS HELL.
WELCOME TO THE 'VERSE, PAL.
I'M JUST SAYING...

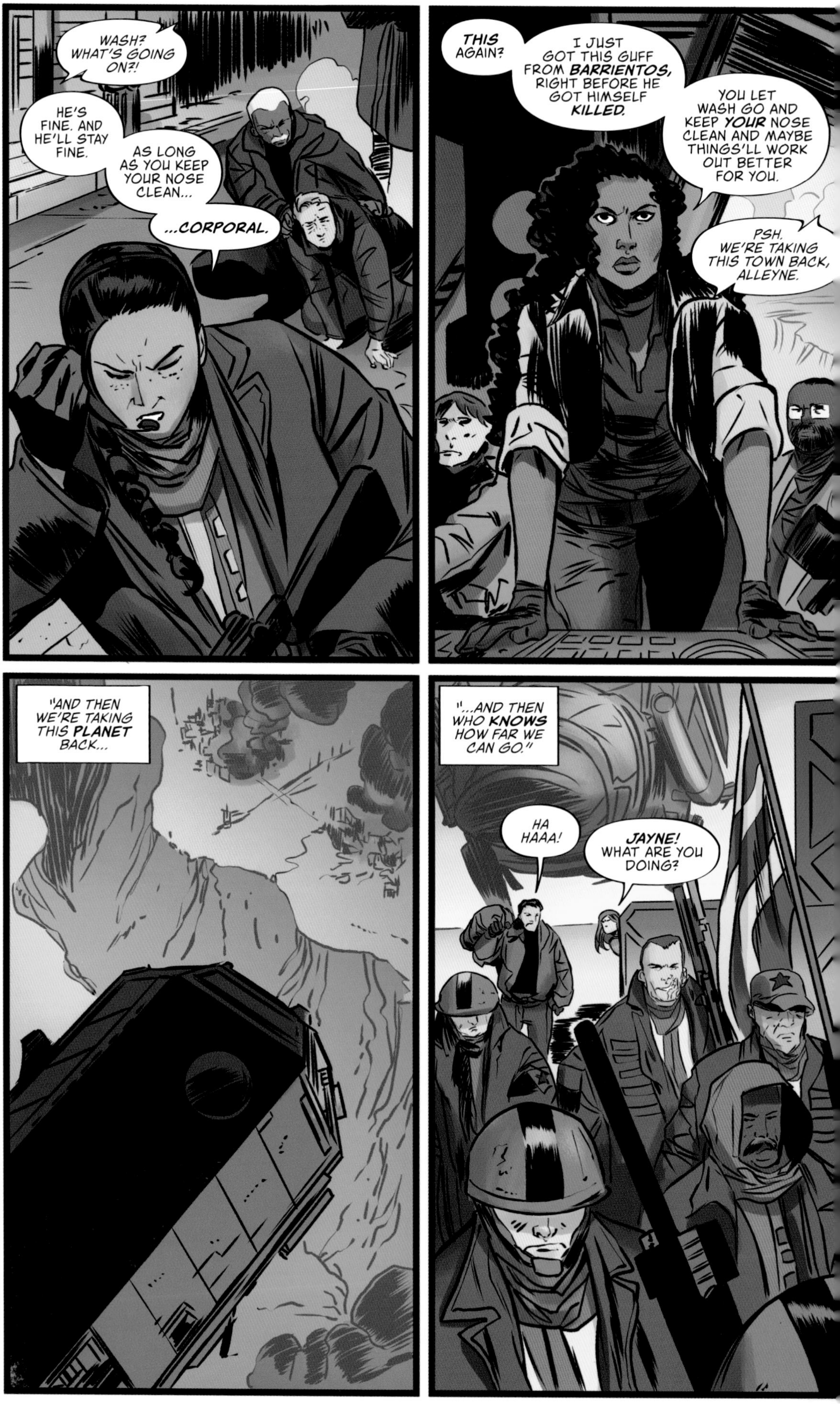
WASH? WHAT'S GOING ON?!
HE'S FINE. AND HE'LL STAY FINE.
AS LONG AS YOU KEEP YOUR NOSE CLEAN...
...CORPORAL.
THIS AGAIN?
I JUST GOT THIS GUFF FROM BARRIENTOS, RIGHT BEFORE HE GOT HIMSELF KILLED.
YOU LET WASH GO AND KEEP YOUR NOSE CLEAN AND MAYBE THINGS'LL WORK OUT BETTER FOR YOU.
PSH. WE'RE TAKING THIS TOWN BACK, ALLEYNE.
"AND THEN WE'RE TAKING THIS PLANET BACK...
"...AND THEN WHO KNOWS HOW FAR WE CAN GO."
HA HAAA!
JAYNE! WHAT ARE YOU DOING?

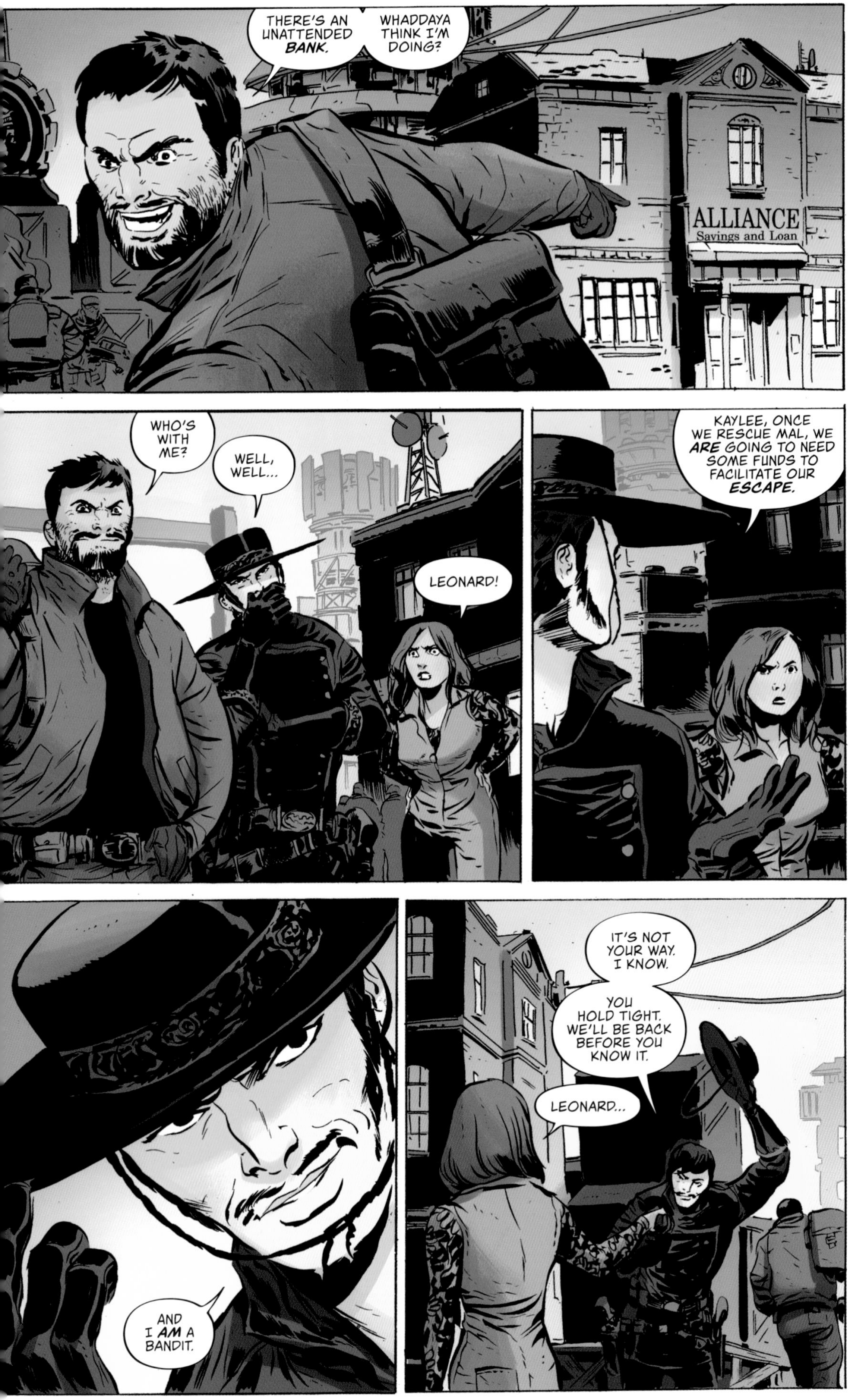
THERE'S AN UNATTENDED BANK.
WHADDAYA THINK I'M DOING?
ALLIANCE Savings and Loan
WHO'S WITH ME?
WELL, WELL...
LEONARD!
KAYLEE, ONCE WE RESCUE MAL, WE ARE GOING TO NEED SOME FUNDS TO FACILITATE OUR ESCAPE.
AND I AM A BANDIT.
IT'S NOT YOUR WAY. I KNOW.
YOU HOLD TIGHT. WE'LL BE BACK BEFORE YOU KNOW IT.
LEONARD...

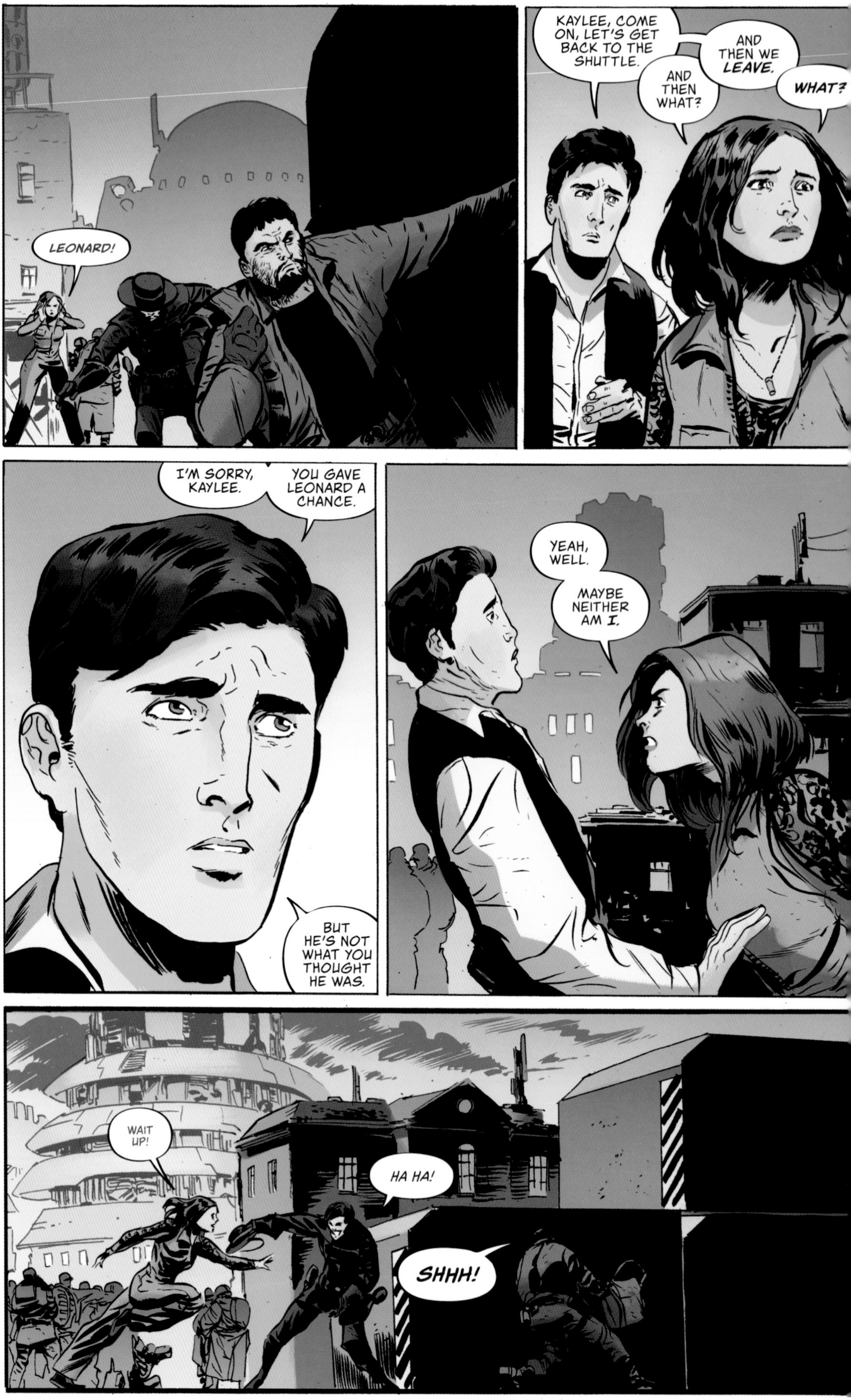
LEONARD!
KAYLEE, COME ON, LET'S GET BACK TO THE SHUTTLE.
AND THEN WHAT?
AND THEN WE LEAVE.
WHAT?
I'M SORRY, KAYLEE.
YOU GAVE LEONARD A CHANCE.
BUT HE'S NOT WHAT YOU THOUGHT HE WAS.
YEAH, WELL.
MAYBE NEITHER AM I.
WAIT UP!
HA HA!
SHHH!

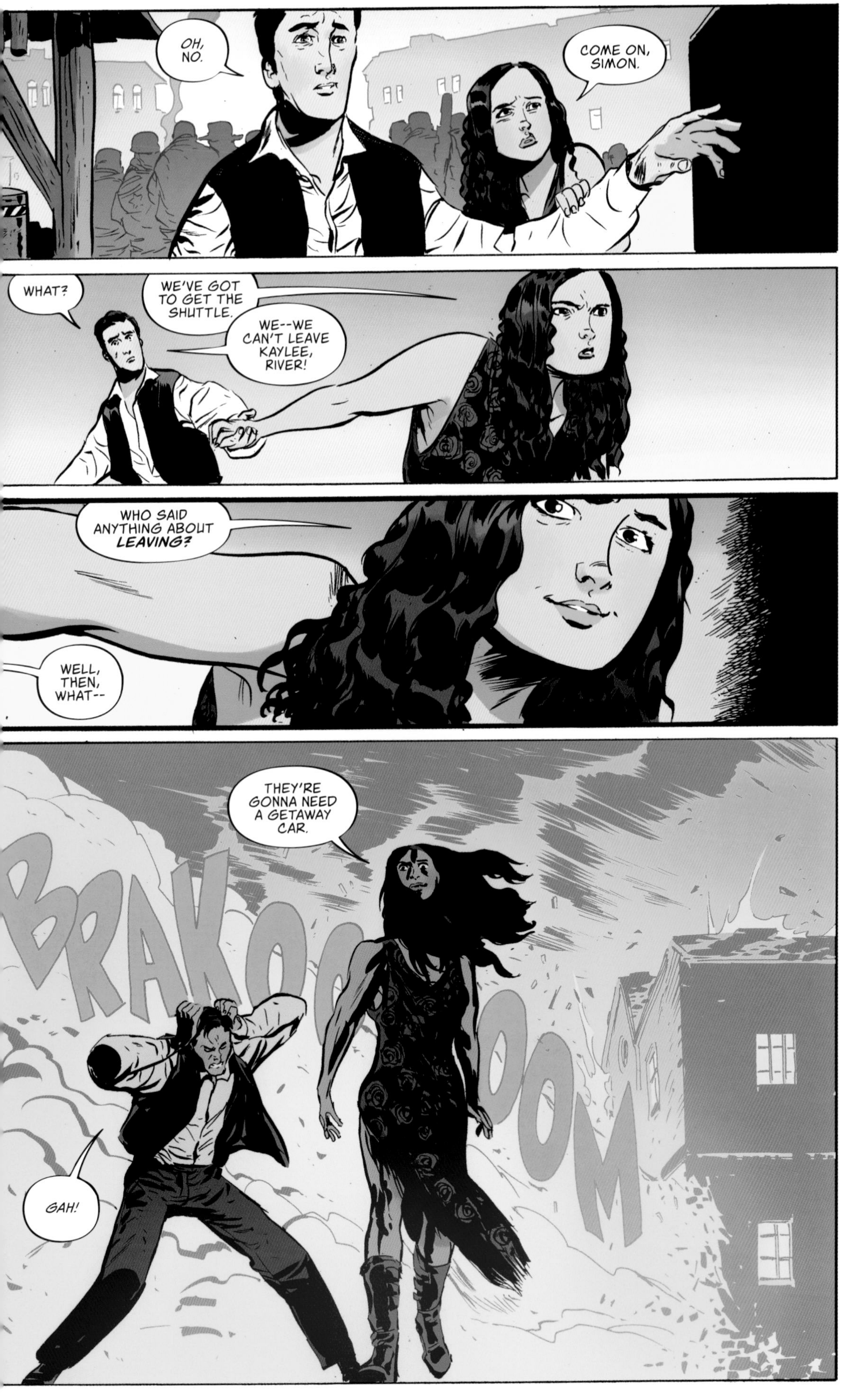
OH, NO.
COME ON, SIMON.
WHAT?
WE'VE GOT TO GET THE SHUTTLE.
WE--WE CAN'T LEAVE KAYLEE, RIVER!
WHO SAID ANYTHING ABOUT *LEAVING?*
WELL, THEN, WHAT--
THEY'RE GONNA NEED A GETAWAY CAR.
BRAKOOOOM
GAH!

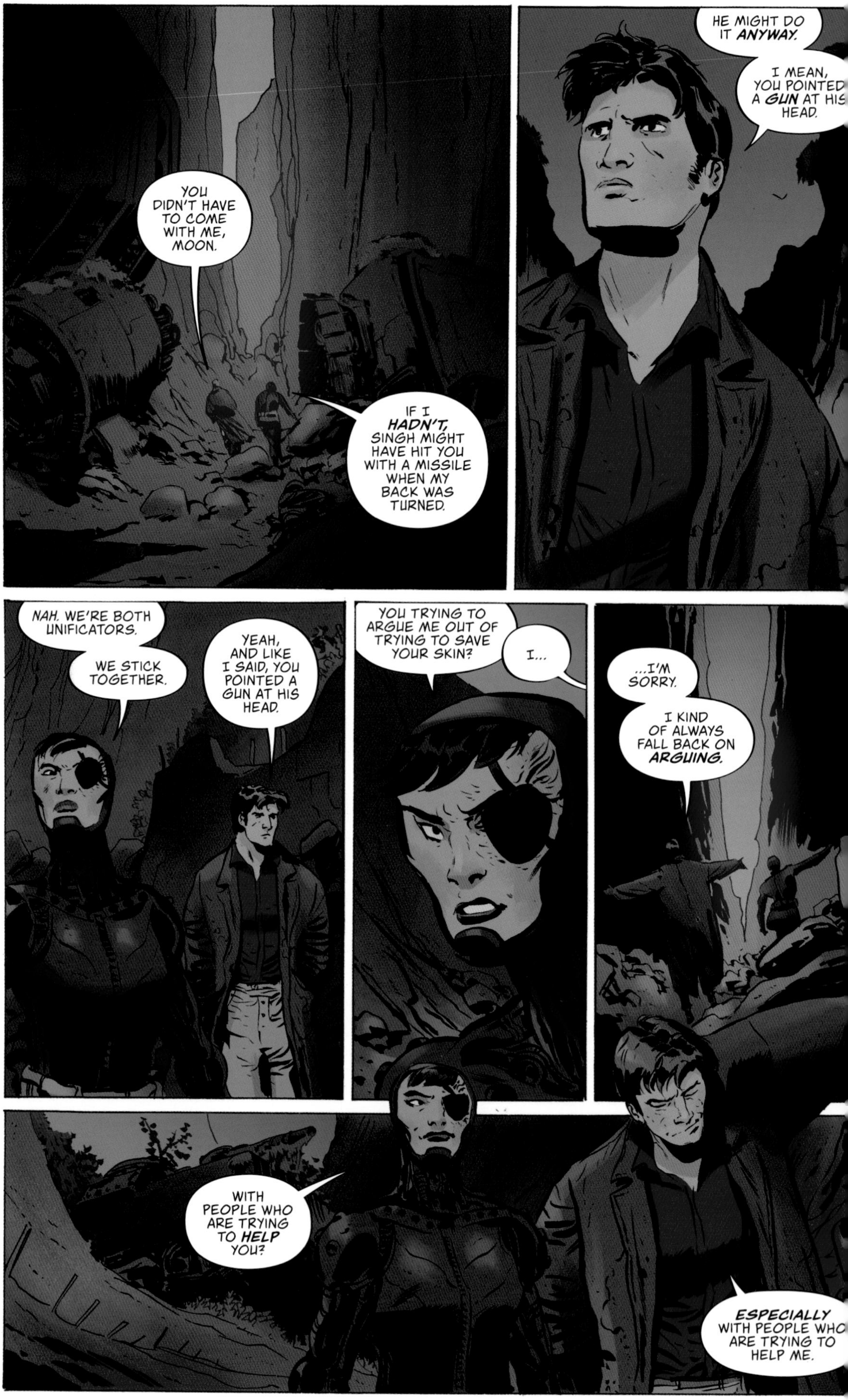

YOU DIDN'T HAVE TO COME WITH ME, MOON.
IF I HADN'T, SINGH MIGHT HAVE HIT YOU WITH A MISSILE WHEN MY BACK WAS TURNED.
HE MIGHT DO IT ANYWAY.
I MEAN, YOU POINTED A GUN AT HIS HEAD.
NAH. WE'RE BOTH UNIFICATORS.
WE STICK TOGETHER.
YEAH, AND LIKE I SAID, YOU POINTED A GUN AT HIS HEAD.
YOU TRYING TO ARGUE ME OUT OF TRYING TO SAVE YOUR SKIN?
I...
...I'M SORRY.
I KIND OF ALWAYS FALL BACK ON ARGUING.
WITH PEOPLE WHO ARE TRYING TO HELP YOU?
ESPECIALLY WITH PEOPLE WHO ARE TRYING TO HELP ME.

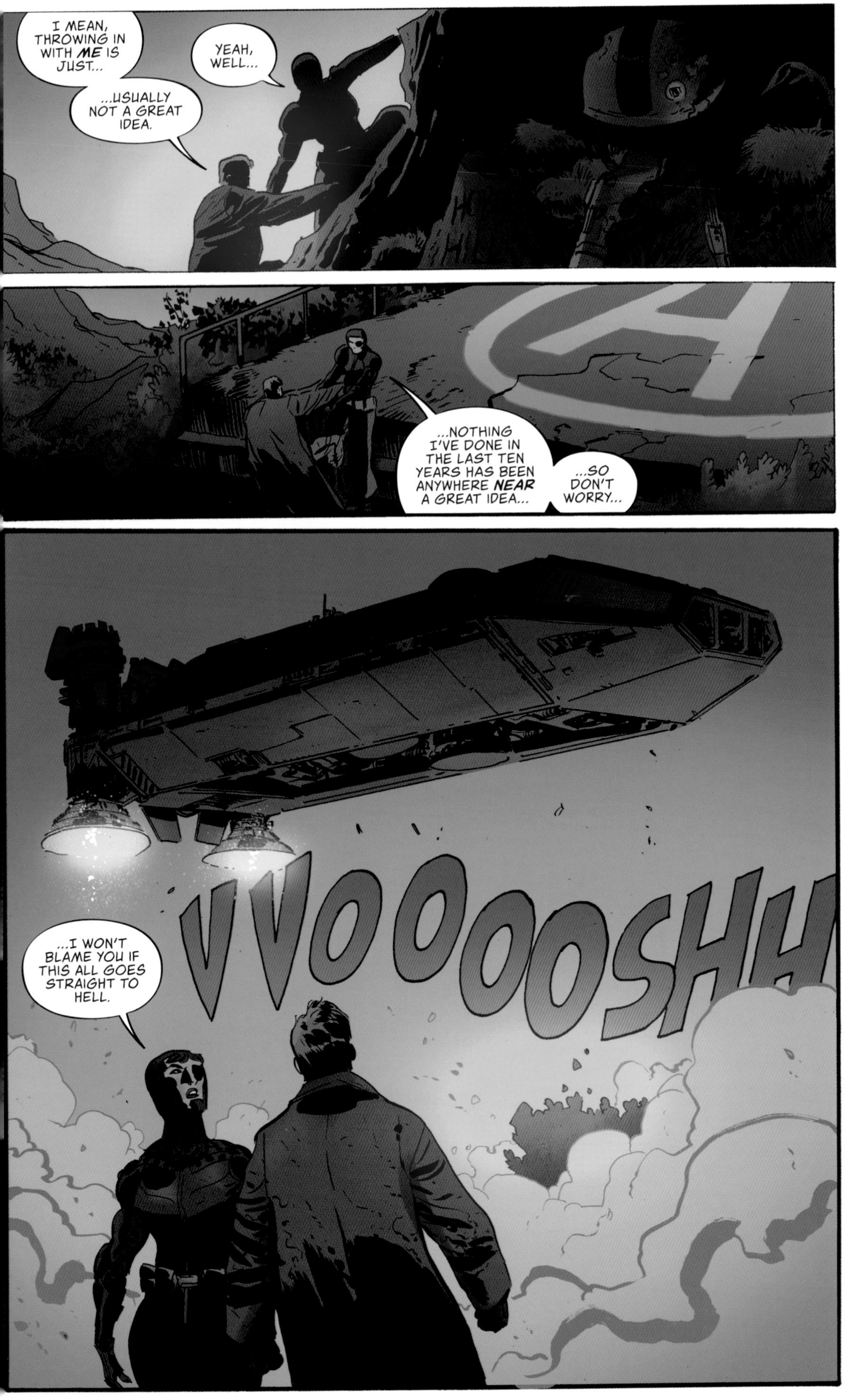
I MEAN, THROWING IN WITH *ME* IS JUST...
YEAH, WELL...
...USUALLY NOT A GREAT IDEA.
...NOTHING I'VE DONE IN THE LAST TEN YEARS HAS BEEN ANYWHERE *NEAR* A GREAT IDEA...
...SO DON'T WORRY...
VVOOOOSHH
...I WON'T BLAME YOU IF THIS ALL GOES STRAIGHT TO HELL.

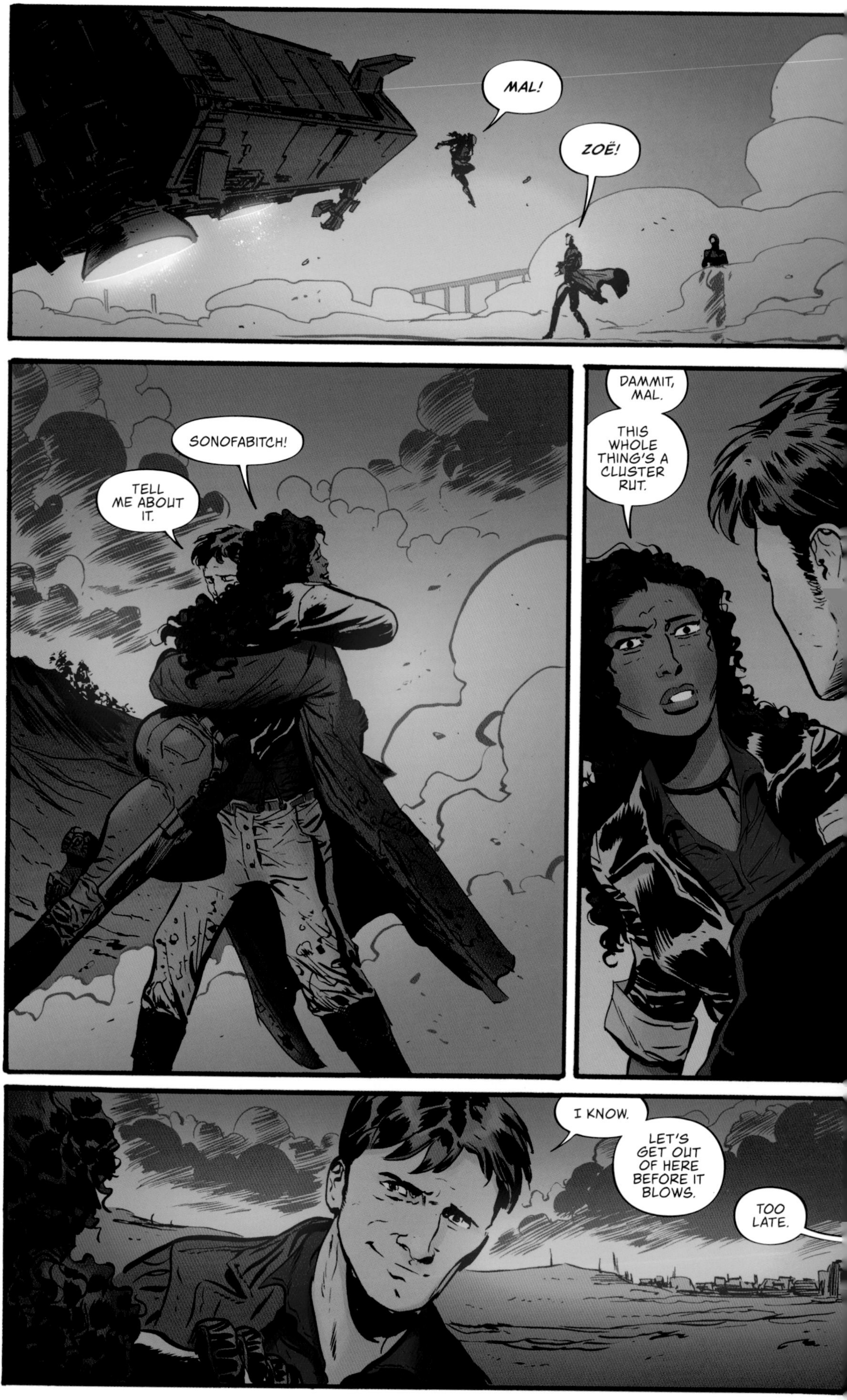
MAL!
ZOË!
SONOFABITCH!
TELL ME ABOUT IT.
DAMMIT, MAL.
THIS WHOLE THING'S A CLUSTER RUT.
I KNOW.
LET'S GET OUT OF HERE BEFORE IT BLOWS.
TOO LATE.

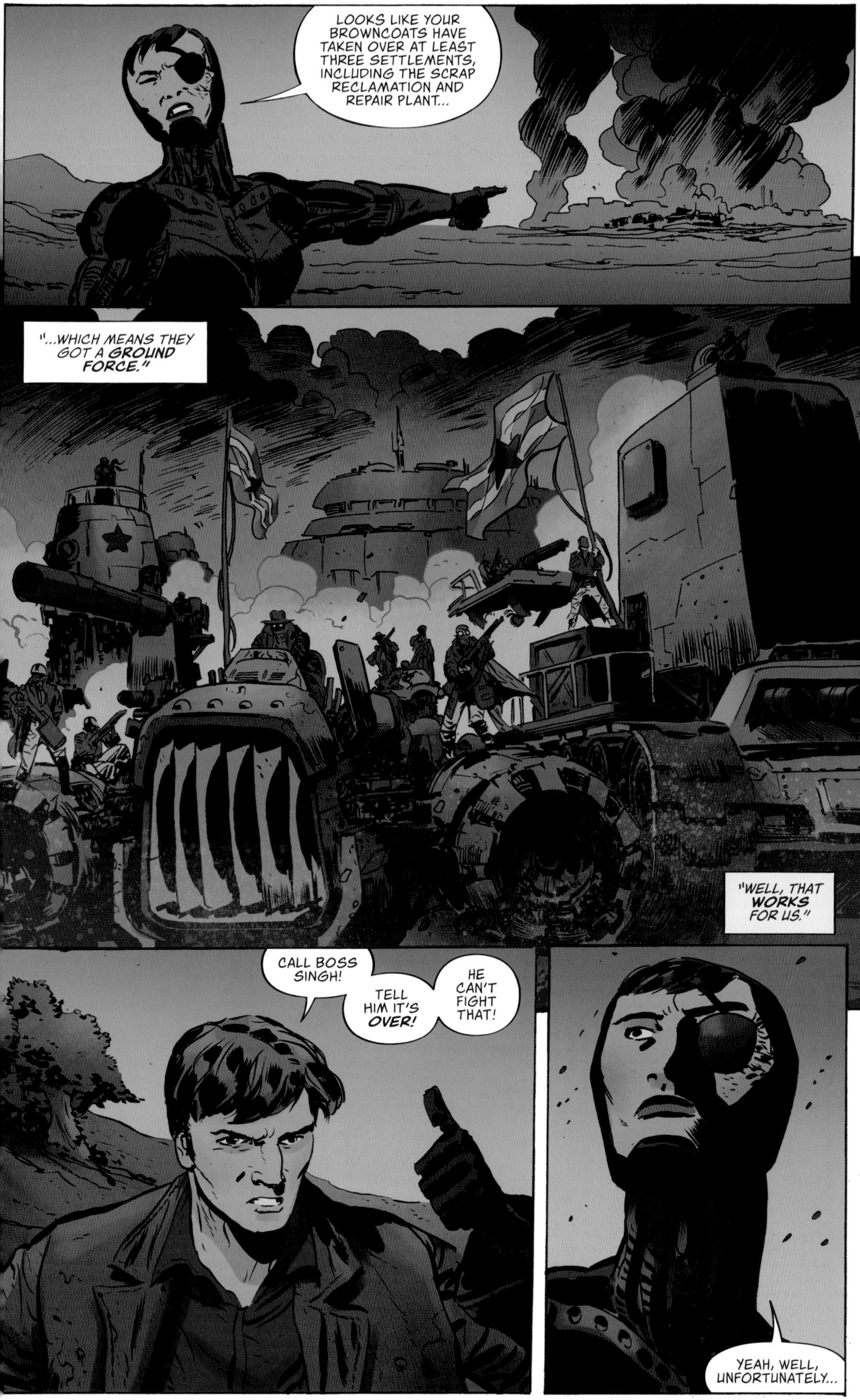
LOOKS LIKE YOUR BROWNCOATS HAVE TAKEN OVER AT LEAST THREE SETTLEMENTS, INCLUDING THE SCRAP RECLAMATION AND REPAIR PLANT...
"...WHICH MEANS THEY GOT A GROUND FORCE."
"WELL, THAT WORKS FOR US."
CALL BOSS SINGH!
TELL HIM IT'S OVER!
HE CAN'T FIGHT THAT!
YEAH, WELL, UNFORTUNATELY...

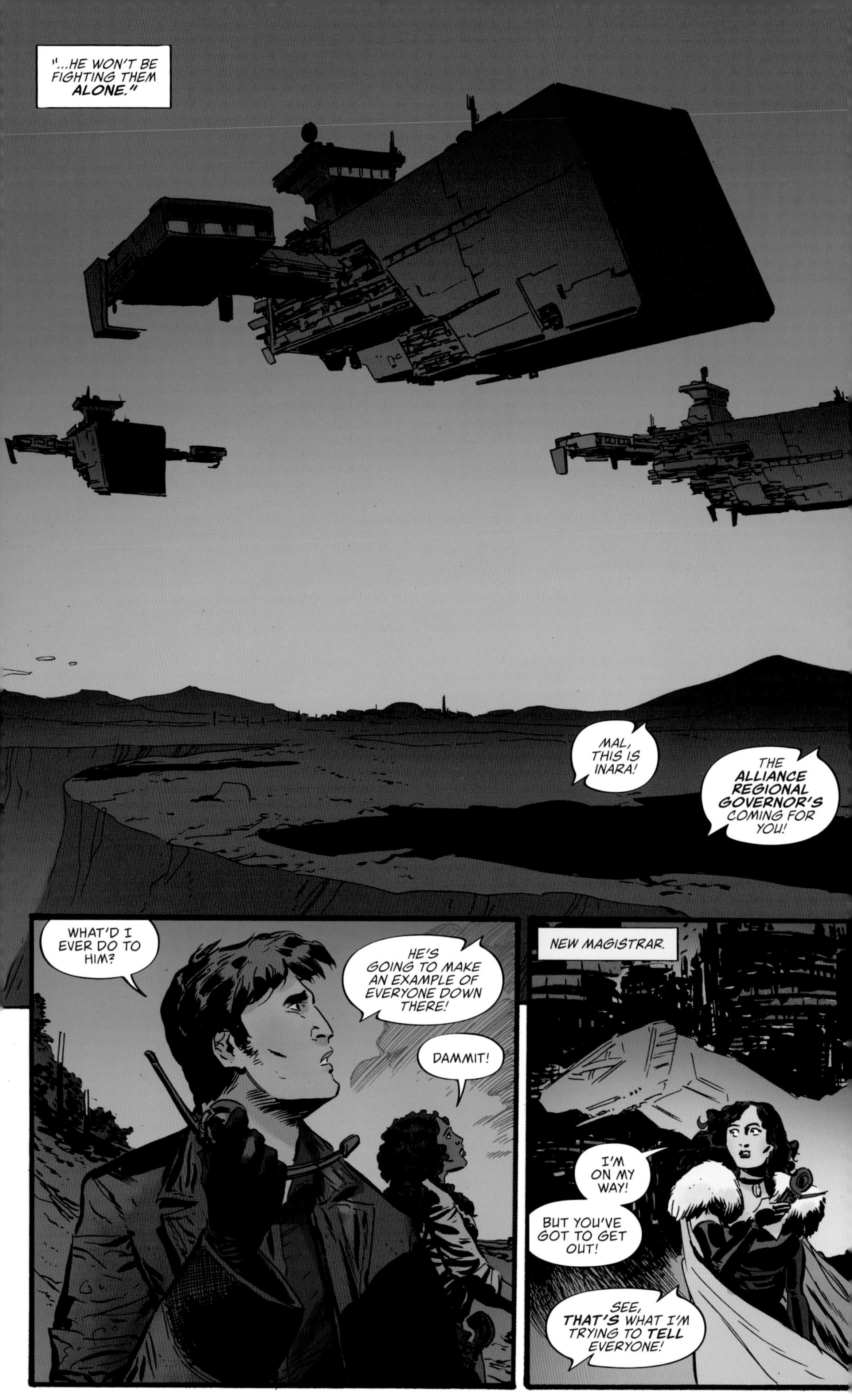
"...HE WON'T BE FIGHTING THEM ALONE."
MAL, THIS IS INARA!
THE ALLIANCE REGIONAL GOVERNOR'S COMING FOR YOU!
WHAT'D I EVER DO TO HIM?
HE'S GOING TO MAKE AN EXAMPLE OF EVERYONE DOWN THERE!
DAMMIT!
NEW MAGISTRAR.
I'M ON MY WAY!
BUT YOU'VE GOT TO GET OUT!
SEE, THAT'S WHAT I'M TRYING TO TELL EVERYONE!

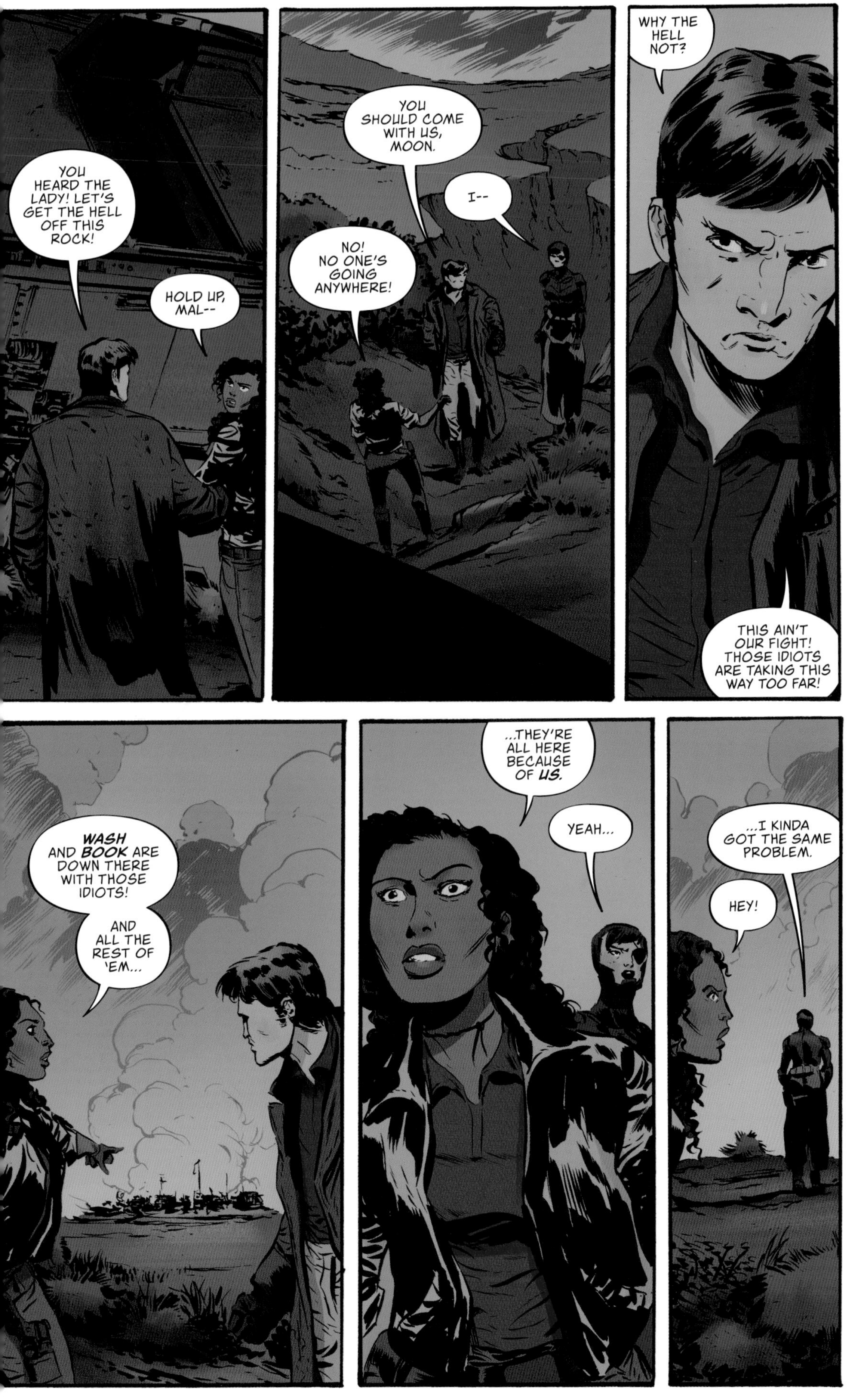
YOU HEARD THE LADY! LET'S GET THE HELL OFF THIS ROCK!
HOLD UP, MAL--
YOU SHOULD COME WITH US, MOON.
I--
NO! NO ONE'S GOING ANYWHERE!
WHY THE HELL NOT?
THIS AIN'T OUR FIGHT! THOSE IDIOTS ARE TAKING THIS WAY TOO FAR!
WASH AND BOOK ARE DOWN THERE WITH THOSE IDIOTS!
AND ALL THE REST OF 'EM...
...THEY'RE ALL HERE BECAUSE OF US.
YEAH...
...I KINDA GOT THE SAME PROBLEM.
HEY!

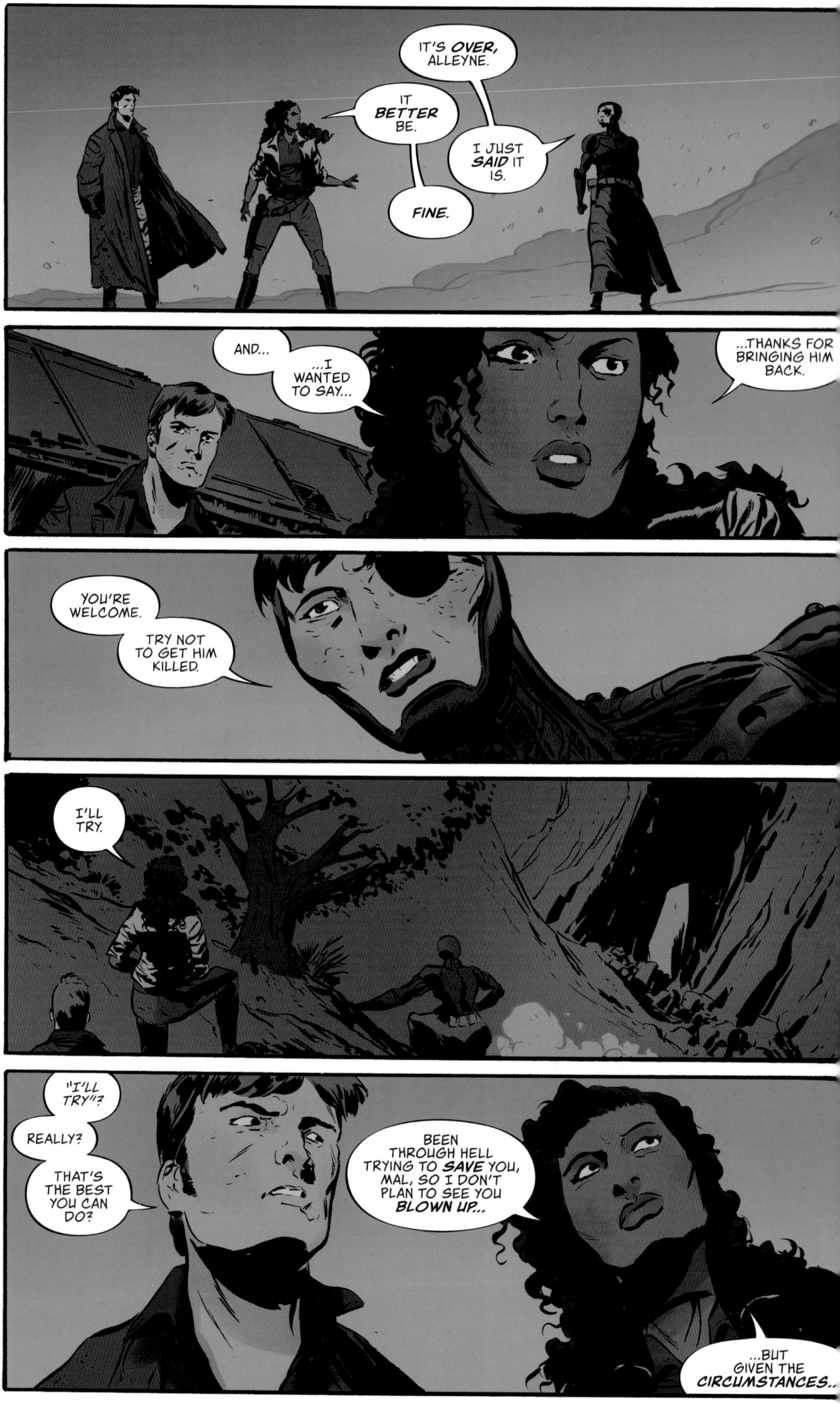

IT'S OVER, ALLEYNE.
IT BETTER BE.
I JUST SAID IT IS.
FINE.
AND...
...I WANTED TO SAY...
...THANKS FOR BRINGING HIM BACK.
YOU'RE WELCOME.
TRY NOT TO GET HIM KILLED.
I'LL TRY.
"I'LL TRY"?
REALLY?
THAT'S THE BEST YOU CAN DO?
BEEN THROUGH HELL TRYING TO SAVE YOU, MAL, SO I DON'T PLAN TO SEE YOU BLOWN UP...
...BUT GIVEN THE CIRCUMSTANCES...

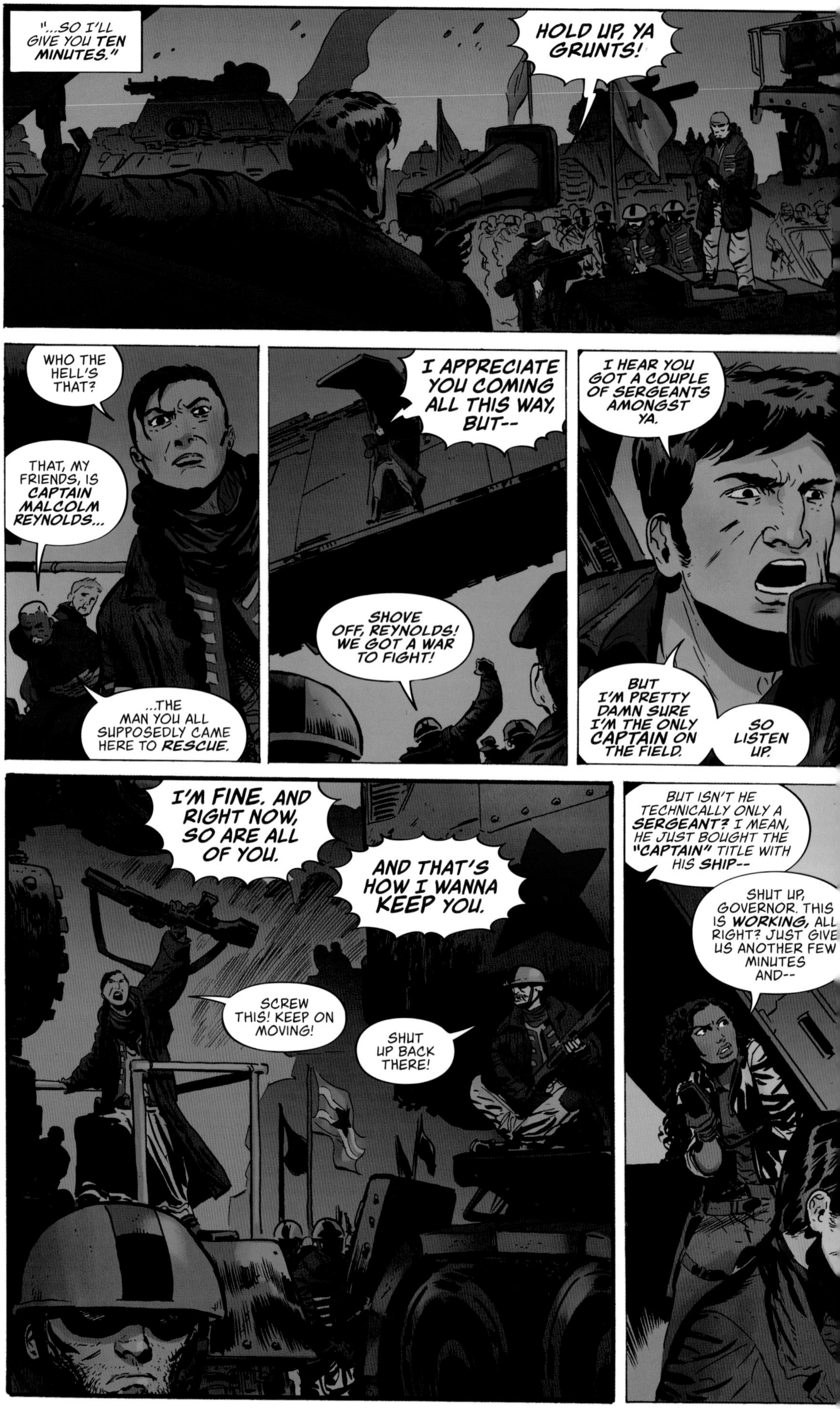
"...SO I'LL GIVE YOU TEN MINUTES."
HOLD UP, YA GRUNTS!
WHO THE HELL'S THAT?
THAT, MY FRIENDS, IS CAPTAIN MALCOLM REYNOLDS...
...THE MAN YOU ALL SUPPOSEDLY CAME HERE TO RESCUE.
I APPRECIATE YOU COMING ALL THIS WAY, BUT--
SHOVE OFF, REYNOLDS! WE GOT A WAR TO FIGHT!
I HEAR YOU GOT A COUPLE OF SERGEANTS AMONGST YA.
BUT I'M PRETTY DAMN SURE I'M THE ONLY CAPTAIN ON THE FIELD.
SO LISTEN UP.
I'M FINE. AND RIGHT NOW, SO ARE ALL OF YOU.
AND THAT'S HOW I WANNA KEEP YOU.
SCREW THIS! KEEP ON MOVING!
SHUT UP BACK THERE!
BUT ISN'T HE TECHNICALLY ONLY A SERGEANT? I MEAN, HE JUST BOUGHT THE "CAPTAIN" TITLE WITH HIS SHIP--
SHUT UP, GOVERNOR. THIS IS WORKING, ALL RIGHT? JUST GIVE US ANOTHER FEW MINUTES AND--

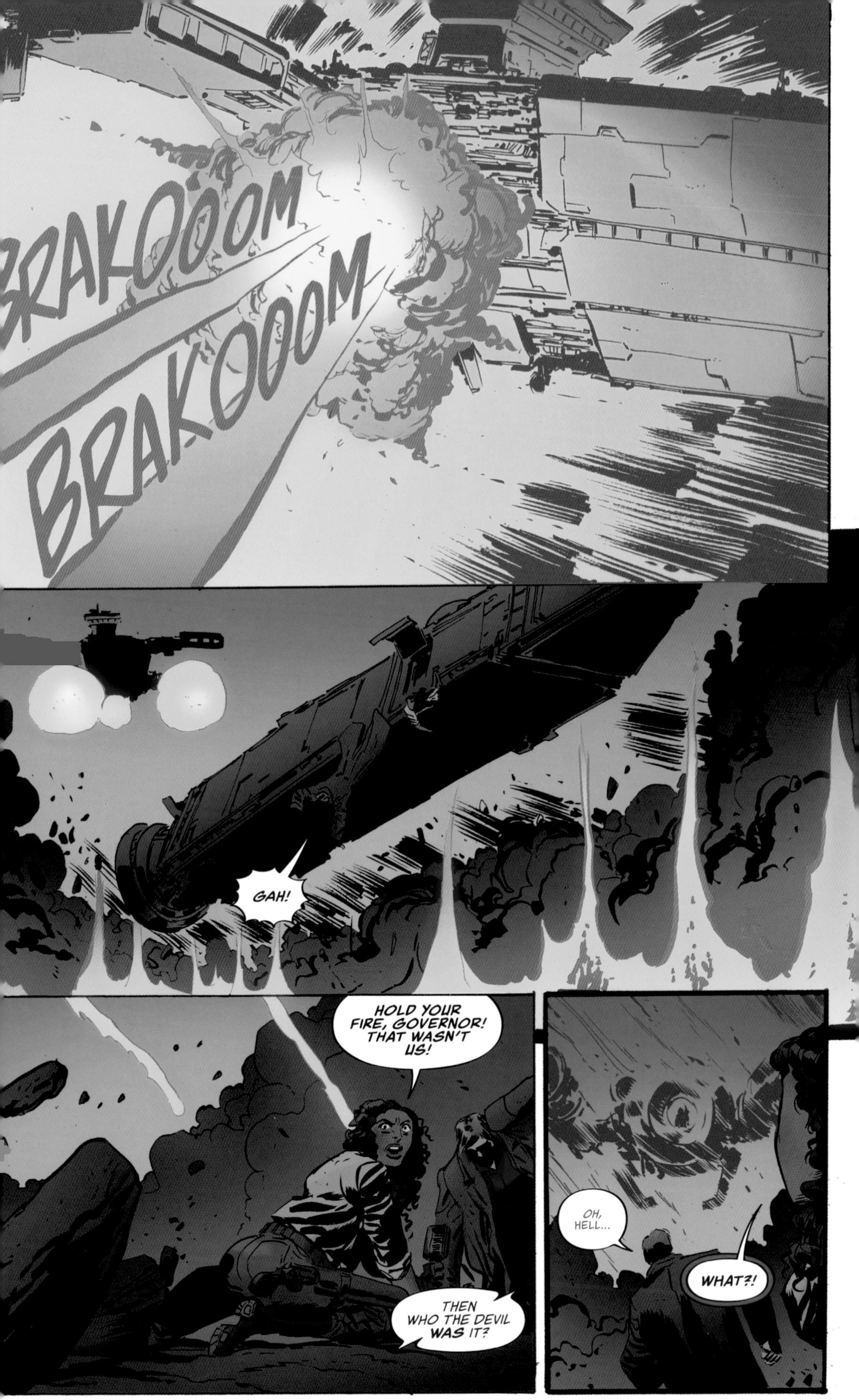
BRAKOOOM
BRAKOOOM
GAH!
HOLD YOUR FIRE, GOVERNOR! THAT WASN'T US!
THEN WHO THE DEVIL WAS IT?
OH, HELL...
WHAT?!

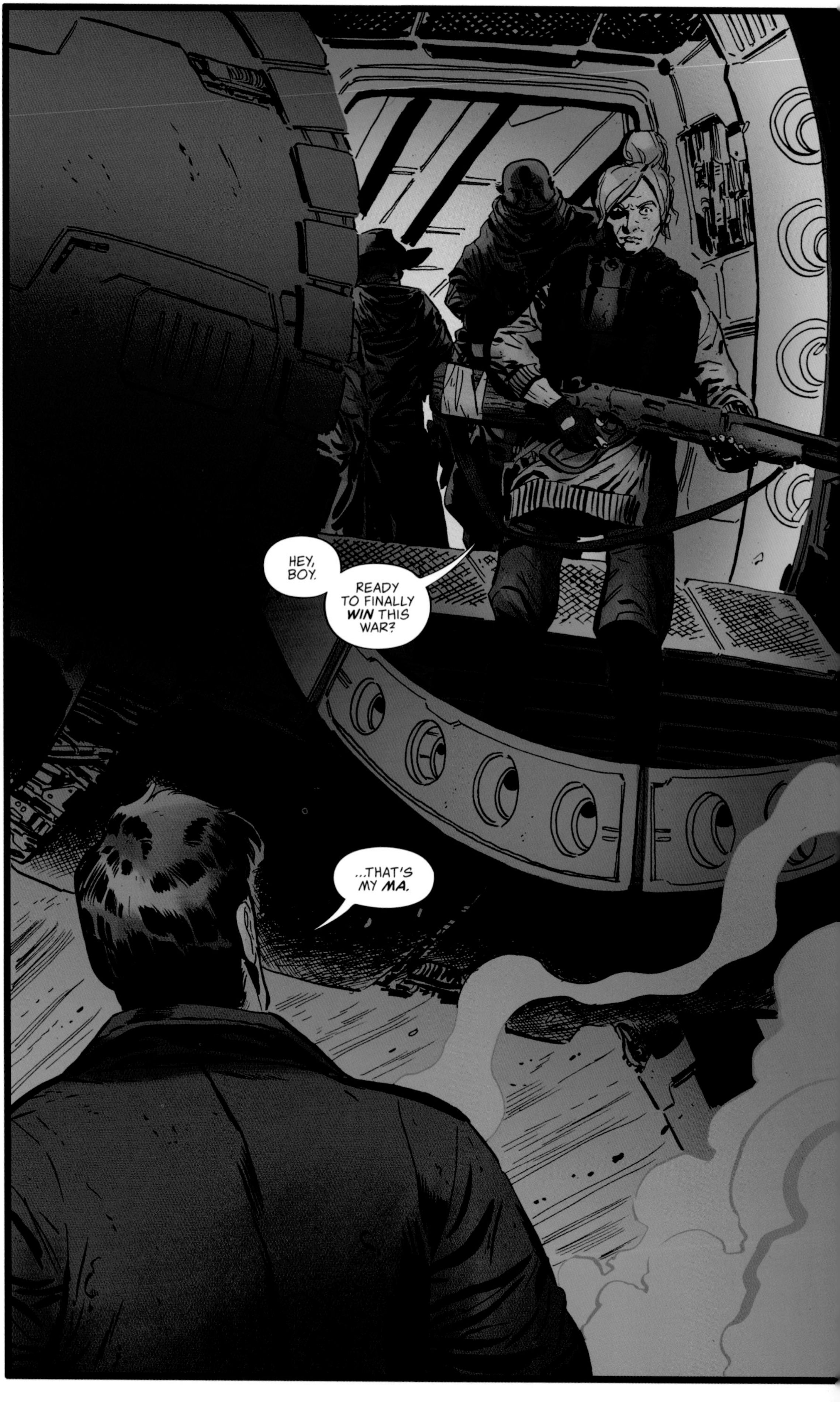
HEY, BOY.
READY TO FINALLY WIN THIS WAR?
...THAT'S MY MA.

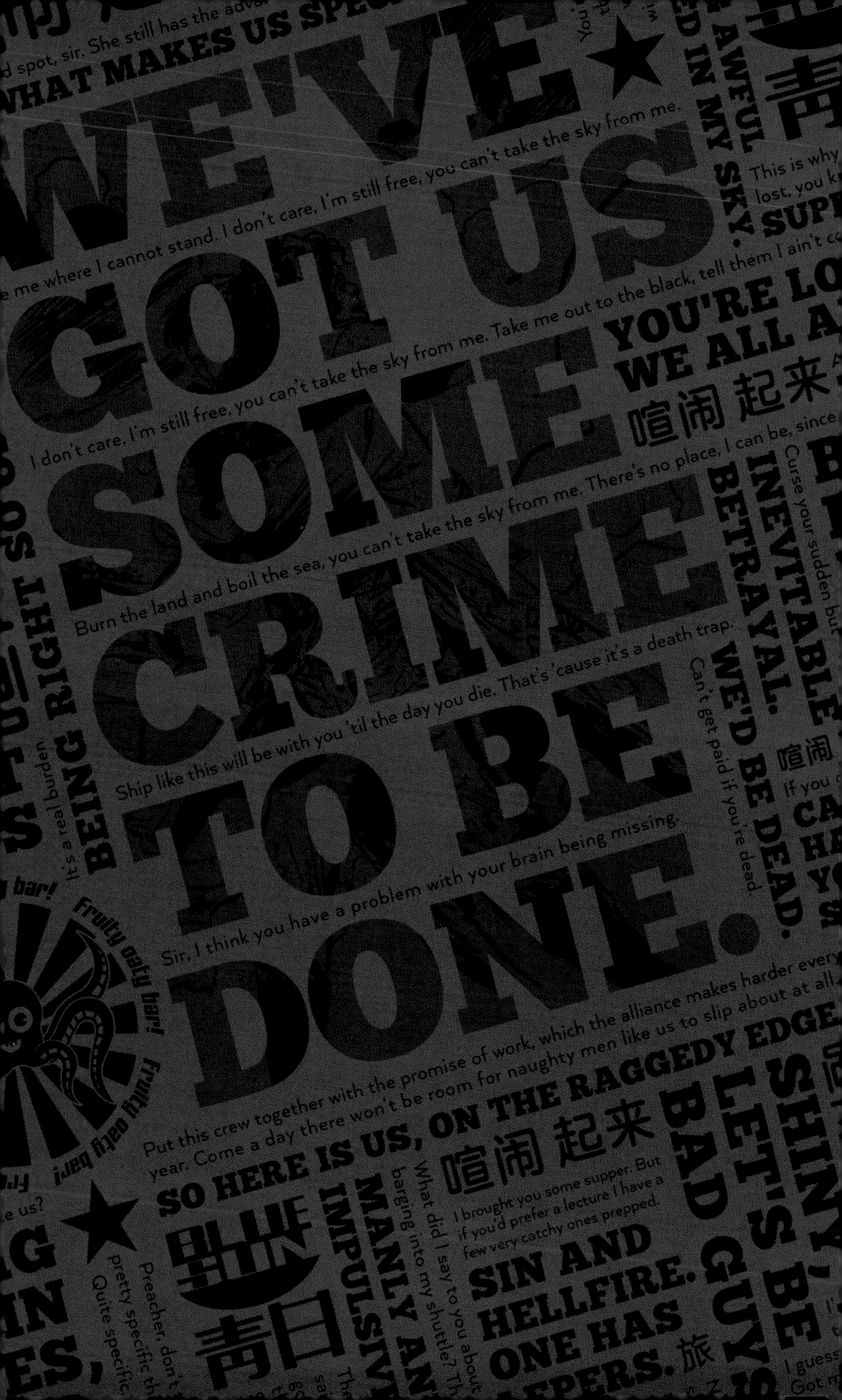
WE'VE GOT US SOME CRIME TO BE DONE.
I don't care, I'm still free, you can't take the sky from me.
I don't care, I'm still free, you can't take the sky from me. Take me out to the black, tell them I ain't co
me where I cannot stand. I don't care, I'm still free, you can't take the sky from me.
Burn the land and boil the sea, you can't take the sky from me. There's no place, I can be, since
Ship like this will be with you 'til the day you die. That's 'cause it's a death trap.
Sir, I think you have a problem with your brain being missing.
Put this crew together with the promise of work, which the alliance makes harder every
year. Come a day there won't be room for naughty men like us to slip about at all.
SO HERE IS US, ON THE RAGGEDY EDGE
喧闹起来
I brought you some supper. But if you'd prefer a lecture I have a few very catchy ones prepped.
SIN AND HELLFIRE.
ONE HAS
WHAT MAKES US SPE
d spot, sir. She still has the adv
YOU'RE LO
WE ALL A
喧闹 起来
IN MY SKY.
AWFUL
This is why
lost, you k
INEVITABLE
BETRAYAL.
Curse your sudden but
WE'D BE DEAD.
Can't get paid if you're dead
It's a real burden
BEING RIGHT
Fruity oaty bar!
What did I say to you about barging into my shuttle?
MANLY AN
IMPULSIV
Preacher, don't
pretty specific
Quite specific
LET'S BE BAD GUY
SHINY,
青日

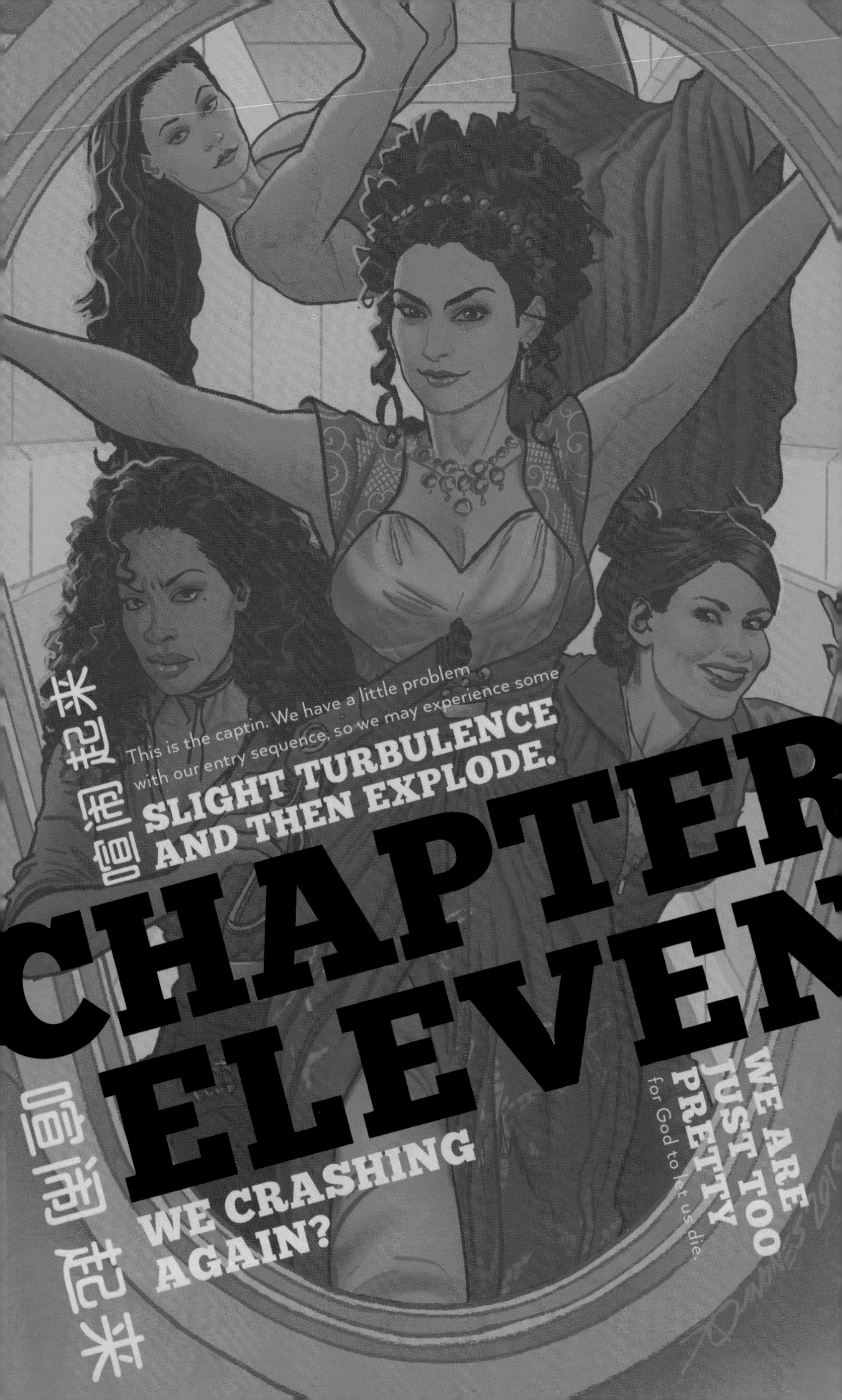
喧闹起来
This is the captin. We have a little problem with our entry sequence, so we may experience some
SLIGHT TURBULENCE AND THEN EXPLODE.
CHAPTER ELEVEN
喧闹起来
WE CRASHING AGAIN?
WE ARE JUST TOO PRETTY
for God to let us die.

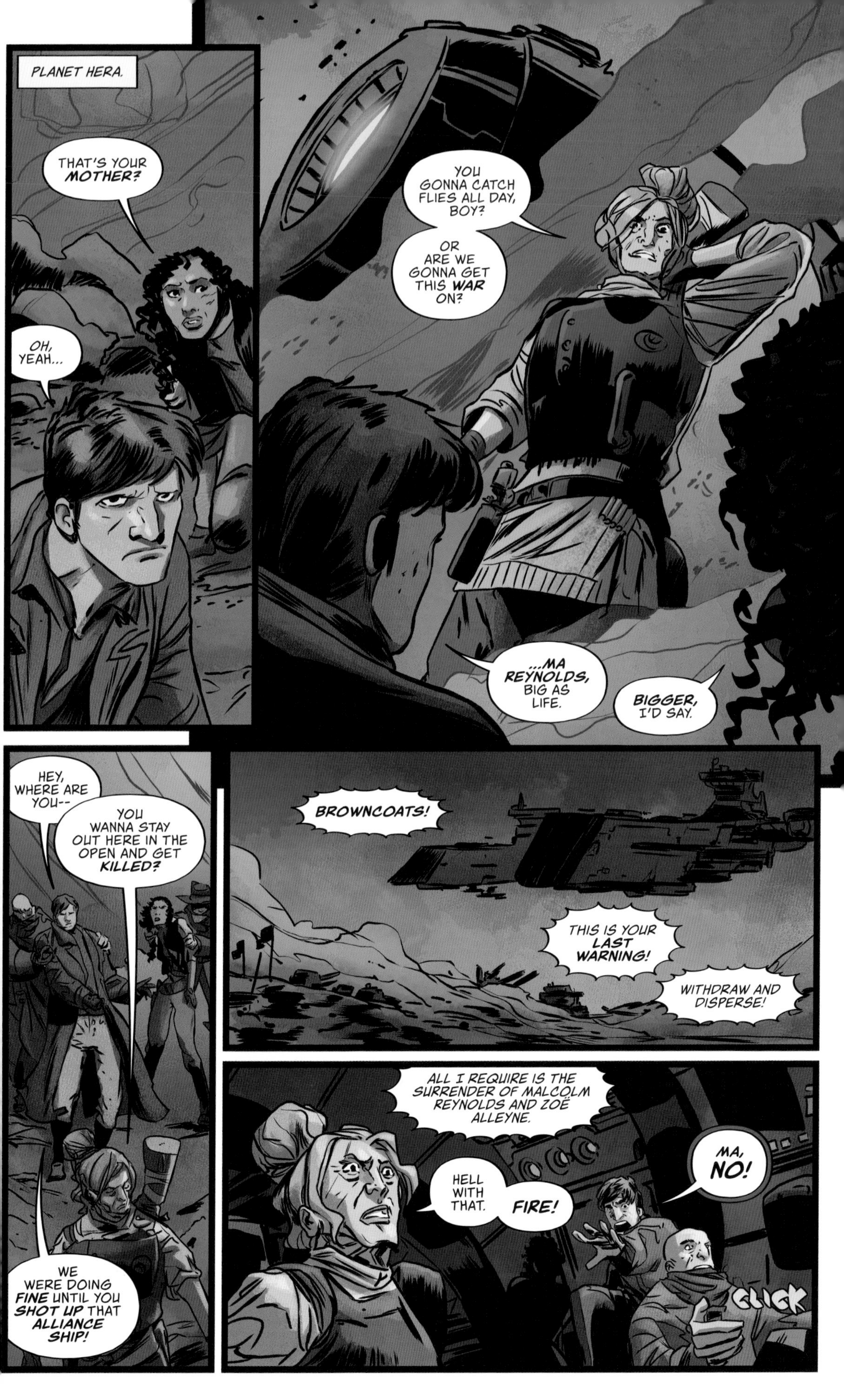
PLANET HERA.
THAT'S YOUR MOTHER?
OH, YEAH...
YOU GONNA CATCH FLIES ALL DAY, BOY?
OR ARE WE GONNA GET THIS WAR ON?
...MA REYNOLDS, BIG AS LIFE.
BIGGER, I'D SAY.
HEY, WHERE ARE YOU--
YOU WANNA STAY OUT HERE IN THE OPEN AND GET KILLED?
WE WERE DOING FINE UNTIL YOU SHOT UP THAT ALLIANCE SHIP!
BROWNCOATS!
THIS IS YOUR LAST WARNING!
WITHDRAW AND DISPERSE!
ALL I REQUIRE IS THE SURRENDER OF MALCOLM REYNOLDS AND ZOË ALLEYNE.
HELL WITH THAT.
FIRE!
MA, NO!
CLICK

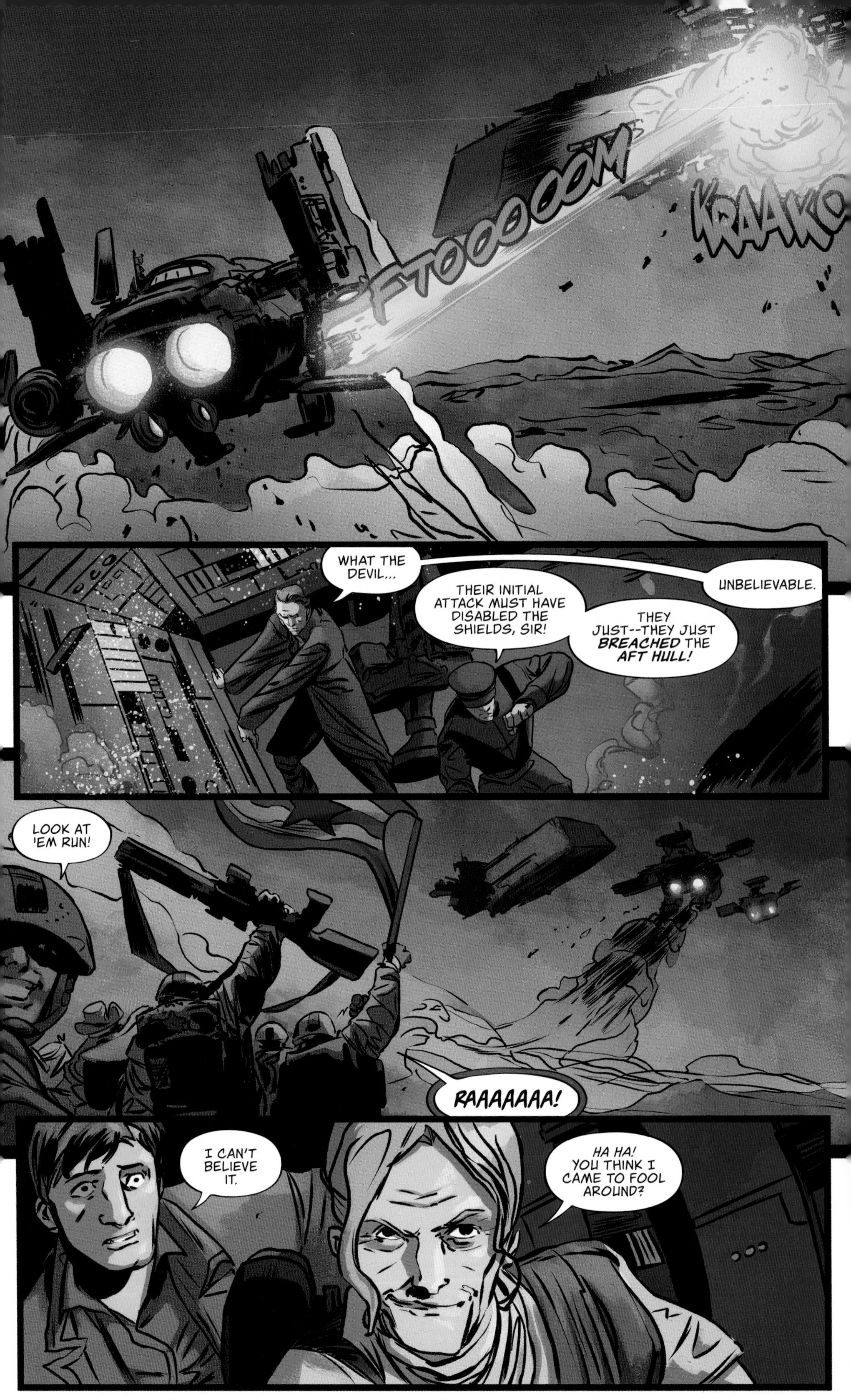
FTOOOOOOM
KRAAKO
WHAT THE DEVIL...
THEIR INITIAL ATTACK MUST HAVE DISABLED THE SHIELDS, SIR!
UNBELIEVABLE.
THEY JUST--THEY JUST BREACHED THE AFT HULL!
LOOK AT 'EM RUN!
RAAAAAAA!
I CAN'T BELIEVE IT.
HA HA! YOU THINK I CAME TO FOOL AROUND?

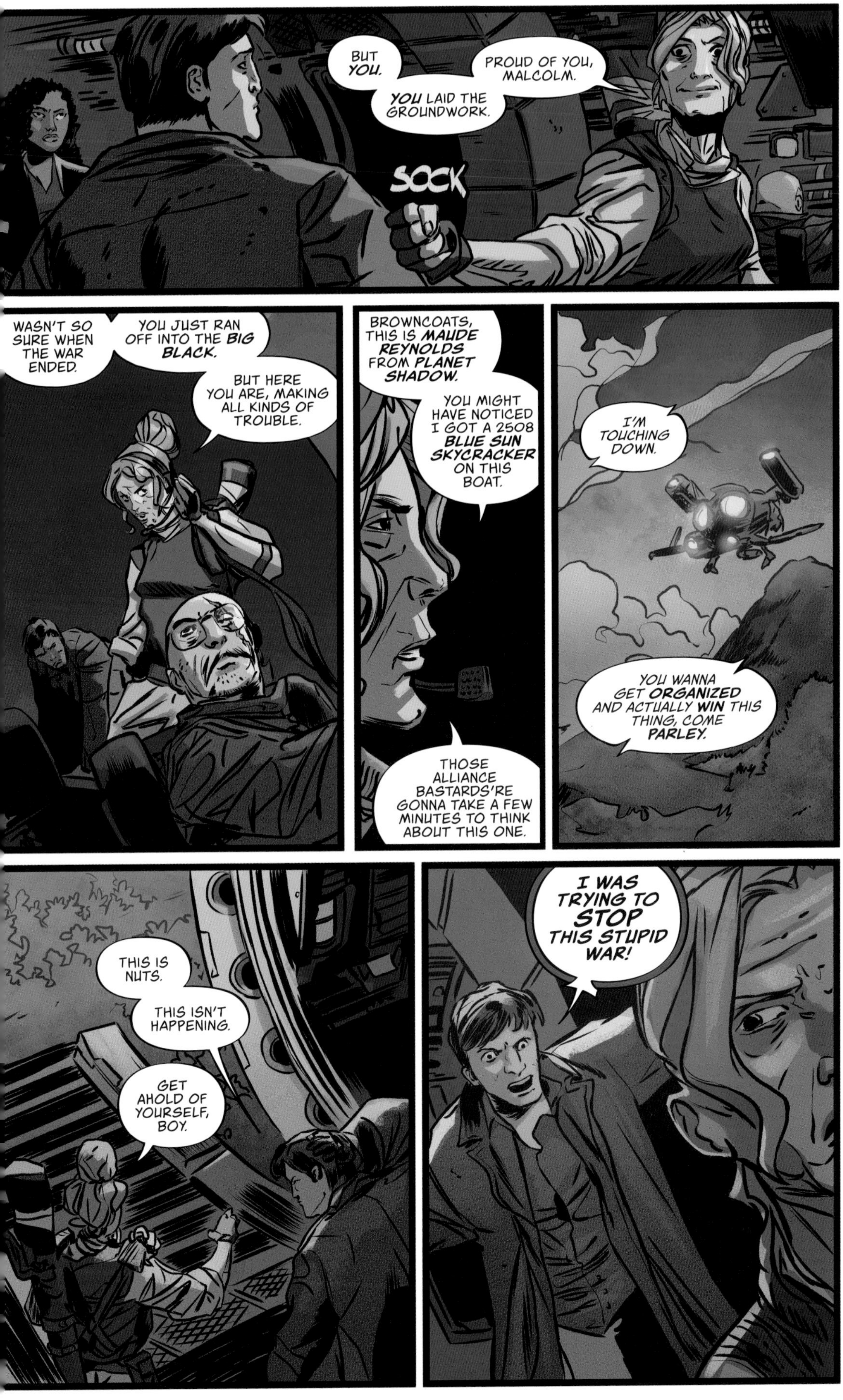
PROUD OF YOU, MALCOLM.
BUT YOU.
YOU LAID THE GROUNDWORK.
SOCK
WASN'T SO SURE WHEN THE WAR ENDED.
YOU JUST RAN OFF INTO THE BIG BLACK.
BUT HERE YOU ARE, MAKING ALL KINDS OF TROUBLE.
BROWNCOATS, THIS IS MAUDE REYNOLDS FROM PLANET SHADOW.
YOU MIGHT HAVE NOTICED I GOT A 2508 BLUE SUN SKYCRACKER ON THIS BOAT.
THOSE ALLIANCE BASTARDS'RE GONNA TAKE A FEW MINUTES TO THINK ABOUT THIS ONE.
I'M TOUCHING DOWN.
YOU WANNA GET ORGANIZED AND ACTUALLY WIN THIS THING, COME PARLEY.
THIS IS NUTS.
THIS ISN'T HAPPENING.
GET AHOLD OF YOURSELF, BOY.
I WAS TRYING TO STOP THIS STUPID WAR!

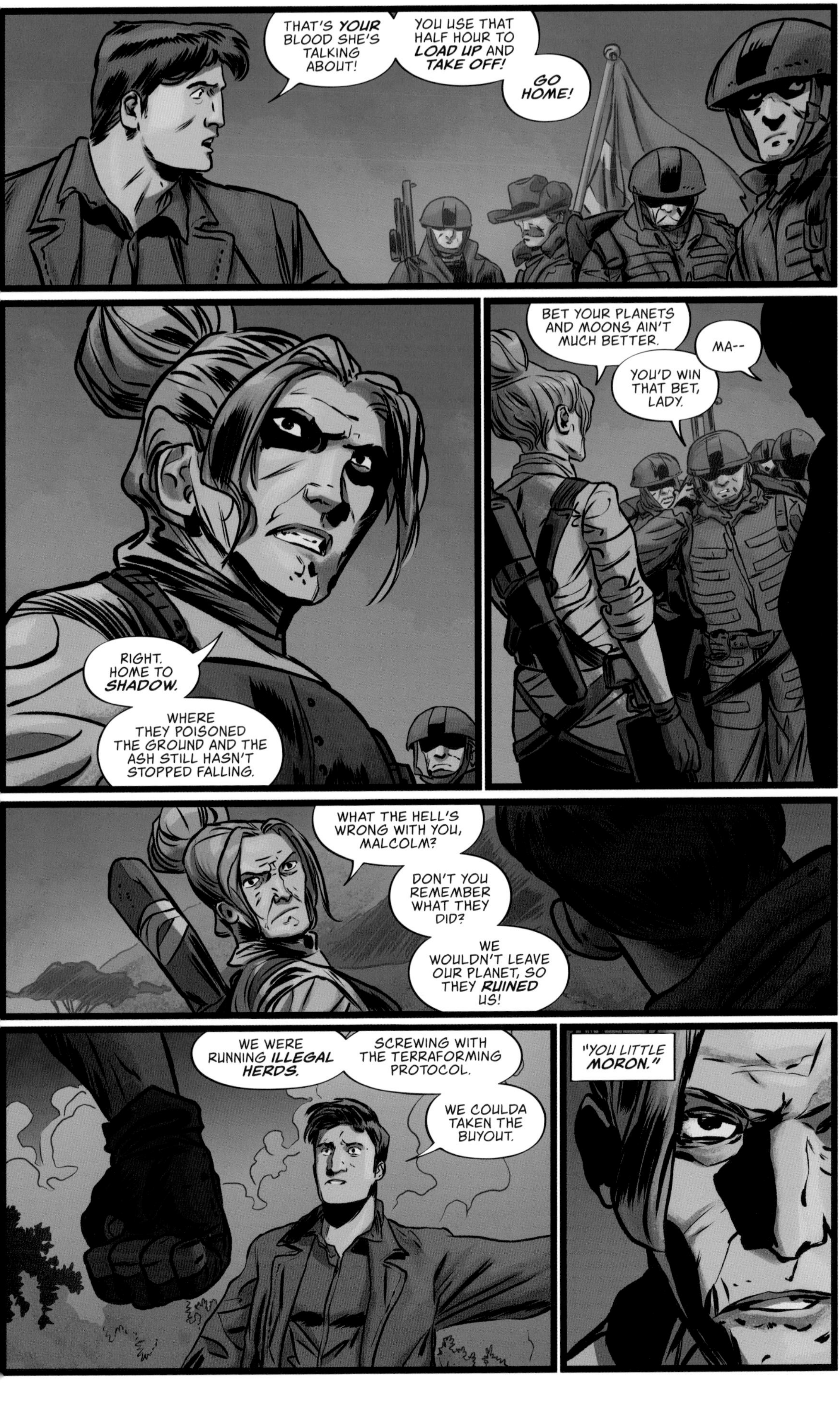

THAT'S YOUR BLOOD SHE'S TALKING ABOUT!
YOU USE THAT HALF HOUR TO LOAD UP AND TAKE OFF!
GO HOME!
RIGHT. HOME TO SHADOW.
WHERE THEY POISONED THE GROUND AND THE ASH STILL HASN'T STOPPED FALLING.
BET YOUR PLANETS AND MOONS AIN'T MUCH BETTER.
MA--
YOU'D WIN THAT BET, LADY.
WHAT THE HELL'S WRONG WITH YOU, MALCOLM?
DON'T YOU REMEMBER WHAT THEY DID?
WE WOULDN'T LEAVE OUR PLANET, SO THEY RUINED US!
WE WERE RUNNING ILLEGAL HERDS.
SCREWING WITH THE TERRAFORMING PROTOCOL.
WE COULDA TAKEN THE BUYOUT.
"YOU LITTLE MORON."

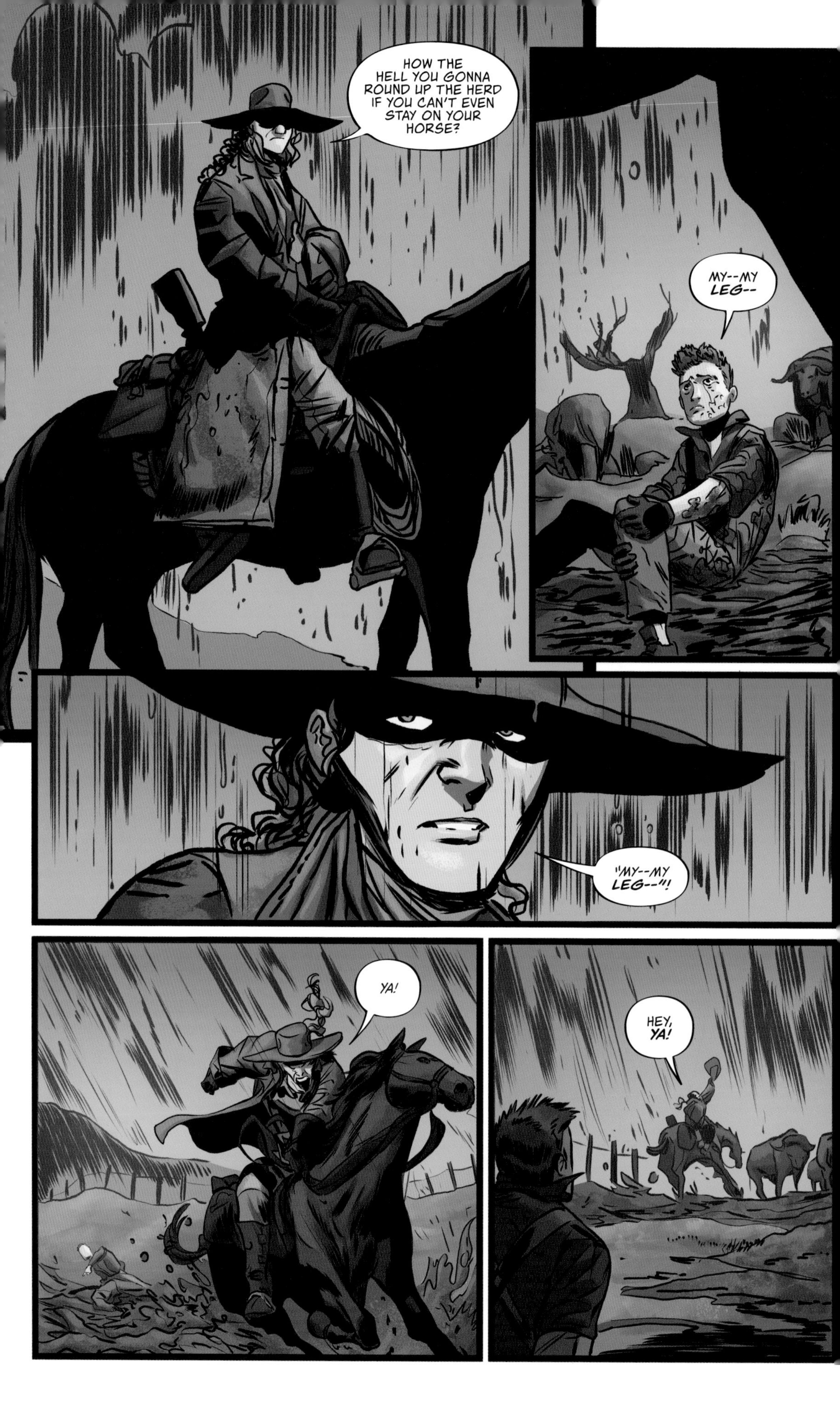
HOW THE HELL YOU GONNA ROUND UP THE HERD IF YOU CAN'T EVEN STAY ON YOUR HORSE?
MY--MY LEG--
"MY--MY LEG--"!
YA!
HEY, YA!

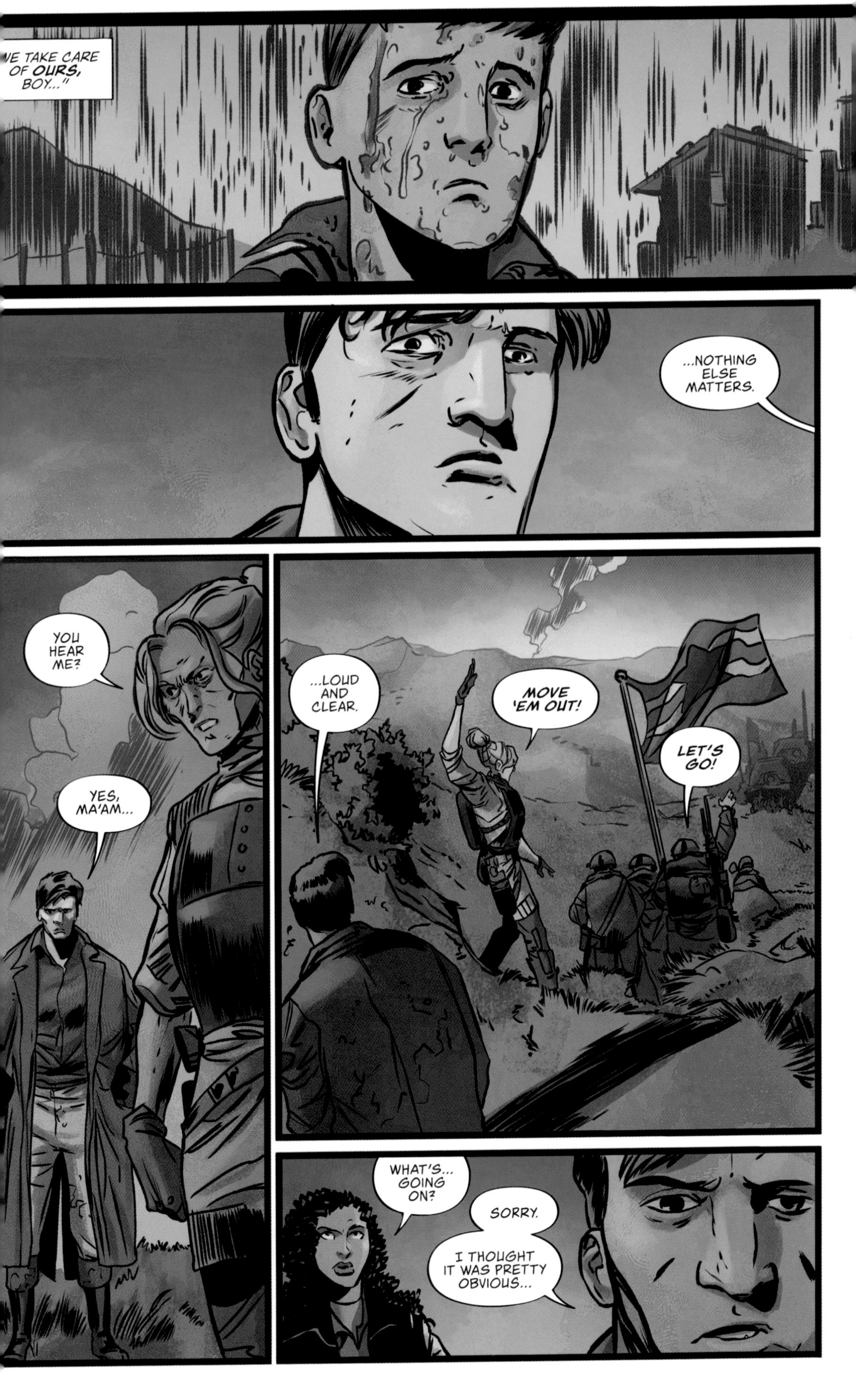

...E TAKE CARE OF OURS, BOY..."
...NOTHING ELSE MATTERS.
YOU HEAR ME?
YES, MA'AM...
...LOUD AND CLEAR.
MOVE 'EM OUT!
LET'S GO!
WHAT'S... GOING ON?
SORRY.
I THOUGHT IT WAS PRETTY OBVIOUS...

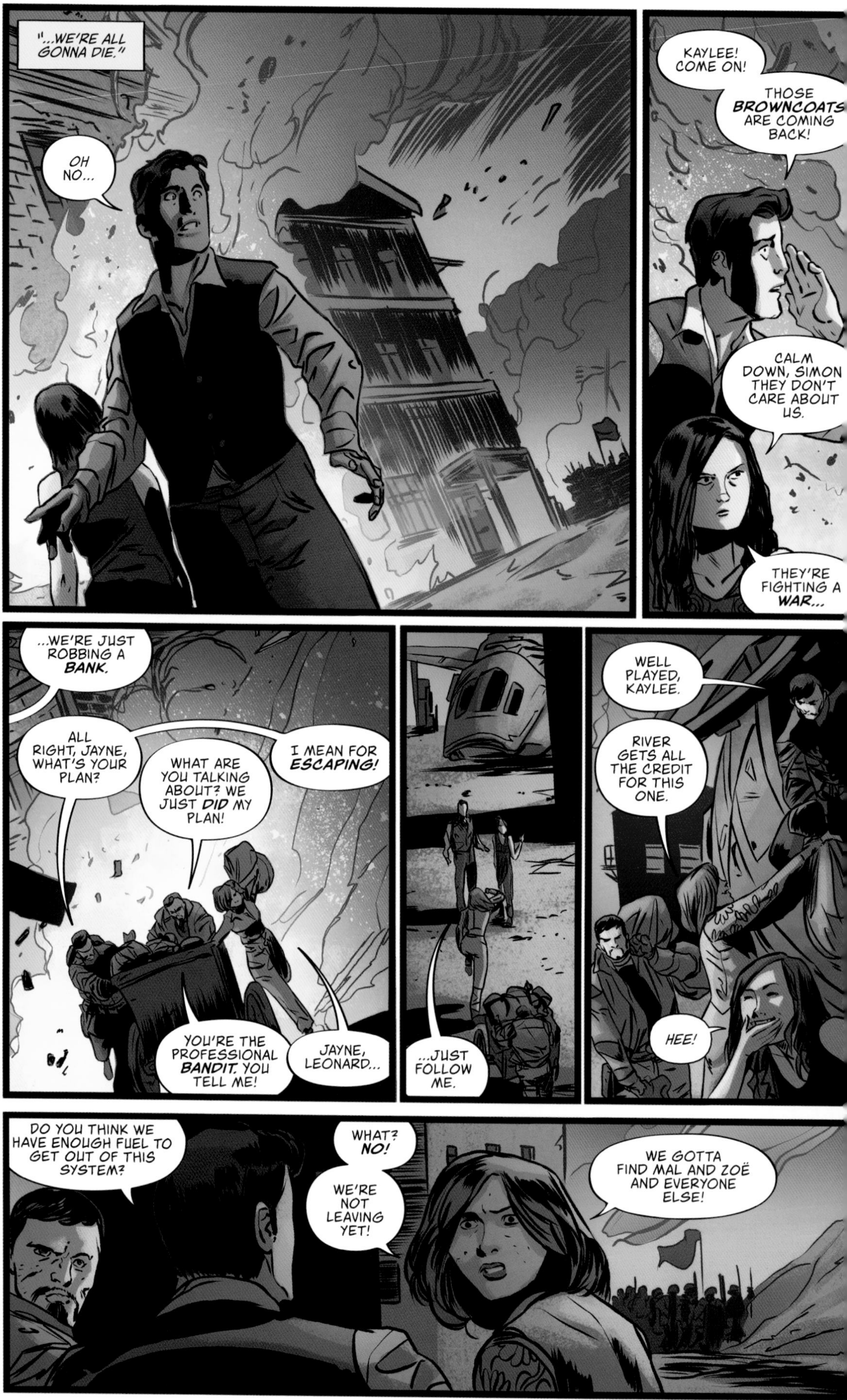
"...WE'RE ALL GONNA DIE."
OH NO...
KAYLEE! COME ON!
THOSE BROWNCOATS ARE COMING BACK!
CALM DOWN, SIMON THEY DON'T CARE ABOUT US.
THEY'RE FIGHTING A WAR...
...WE'RE JUST ROBBING A BANK.
ALL RIGHT, JAYNE, WHAT'S YOUR PLAN?
WHAT ARE YOU TALKING ABOUT? WE JUST DID MY PLAN!
I MEAN FOR ESCAPING!
YOU'RE THE PROFESSIONAL BANDIT. YOU TELL ME!
JAYNE, LEONARD...
...JUST FOLLOW ME.
WELL PLAYED, KAYLEE.
RIVER GETS ALL THE CREDIT FOR THIS ONE.
HEE!
DO YOU THINK WE HAVE ENOUGH FUEL TO GET OUT OF THIS SYSTEM?
WHAT? NO!
WE'RE NOT LEAVING YET!
WE GOTTA FIND MAL AND ZOË AND EVERYONE ELSE!

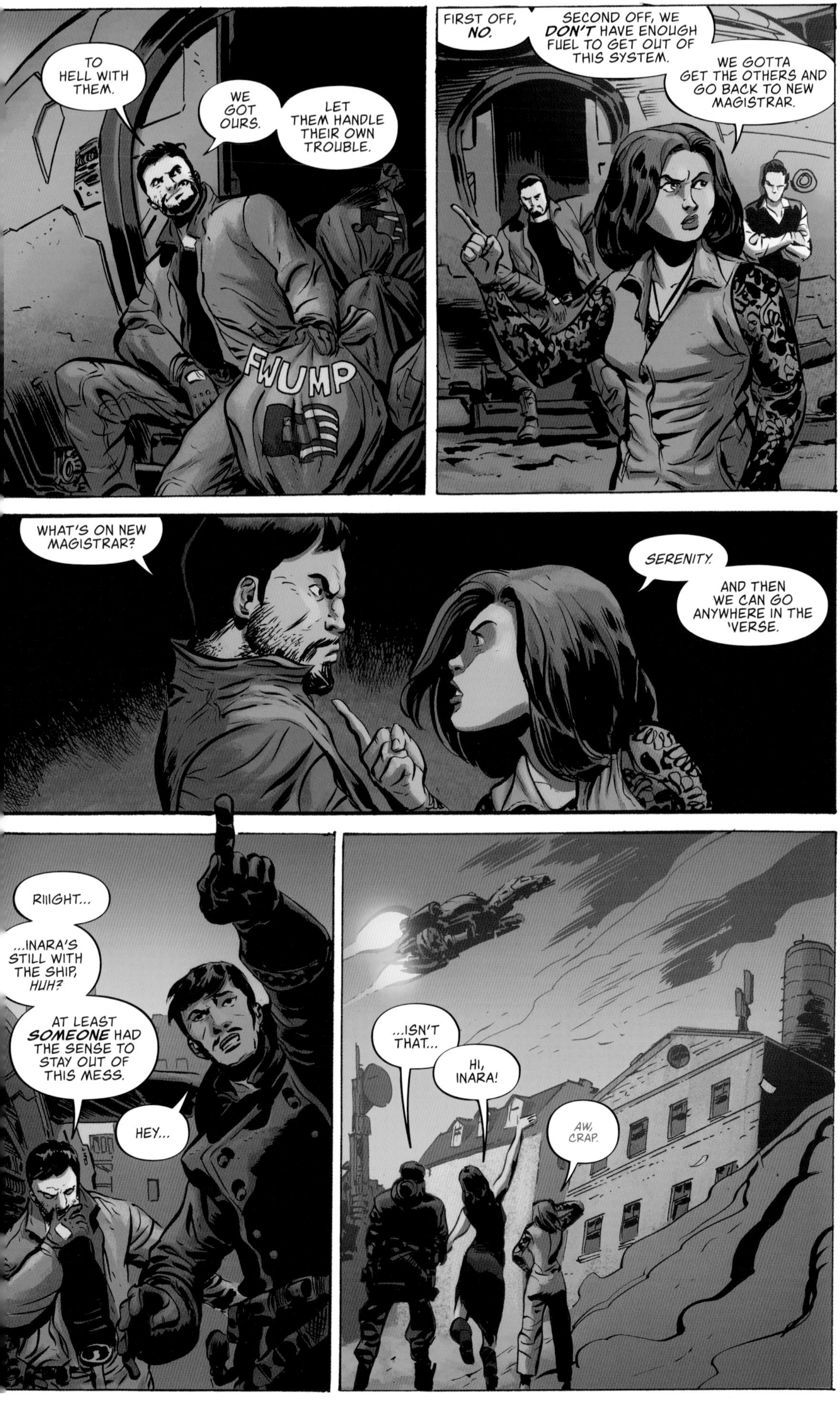
TO HELL WITH THEM.
WE GOT OURS.
LET THEM HANDLE THEIR OWN TROUBLE.
FWUMP
FIRST OFF, NO.
SECOND OFF, WE DON'T HAVE ENOUGH FUEL TO GET OUT OF THIS SYSTEM.
WE GOTTA GET THE OTHERS AND GO BACK TO NEW MAGISTRAR.
WHAT'S ON NEW MAGISTRAR?
SERENITY.
AND THEN WE CAN GO ANYWHERE IN THE 'VERSE.
RIIIGHT...
...INARA'S STILL WITH THE SHIP, HUH?
AT LEAST SOMEONE HAD THE SENSE TO STAY OUT OF THIS MESS.
HEY...
...ISN'T THAT...
HI, INARA!
AW, CRAP.

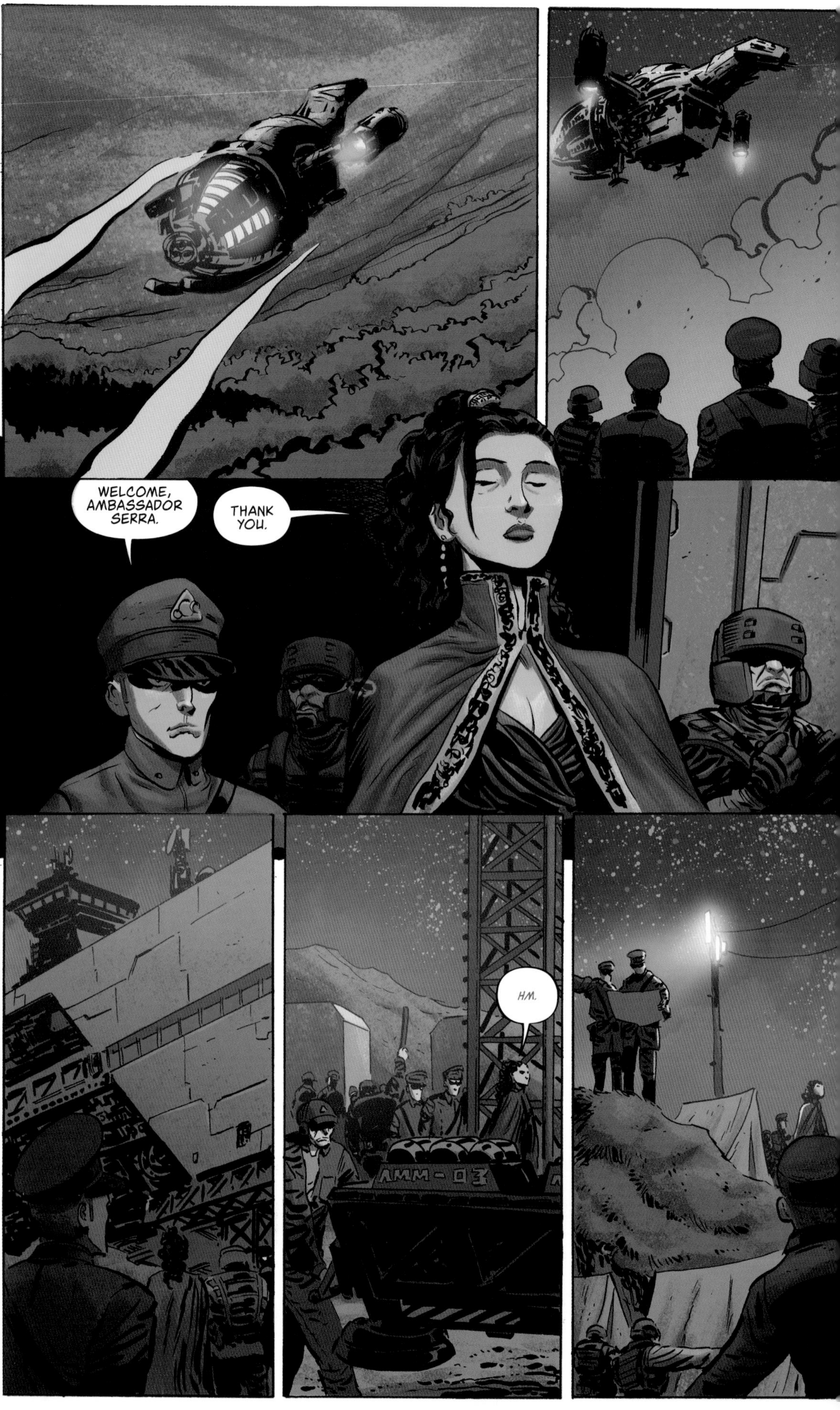
WELCOME, AMBASSADOR SERRA.
THANK YOU.
HM.
AMM-03

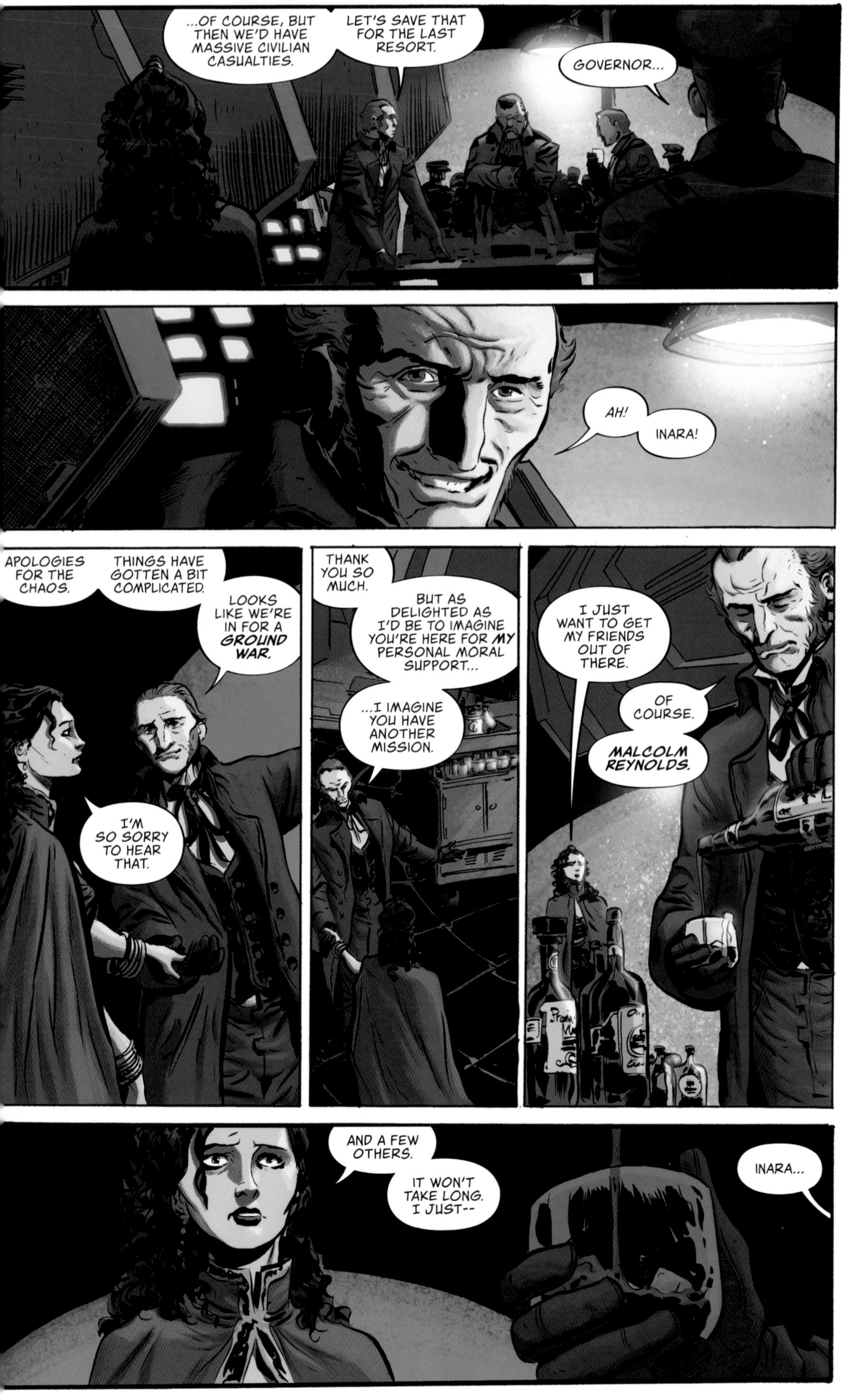
...OF COURSE, BUT THEN WE'D HAVE MASSIVE CIVILIAN CASUALTIES.
LET'S SAVE THAT FOR THE LAST RESORT.
GOVERNOR...
AH!
INARA!
APOLOGIES FOR THE CHAOS.
THINGS HAVE GOTTEN A BIT COMPLICATED.
LOOKS LIKE WE'RE IN FOR A GROUND WAR.
I'M SO SORRY TO HEAR THAT.
THANK YOU SO MUCH.
BUT AS DELIGHTED AS I'D BE TO IMAGINE YOU'RE HERE FOR MY PERSONAL MORAL SUPPORT...
...I IMAGINE YOU HAVE ANOTHER MISSION.
I JUST WANT TO GET MY FRIENDS OUT OF THERE.
OF COURSE.
MALCOLM REYNOLDS.
AND A FEW OTHERS.
IT WON'T TAKE LONG. I JUST--
INARA...

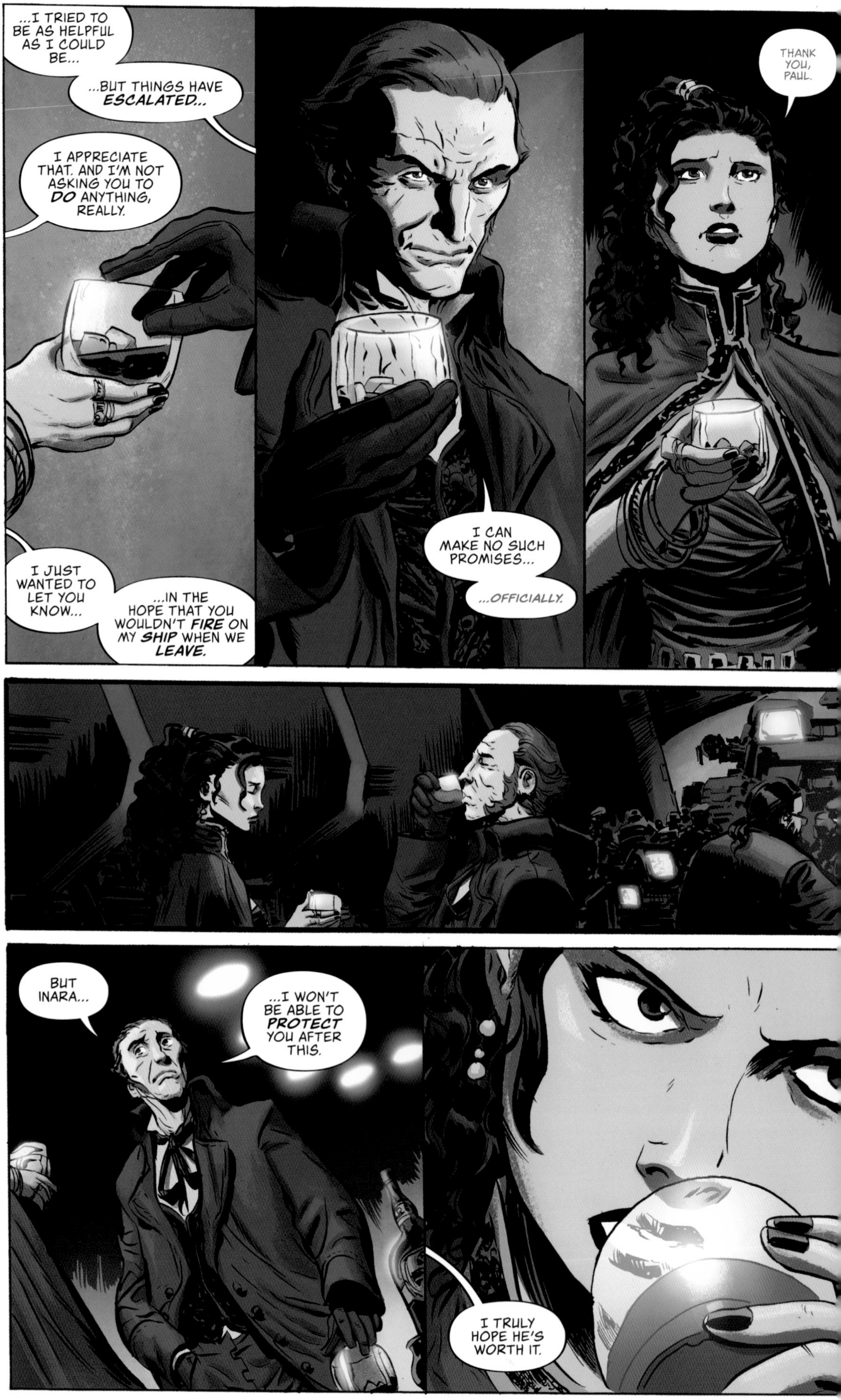

...I TRIED TO BE AS HELPFUL AS I COULD BE...
...BUT THINGS HAVE ESCALATED...
I APPRECIATE THAT. AND I'M NOT ASKING YOU TO DO ANYTHING, REALLY.
I JUST WANTED TO LET YOU KNOW...
...IN THE HOPE THAT YOU WOULDN'T FIRE ON MY SHIP WHEN WE LEAVE.
I CAN MAKE NO SUCH PROMISES...
...OFFICIALLY.
THANK YOU, PAUL.
BUT INARA...
...I WON'T BE ABLE TO PROTECT YOU AFTER THIS.
I TRULY HOPE HE'S WORTH IT.

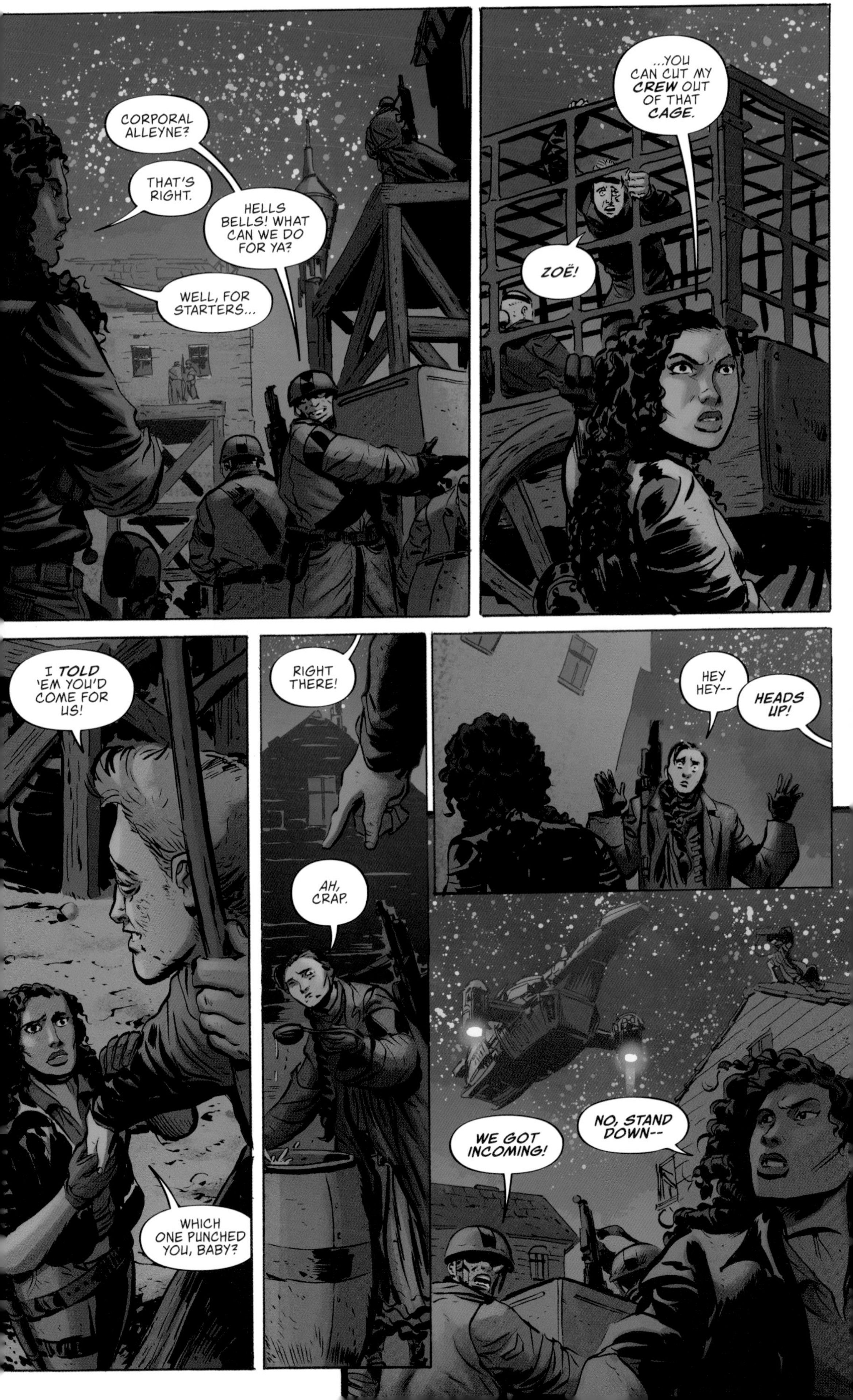
CORPORAL ALLEYNE?
THAT'S RIGHT.
HELLS BELLS! WHAT CAN WE DO FOR YA?
WELL, FOR STARTERS...
...YOU CAN CUT MY CREW OUT OF THAT CAGE.
ZOË!
I TOLD 'EM YOU'D COME FOR US!
WHICH ONE PUNCHED YOU, BABY?
RIGHT THERE!
AH, CRAP.
HEY HEY--
HEADS UP!
WE GOT INCOMING!
NO, STAND DOWN--

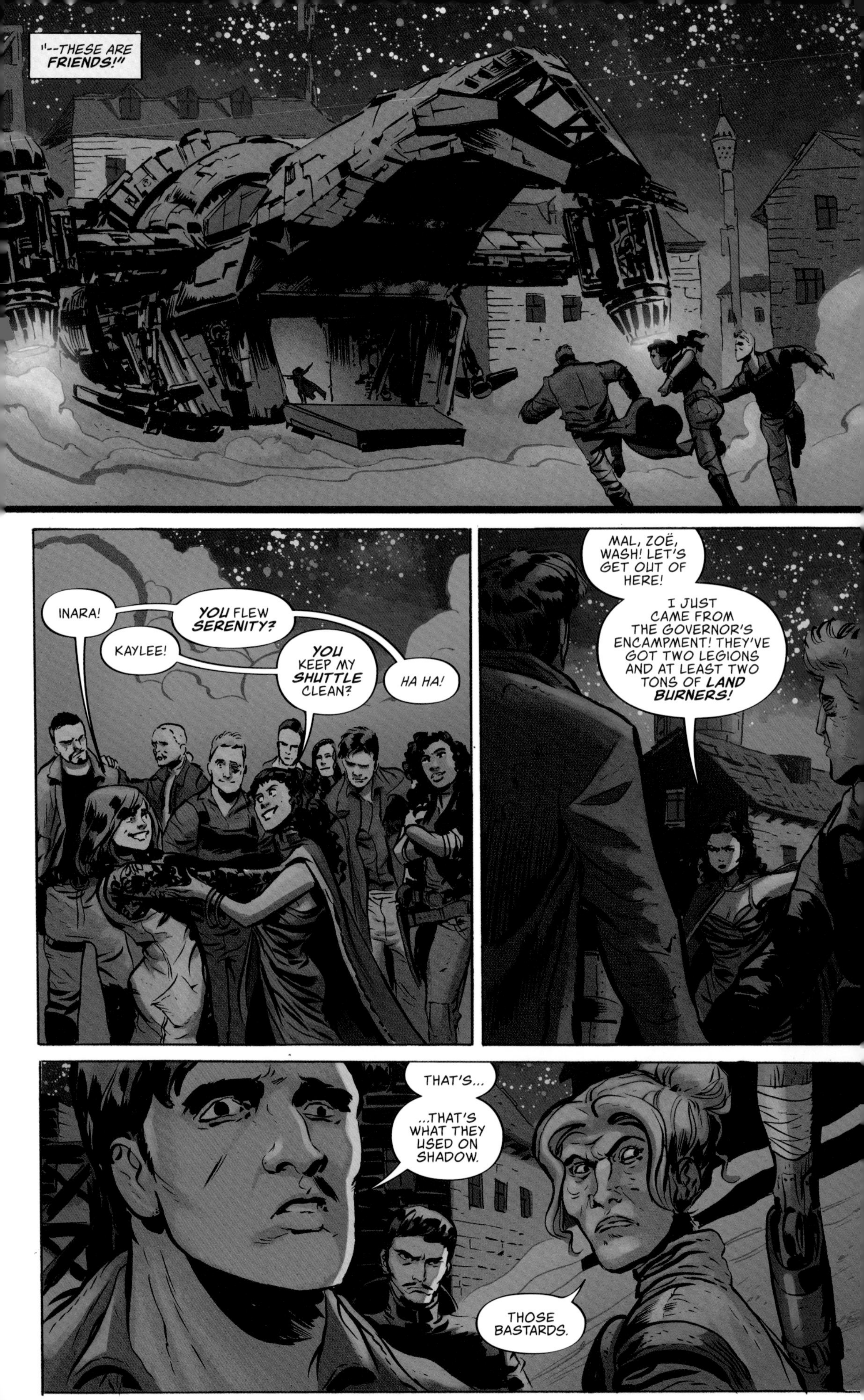
"--THESE ARE FRIENDS!"
INARA!
YOU FLEW SERENITY?
KAYLEE!
YOU KEEP MY SHUTTLE CLEAN?
HA HA!
MAL, ZOË, WASH! LET'S GET OUT OF HERE!
I JUST CAME FROM THE GOVERNOR'S ENCAMPMENT! THEY'VE GOT TWO LEGIONS AND AT LEAST TWO TONS OF LAND BURNERS!
THAT'S...
...THAT'S WHAT THEY USED ON SHADOW.
THOSE BASTARDS.

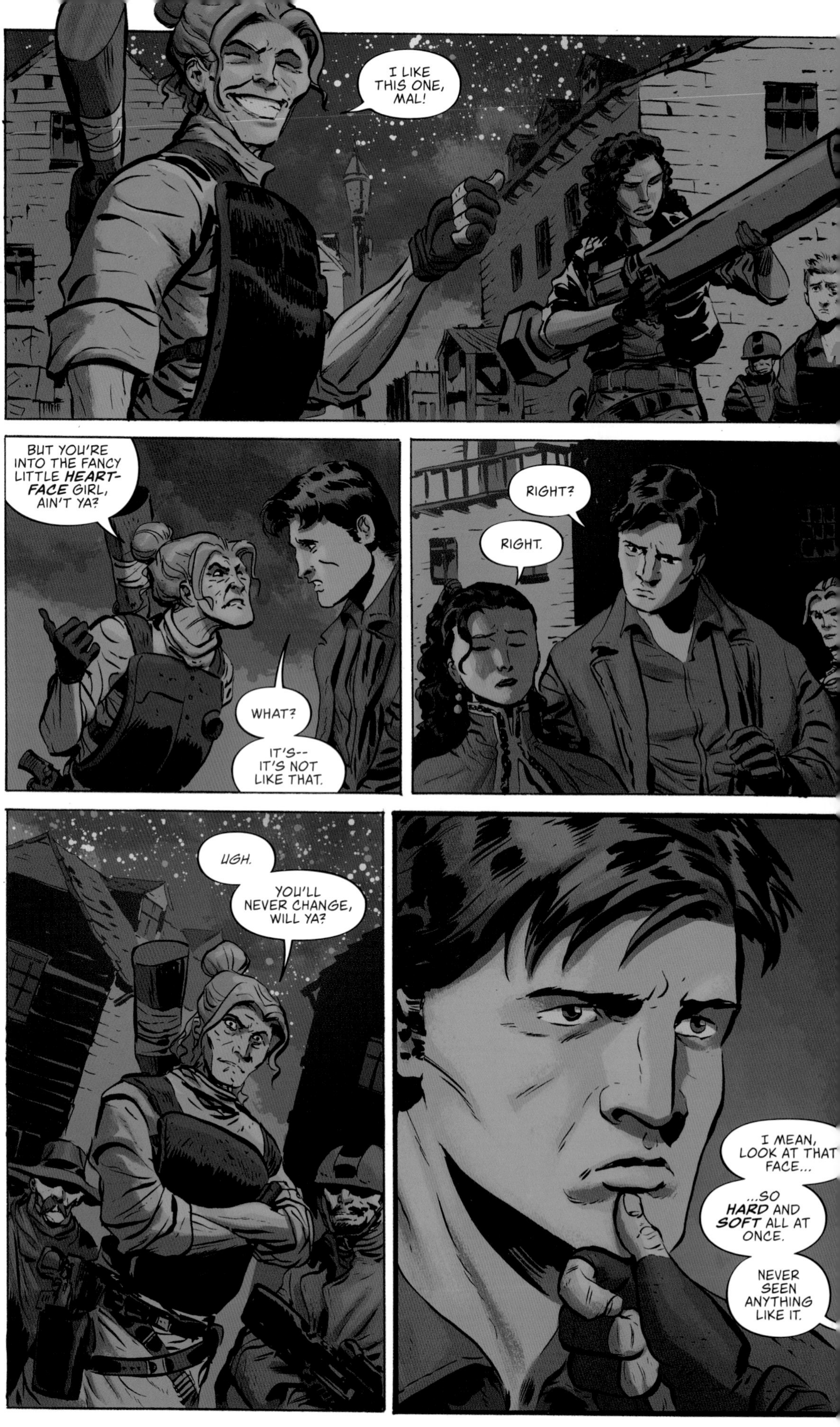
I LIKE THIS ONE, MAL!
BUT YOU'RE INTO THE FANCY LITTLE HEART-FACE GIRL, AIN'T YA?
WHAT?
IT'S-- IT'S NOT LIKE THAT.
RIGHT?
RIGHT.
UGH.
YOU'LL NEVER CHANGE, WILL YA?
I MEAN, LOOK AT THAT FACE...
...SO HARD AND SOFT ALL AT ONCE.
NEVER SEEN ANYTHING LIKE IT.

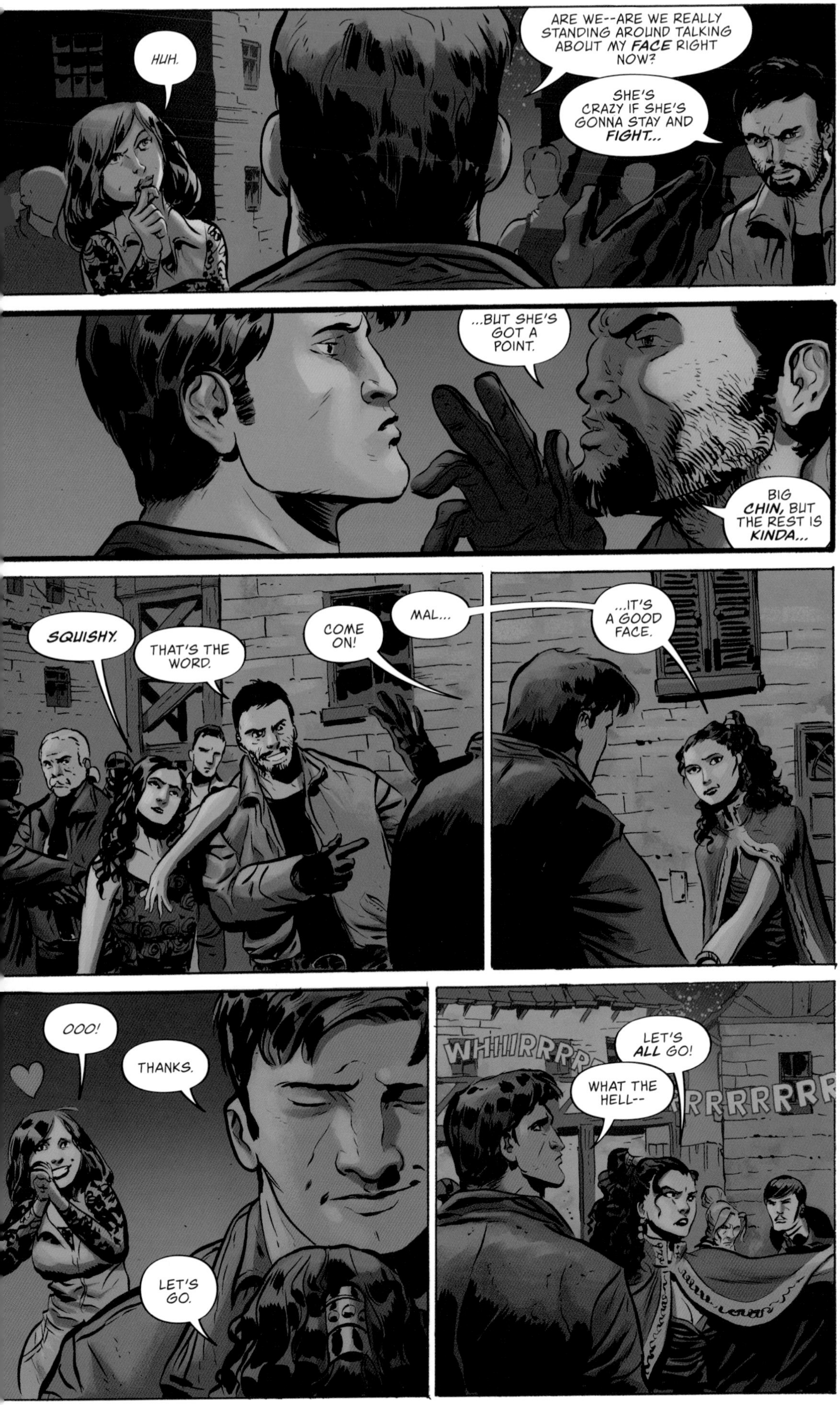
HUH.
ARE WE--ARE WE REALLY STANDING AROUND TALKING ABOUT MY **FACE** RIGHT NOW?
SHE'S CRAZY IF SHE'S GONNA STAY AND **FIGHT...**
...BUT SHE'S GOT A POINT.
BIG **CHIN,** BUT THE REST IS **KINDA...**
SQUISHY.
THAT'S THE WORD.
COME ON!
MAL...
...IT'S A GOOD FACE.
OOO!
THANKS.
LET'S GO.
WHHIIRRRR
LET'S **ALL** GO!
WHAT THE HELL--
RRRRRRRR

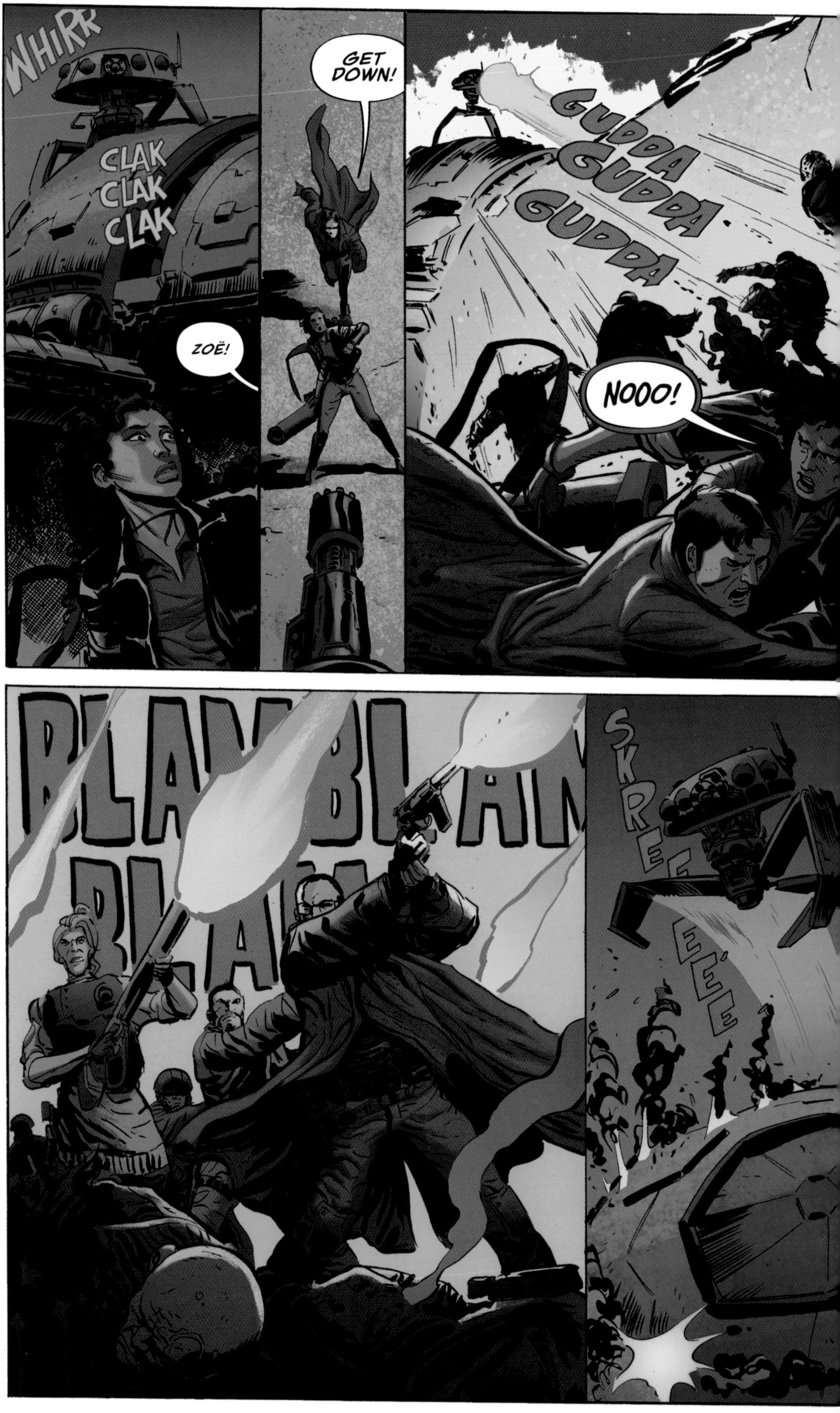
WHIRR
CLAK
CLAK
CLAK
ZOË!
GET DOWN!
GUDDA
GUDDA
GUDDA
NOOO!
SKREEEEE

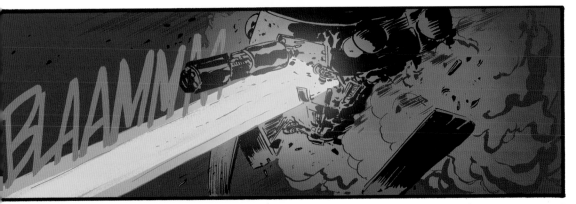

BLAAMMM

SKLANG

AAAAGH!

HANG IN THERE, WE'VE GOT YOU...

AH, HELL...

WHERE'D YOU SAY YOU CAME FROM?

THE GOVERNOR. BUT HE...HE SAID--

HE USED YOU, GIRL.

OH, NO...

I...

SURE, WE COULD RUN LIKE COCK-ROACHES...

...BUT THAT GOVERNOR'S GOT A PLAN TO MAKE HIMSELF IMPORTANT!

HE WANTS A FIGHT!

LET'S GIVE IT TO HIM.

ZOË, NO!

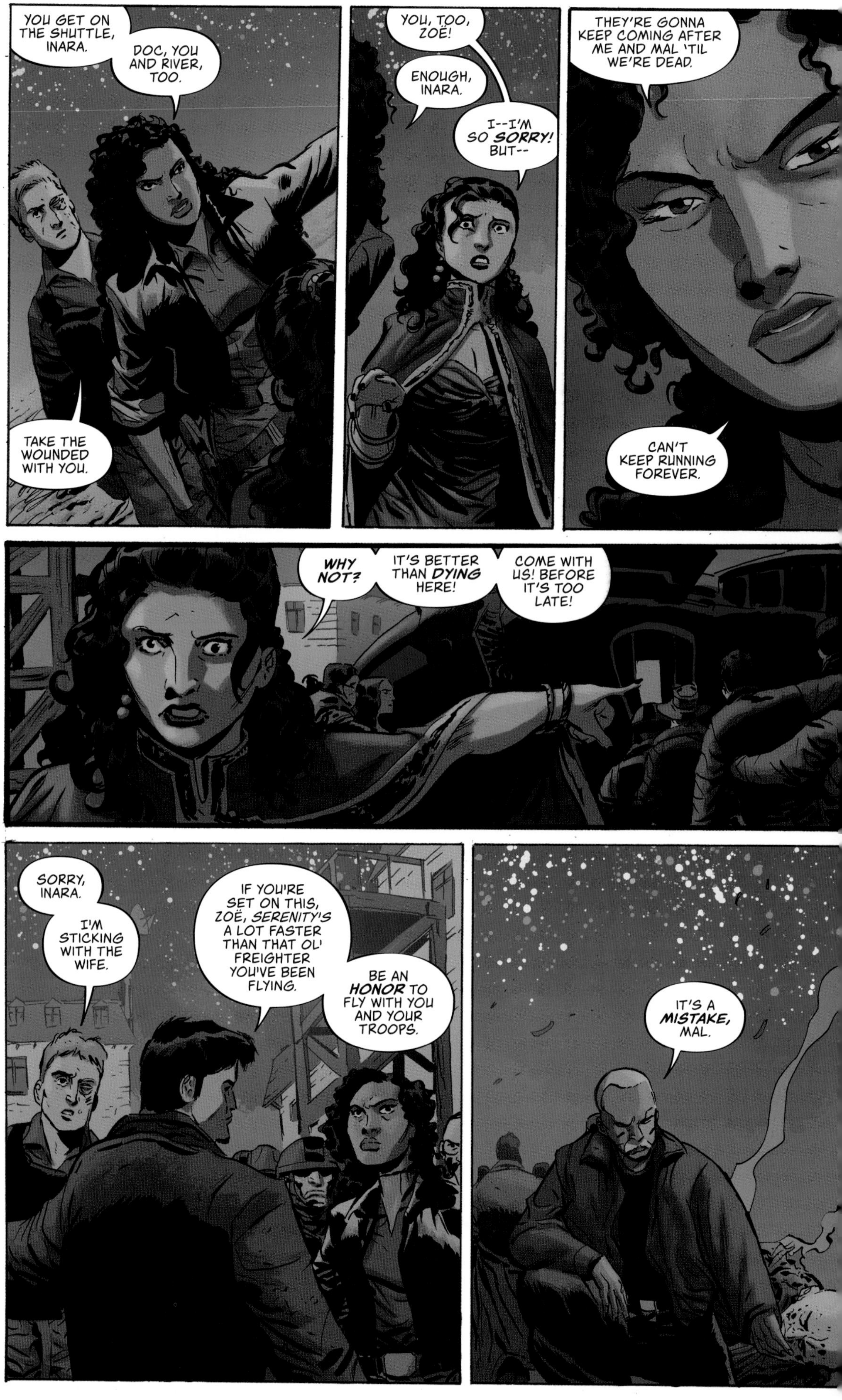

YOU GET ON THE SHUTTLE, INARA.
DOC, YOU AND RIVER, TOO.
TAKE THE WOUNDED WITH YOU.
YOU, TOO, ZOË!
ENOUGH, INARA.
I--I'M SO SORRY! BUT--
THEY'RE GONNA KEEP COMING AFTER ME AND MAL 'TIL WE'RE DEAD.
CAN'T KEEP RUNNING FOREVER.
WHY NOT?
IT'S BETTER THAN DYING HERE!
COME WITH US! BEFORE IT'S TOO LATE!
SORRY, INARA.
I'M STICKING WITH THE WIFE.
IF YOU'RE SET ON THIS, ZOË, SERENITY'S A LOT FASTER THAN THAT OL' FREIGHTER YOU'VE BEEN FLYING.
BE AN HONOR TO FLY WITH YOU AND YOUR TROOPS.
IT'S A MISTAKE, MAL.

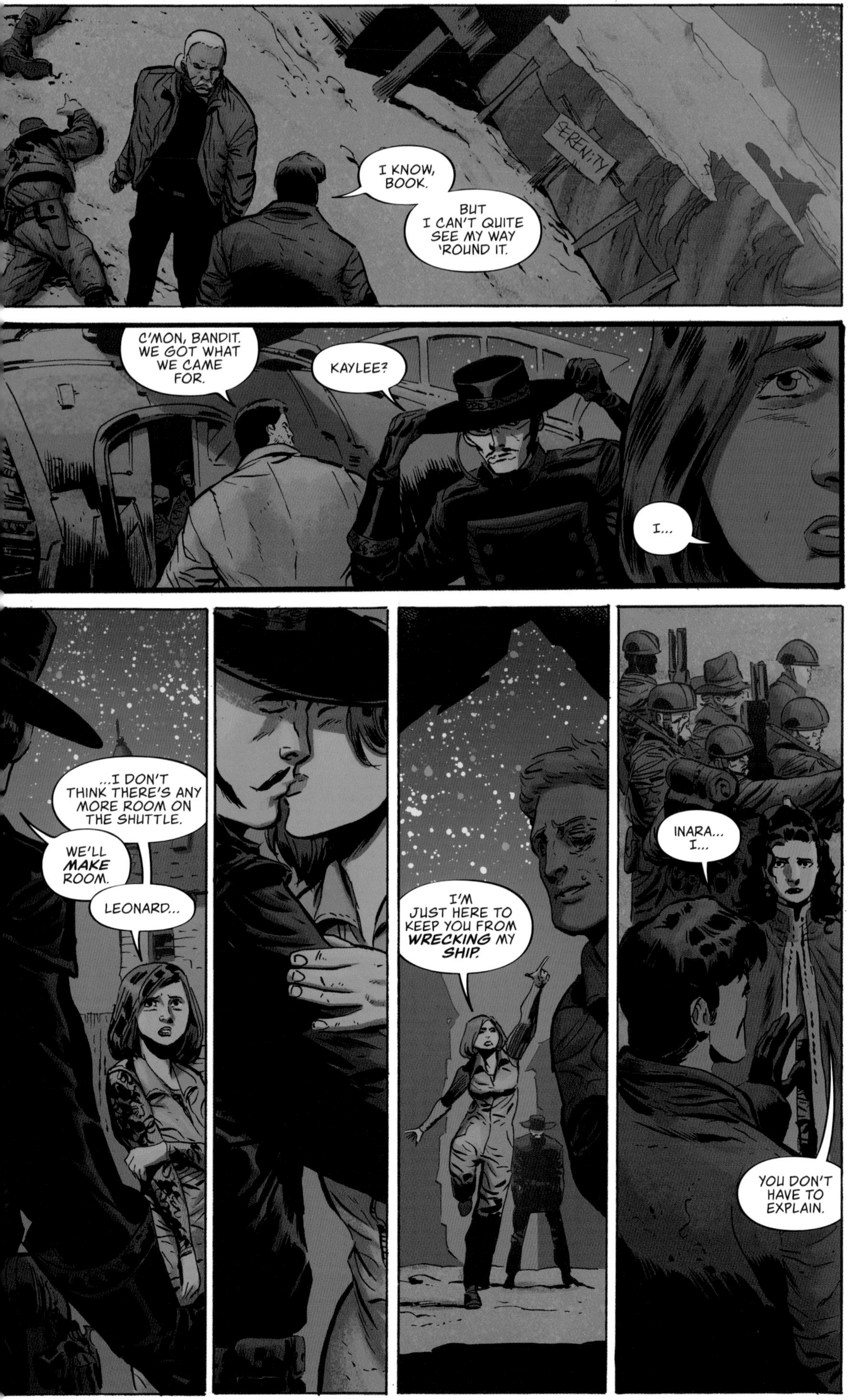
I KNOW, BOOK.
BUT I CAN'T QUITE SEE MY WAY 'ROUND IT.
C'MON, BANDIT. WE GOT WHAT WE CAME FOR.
KAYLEE?
I...
...I DON'T THINK THERE'S ANY MORE ROOM ON THE SHUTTLE.
WE'LL MAKE ROOM.
LEONARD...
I'M JUST HERE TO KEEP YOU FROM WRECKING MY SHIP.
INARA... I...
YOU DON'T HAVE TO EXPLAIN.

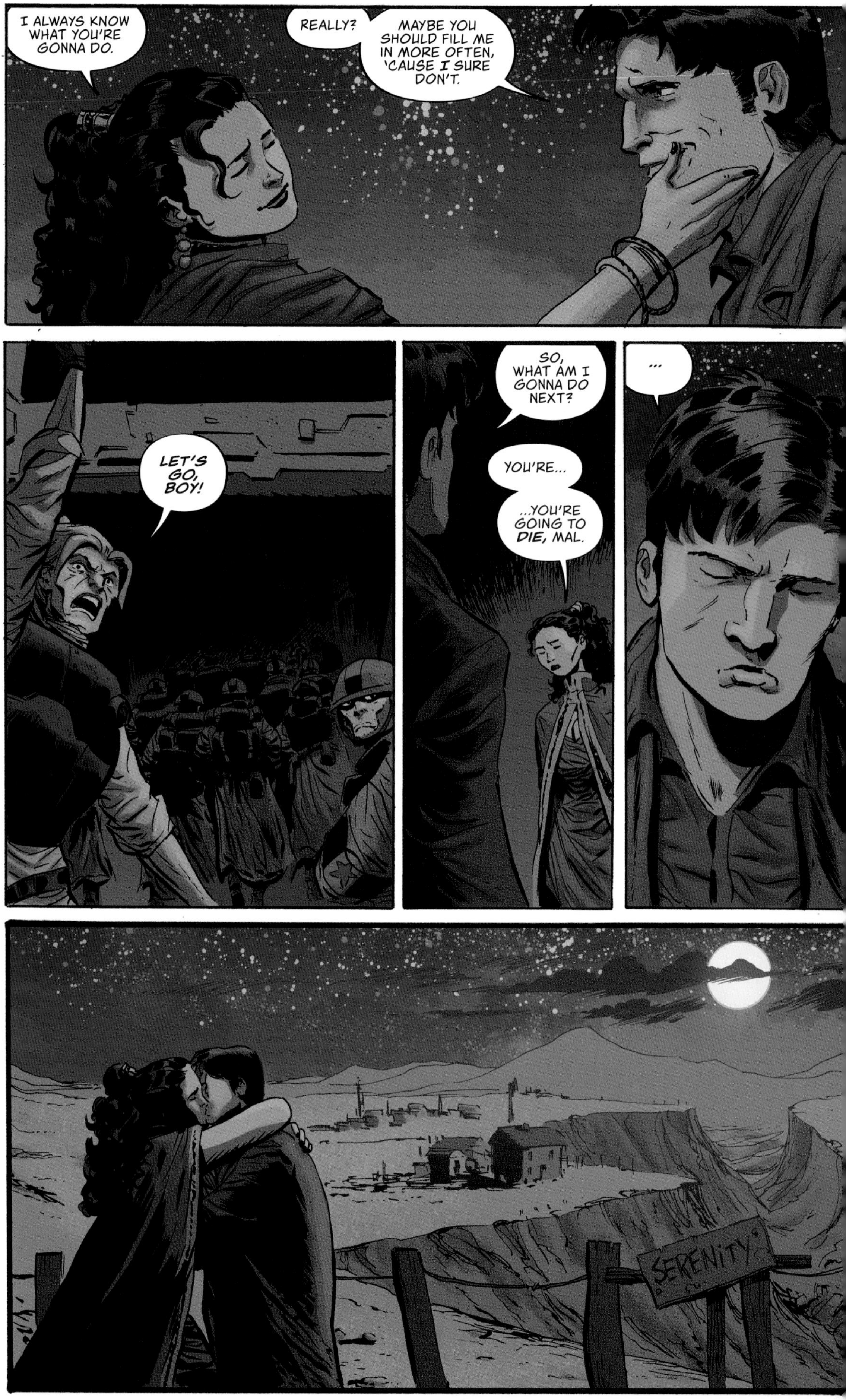
I ALWAYS KNOW WHAT YOU'RE GONNA DO.
REALLY?
MAYBE YOU SHOULD FILL ME IN MORE OFTEN, 'CAUSE I SURE DON'T.
LET'S GO, BOY!
SO, WHAT AM I GONNA DO NEXT?
YOU'RE...
...YOU'RE GOING TO DIE, MAL.
...
SERENITY

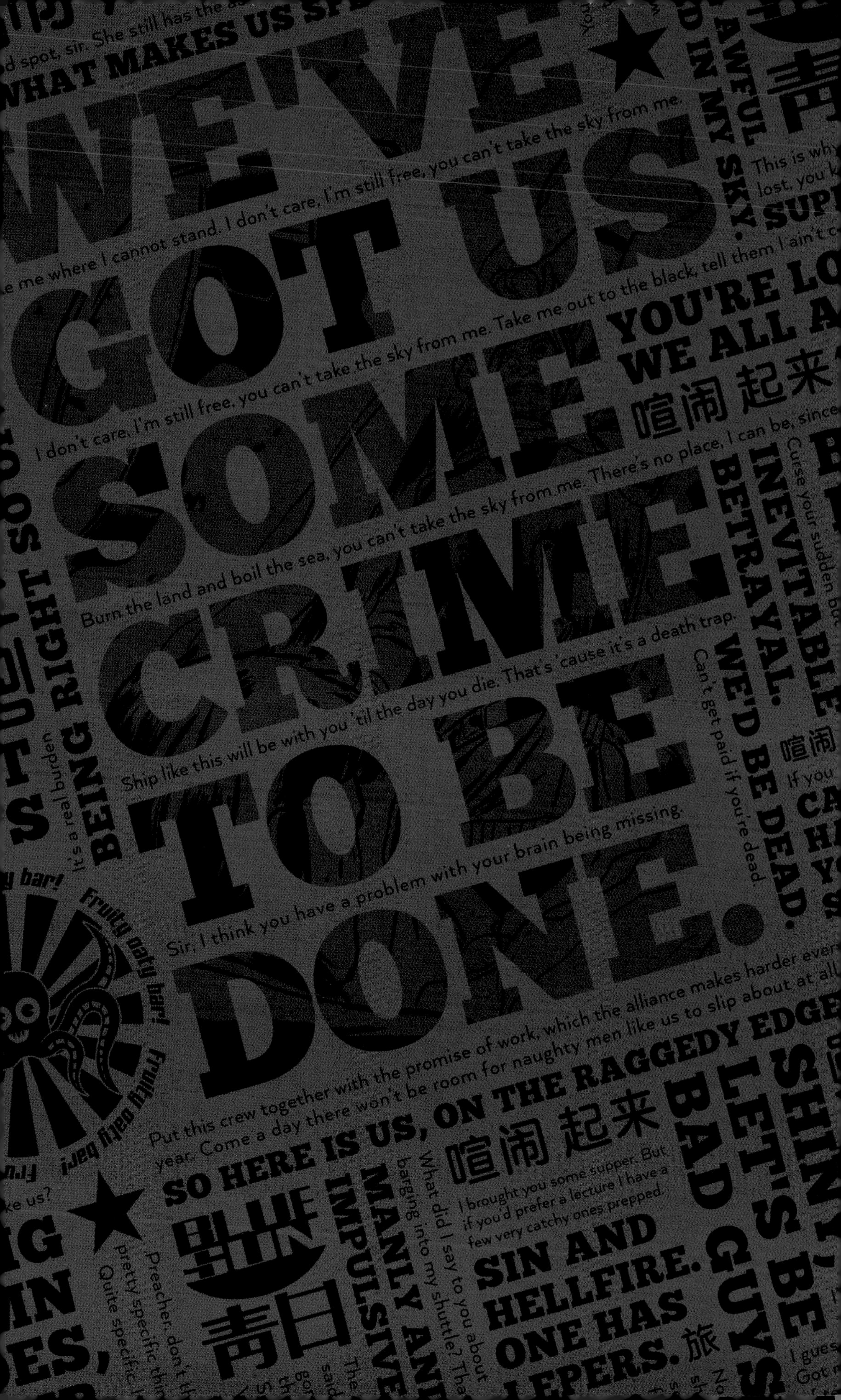
WE'VE GOT US SOME CRIME TO BE DONE.
WHAT MAKES US
I don't care. I'm still free, you can't take the sky from me.
I don't care. I'm still free, you can't take the sky from me. Take me out to the black, tell them I ain't c
Burn the land and boil the sea, you can't take the sky from me. There's no place, I can be, since
Ship like this will be with you 'til the day you die. That's 'cause it's a death trap.
Sir, I think you have a problem with your brain being missing.
Put this crew together with the promise of work, which the alliance makes harder eve
year. Come a day there won't be room for naughty men like us to slip about at all
SO HERE IS US, ON THE RAGGEDY EDGE
喧闹 起来
YOU'RE LO
WE ALL A
喧闹 起来
AWFUL IN MY SKY.
This is why
lost, you k
SUP
INEVITABLE BETRAYAL.
WE'D BE DEAD.
Can't get paid if you're dead.
Curse your sudden but
BEING RIGHT
It's a real burden
Fruity Oaty bar!
BLUE SUN
青日
IMPULSIVE
MANLY AND
What did I say to you about barging into my shuttle?
I brought you some supper. But if you'd prefer a lecture I have a few very catchy ones prepped.
SIN AND HELLFIRE. ONE HAS LEPERS.
旅
LET'S BE BAD GUYS
Preacher, don't th
pretty specific
Quite specific.
喧闹
If you

CHAPTER TWELVE

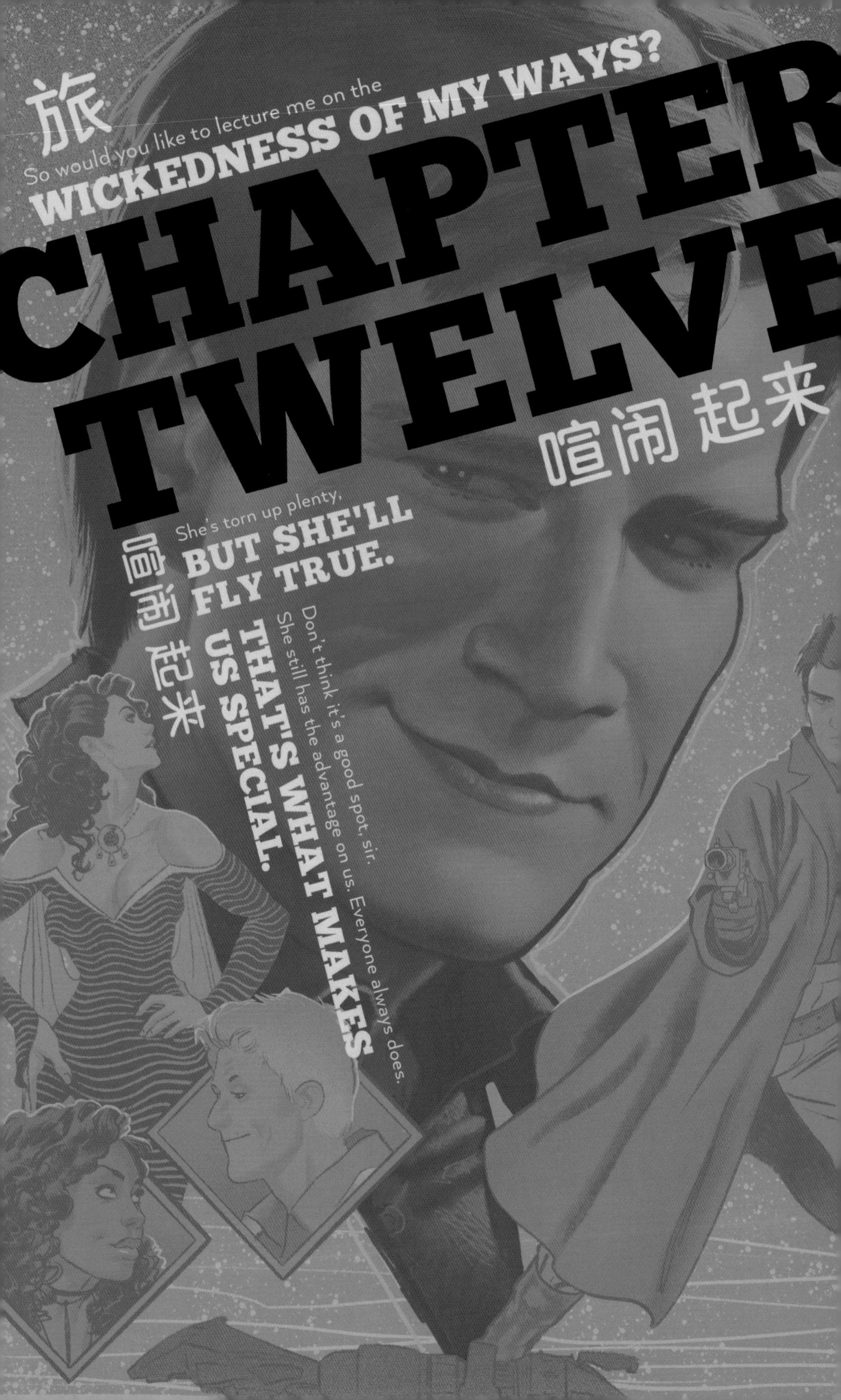

旅
So would you like to lecture me on the
WICKEDNESS OF MY WAYS?
喧闹 起来
She's torn up plenty,
BUT SHE'LL
FLY TRUE.
喧闹 起来
Don't think it's a good spot, sir.
She still has the advantage on us. Everyone always does.
THAT'S WHAT MAKES
US SPECIAL.

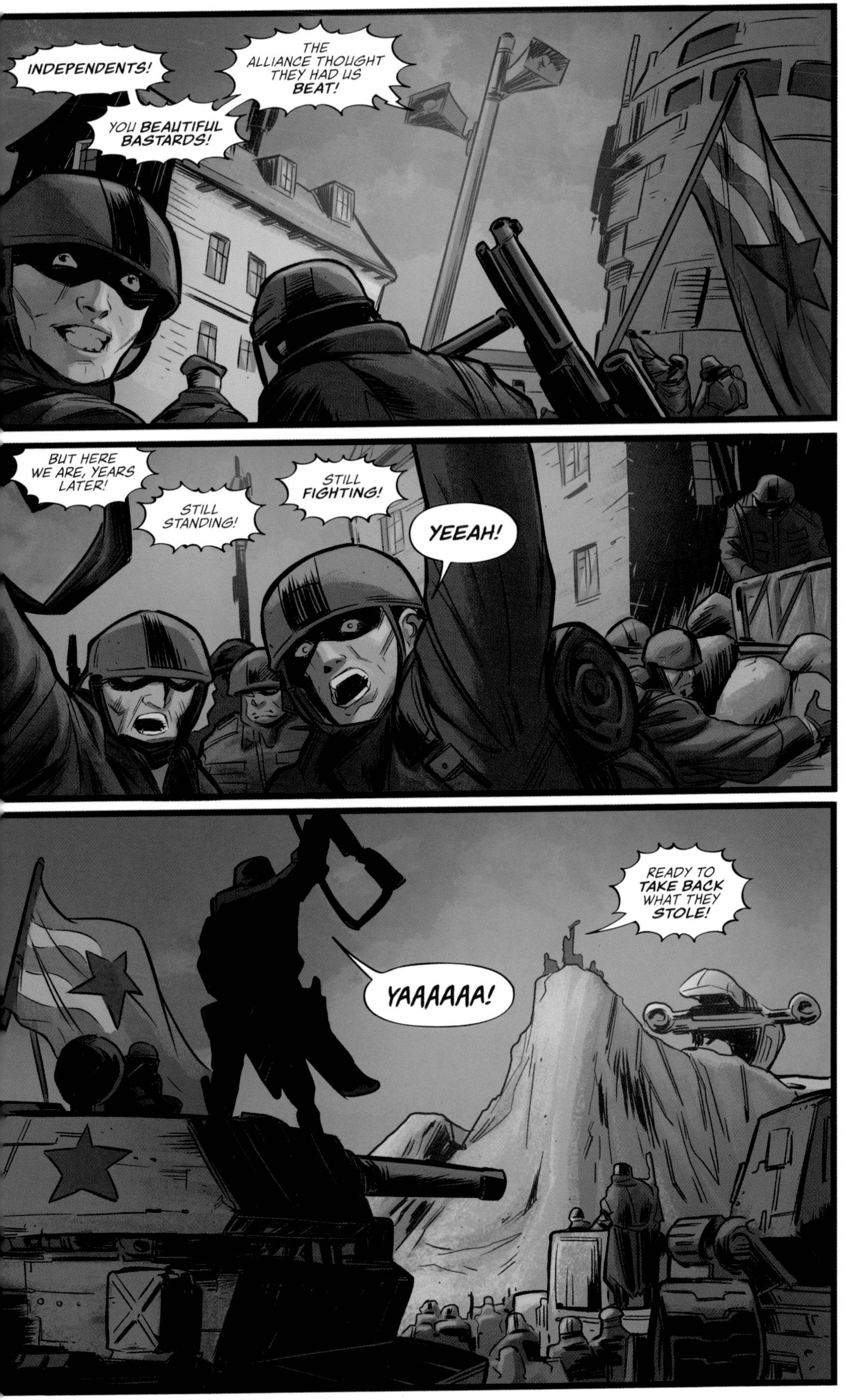
INDEPENDENTS!
THE ALLIANCE THOUGHT THEY HAD US BEAT!
YOU BEAUTIFUL BASTARDS!
BUT HERE WE ARE, YEARS LATER!
STILL STANDING!
STILL FIGHTING!
YEEAH!
READY TO TAKE BACK WHAT THEY STOLE!
YAAAAAA!

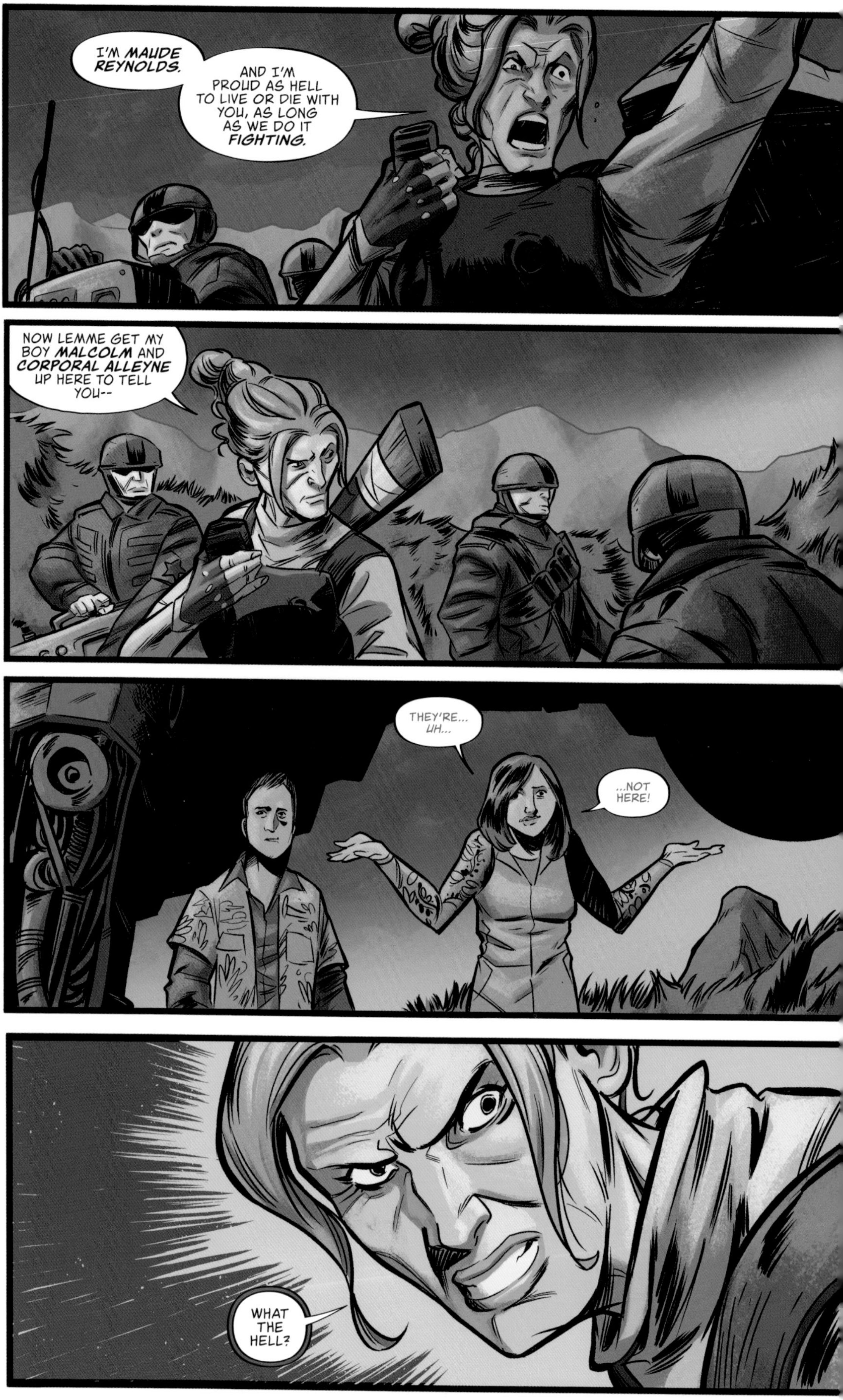
I'M MAUDE REYNOLDS.
AND I'M PROUD AS HELL TO LIVE OR DIE WITH YOU, AS LONG AS WE DO IT FIGHTING.
NOW LEMME GET MY BOY MALCOLM AND CORPORAL ALLEYNE UP HERE TO TELL YOU--
THEY'RE... UH...
...NOT HERE!
WHAT THE HELL?

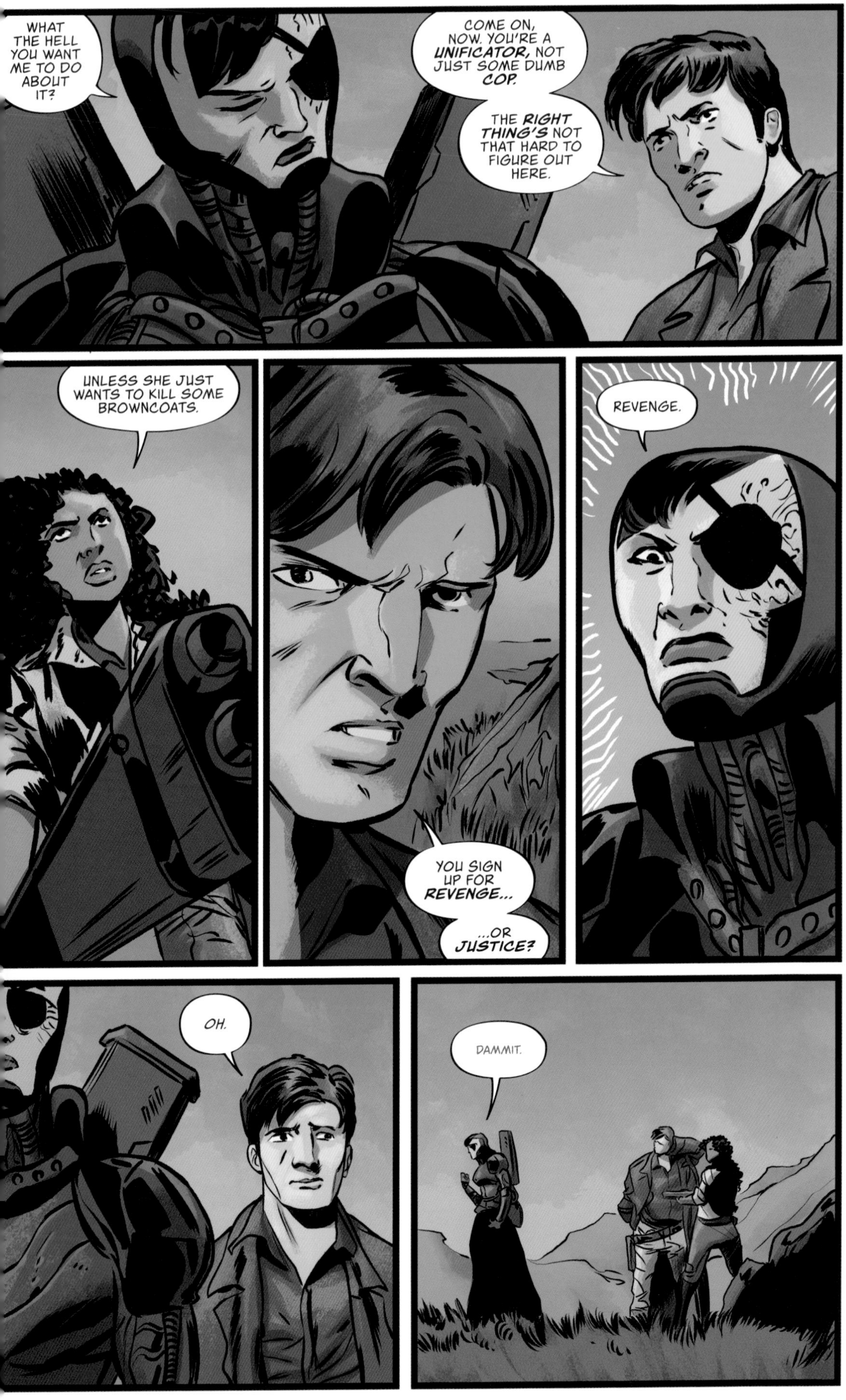

WHAT THE HELL YOU WANT ME TO DO ABOUT IT?
COME ON, NOW. YOU'RE A UNIFICATOR, NOT JUST SOME DUMB COP.
THE RIGHT THING'S NOT THAT HARD TO FIGURE OUT HERE.
UNLESS SHE JUST WANTS TO KILL SOME BROWNCOATS.
YOU SIGN UP FOR REVENGE...
...OR JUSTICE?
REVENGE.
OH.
DAMMIT.

NINETEEN MINUTES LATER...

UFF.

WHAT?

NOTHING. IT'S JUST A LITTLE *TIGHT*...

...IN THE *HINDER* REGIONS.

YOU MEAN YOU'RE A LITTLE *BROAD* IN THE HINDER--

SHHH.

HOW'S IT LOOKING, SOLDIER?

WHO WANTS TO KNOW?

BOSS MOON, UNIFICATOR I.D. 44454.

CHECKING ON THE STATUS OF THE *LAND BURNERS*.

OH, THEY'RE ALREADY LOADED, BOSS.

GREAT. WHICH SHIP?

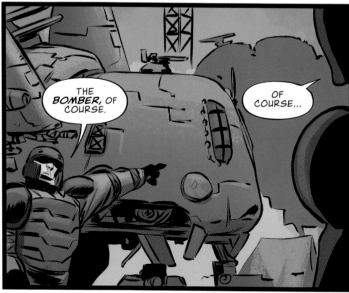

THE *BOMBER*, OF COURSE.

OF COURSE...

SO...WHAT DO YOU UNIFICATORS HAVE TO DO WITH--

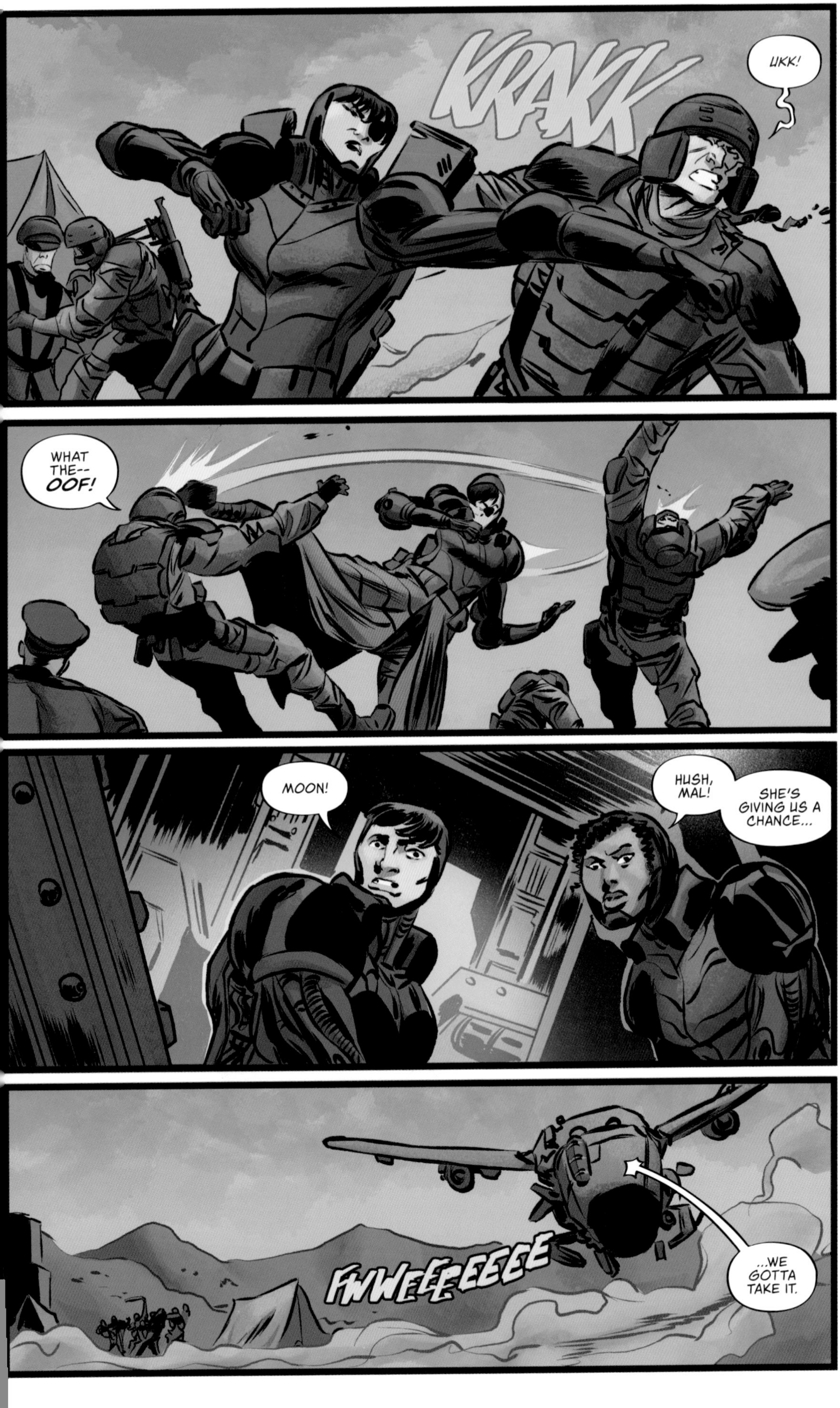
KRAKK
UKK!
WHAT THE-- OOF!
MOON!
HUSH, MAL!
SHE'S GIVING US A CHANCE...
FWWEEEEEEE
...WE GOTTA TAKE IT.

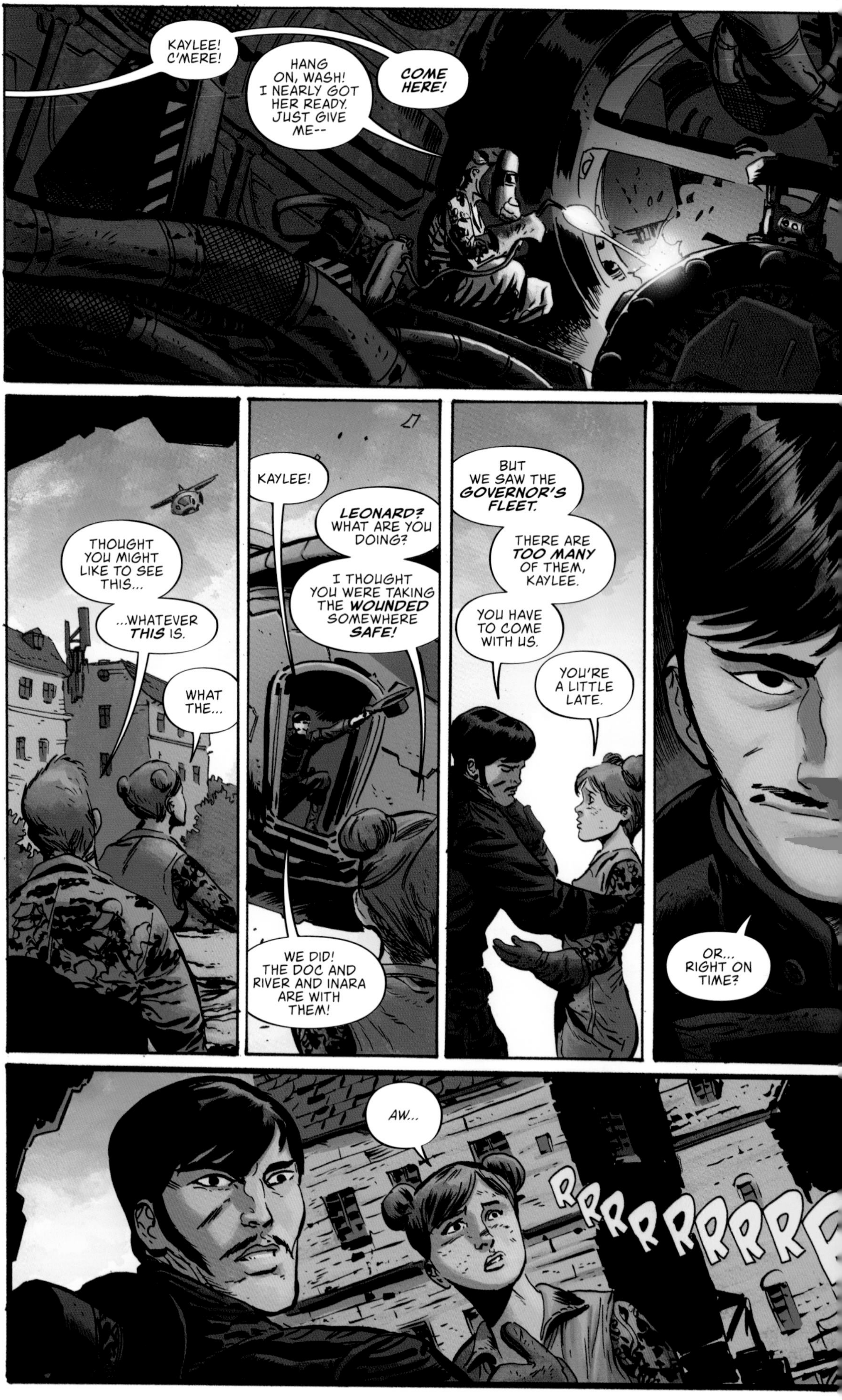

KAYLEE! C'MERE!
HANG ON, WASH! I NEARLY GOT HER READY. JUST GIVE ME--
COME HERE!
THOUGHT YOU MIGHT LIKE TO SEE THIS...
...WHATEVER THIS IS.
WHAT THE...
KAYLEE!
LEONARD? WHAT ARE YOU DOING?
I THOUGHT YOU WERE TAKING THE WOUNDED SOMEWHERE SAFE!
WE DID! THE DOC AND RIVER AND INARA ARE WITH THEM!
BUT WE SAW THE GOVERNOR'S FLEET.
THERE ARE TOO MANY OF THEM, KAYLEE.
YOU HAVE TO COME WITH US.
YOU'RE A LITTLE LATE.
OR... RIGHT ON TIME?
AW...
RRRRRRRRR

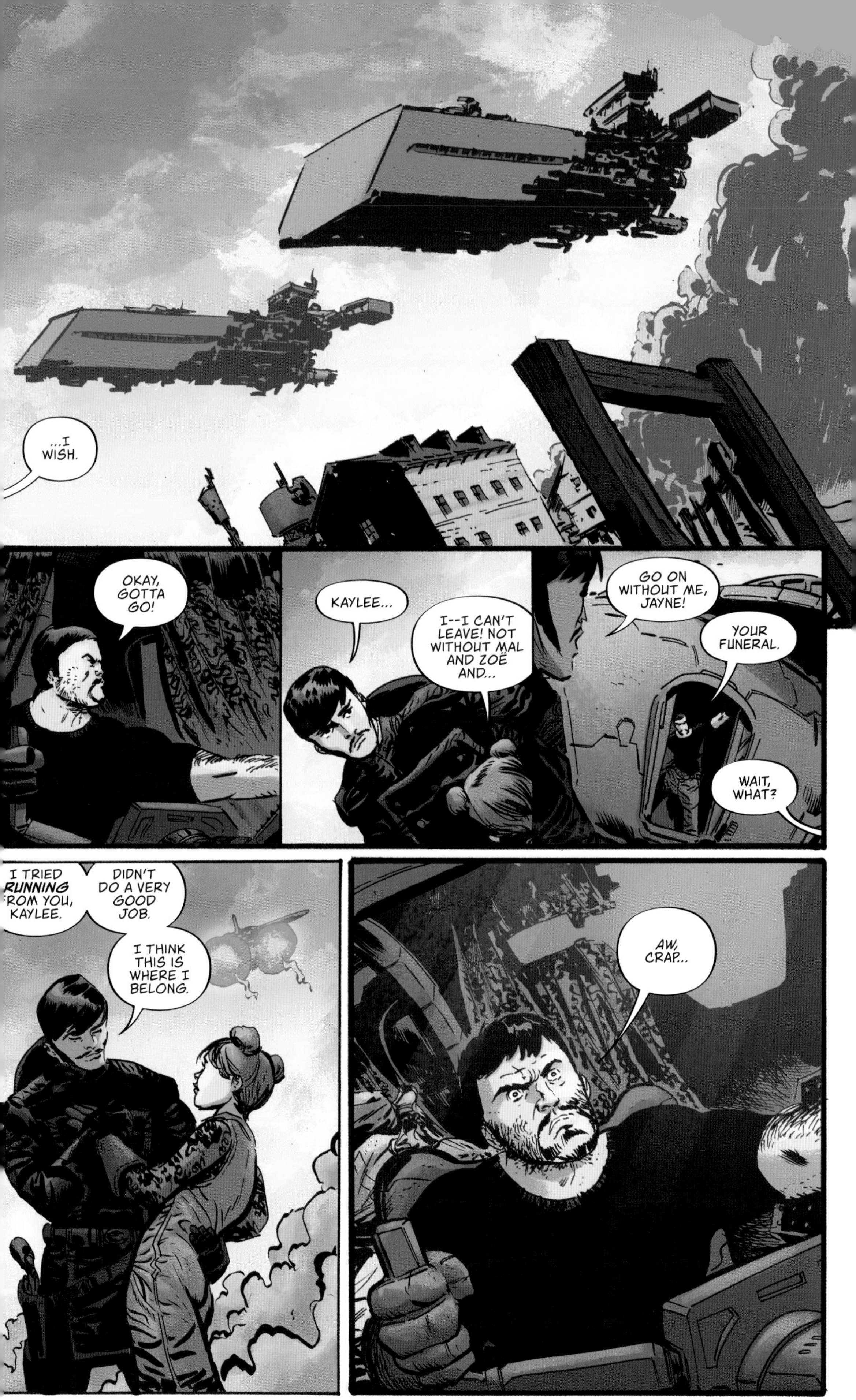
...I WISH.
OKAY, GOTTA GO!
KAYLEE...
I--I CAN'T LEAVE! NOT WITHOUT MAL AND ZOË AND...
GO ON WITHOUT ME, JAYNE!
YOUR FUNERAL.
WAIT, WHAT?
I TRIED RUNNING FROM YOU, KAYLEE.
DIDN'T DO A VERY GOOD JOB.
I THINK THIS IS WHERE I BELONG.
AW, CRAP...

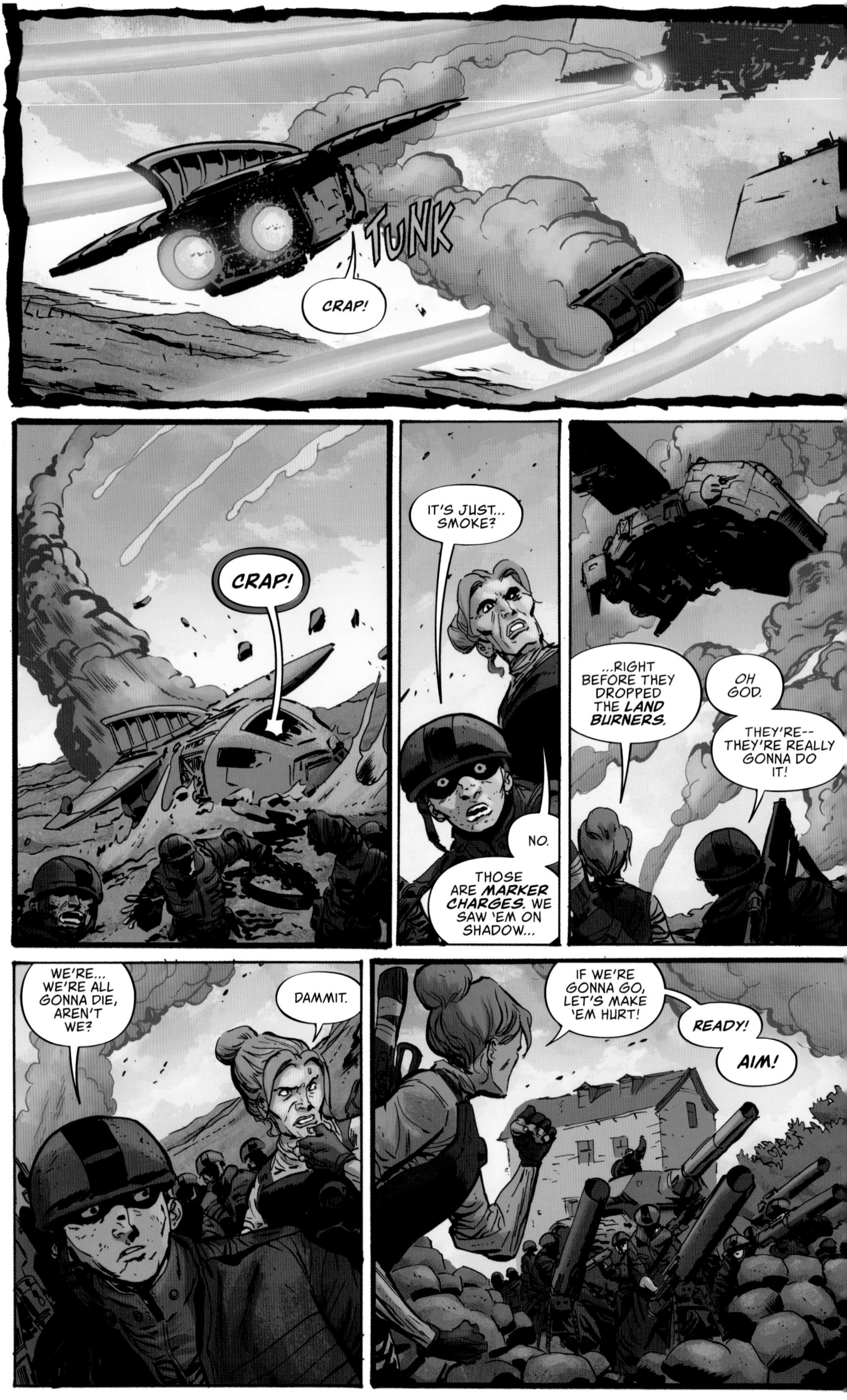
TUNK
CRAP!
CRAP!
IT'S JUST... SMOKE?
NO.
THOSE ARE MARKER CHARGES. WE SAW 'EM ON SHADOW...
...RIGHT BEFORE THEY DROPPED THE LAND BURNERS.
OH GOD.
THEY'RE-- THEY'RE REALLY GONNA DO IT!
WE'RE... WE'RE ALL GONNA DIE, AREN'T WE?
DAMMIT.
IF WE'RE GONNA GO, LET'S MAKE 'EM HURT!
READY!
AIM!

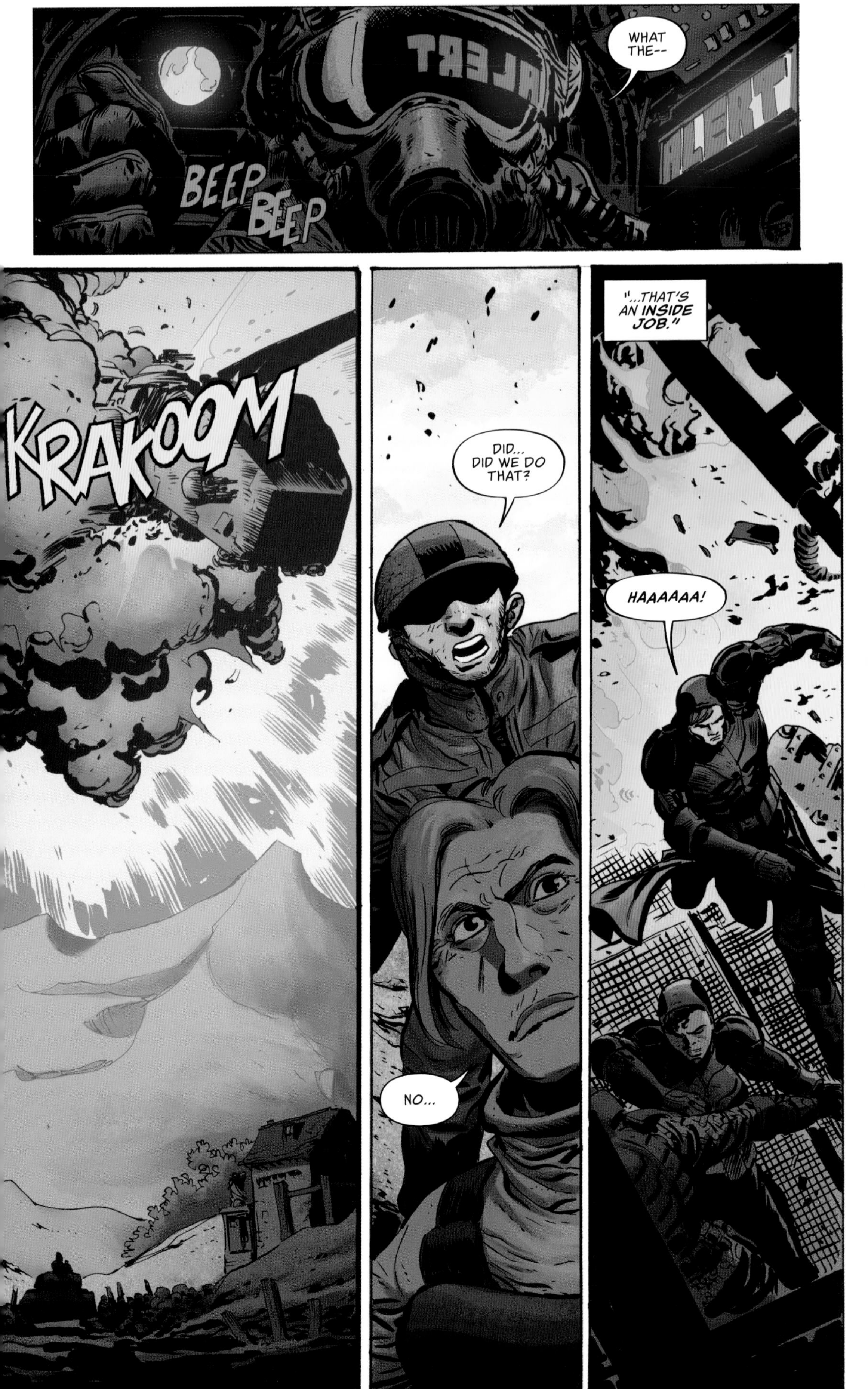
BEEP
BEEP
WHAT THE--
KRAKOOM
DID... DID WE DO THAT?
NO...
"...THAT'S AN INSIDE JOB."
HAAAAAA!

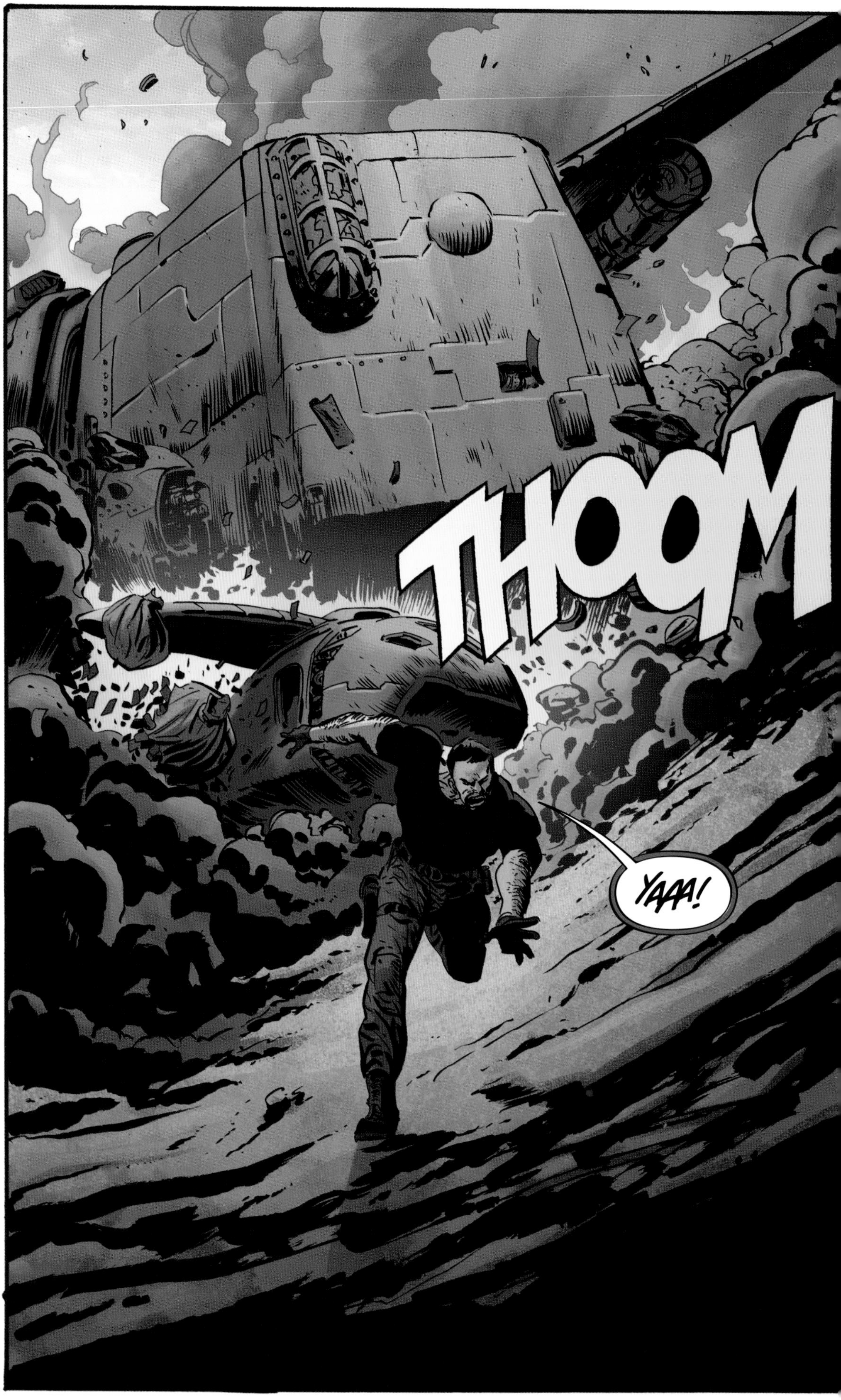
THOOM
YAAA!

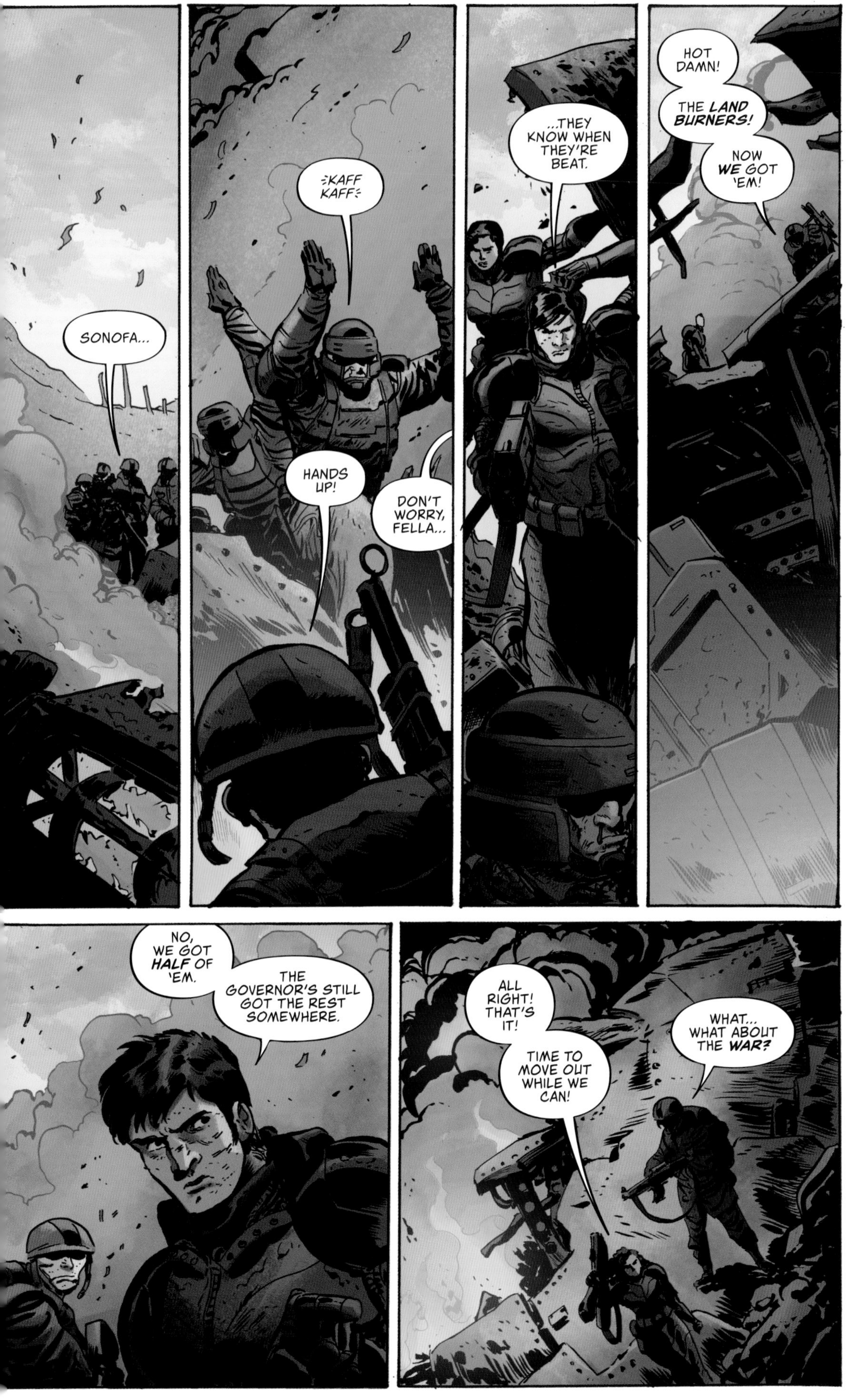
SONOFA...
KAFF KAFF
HANDS UP!
DON'T WORRY, FELLA...
...THEY KNOW WHEN THEY'RE BEAT.
HOT DAMN!
THE LAND BURNERS!
NOW WE GOT 'EM!
NO, WE GOT HALF OF 'EM.
THE GOVERNOR'S STILL GOT THE REST SOMEWHERE.
ALL RIGHT! THAT'S IT!
TIME TO MOVE OUT WHILE WE CAN!
WHAT... WHAT ABOUT THE WAR?

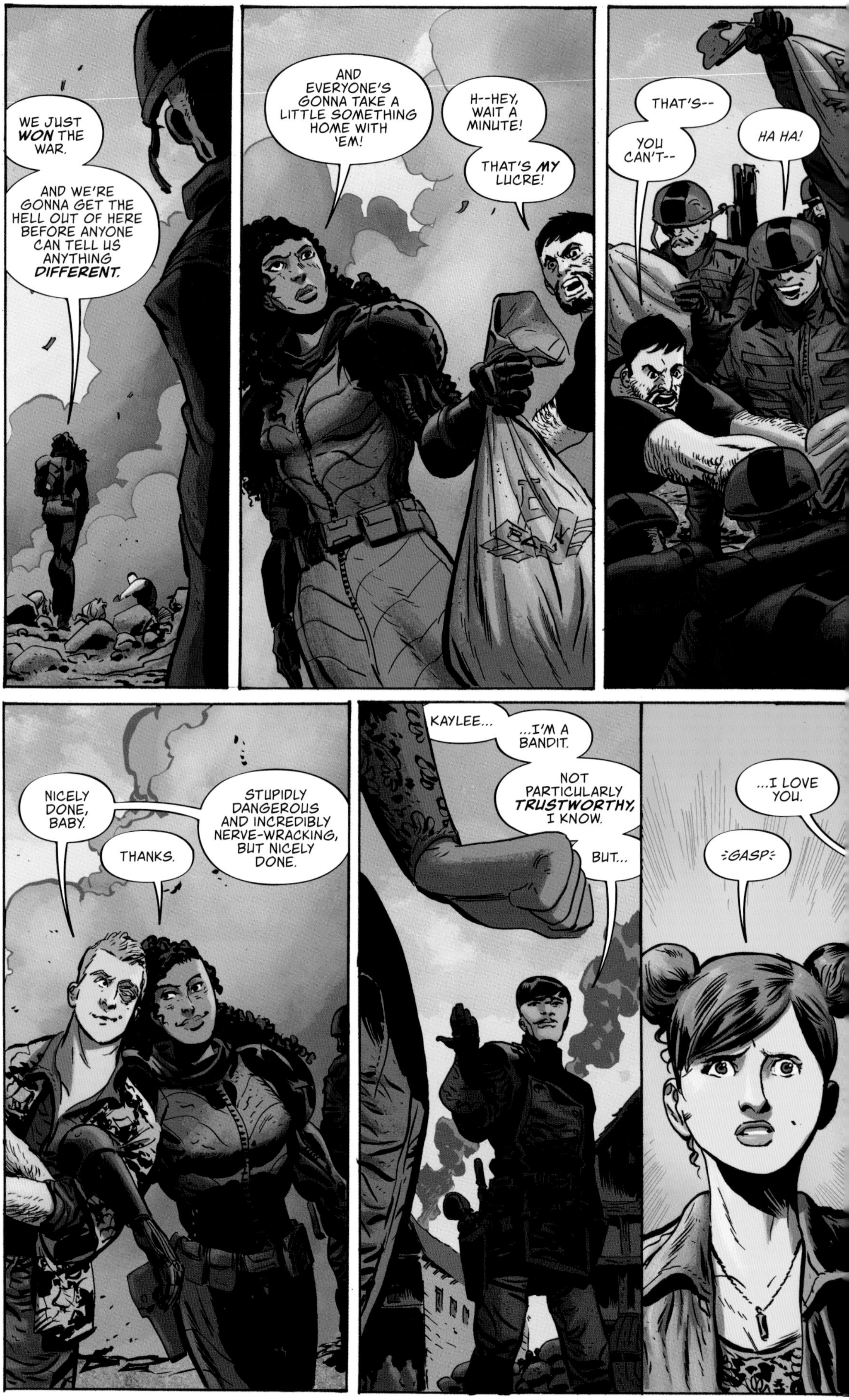

WE JUST WON THE WAR.
AND WE'RE GONNA GET THE HELL OUT OF HERE BEFORE ANYONE CAN TELL US ANYTHING DIFFERENT.
AND EVERYONE'S GONNA TAKE A LITTLE SOMETHING HOME WITH 'EM!
H--HEY, WAIT A MINUTE!
THAT'S MY LUCRE!
THAT'S--
YOU CAN'T--
HA HA!
NICELY DONE, BABY.
THANKS.
STUPIDLY DANGEROUS AND INCREDIBLY NERVE-WRACKING, BUT NICELY DONE.
KAYLEE...
...I'M A BANDIT.
NOT PARTICULARLY TRUSTWORTHY, I KNOW.
BUT...
...I LOVE YOU.
GASP

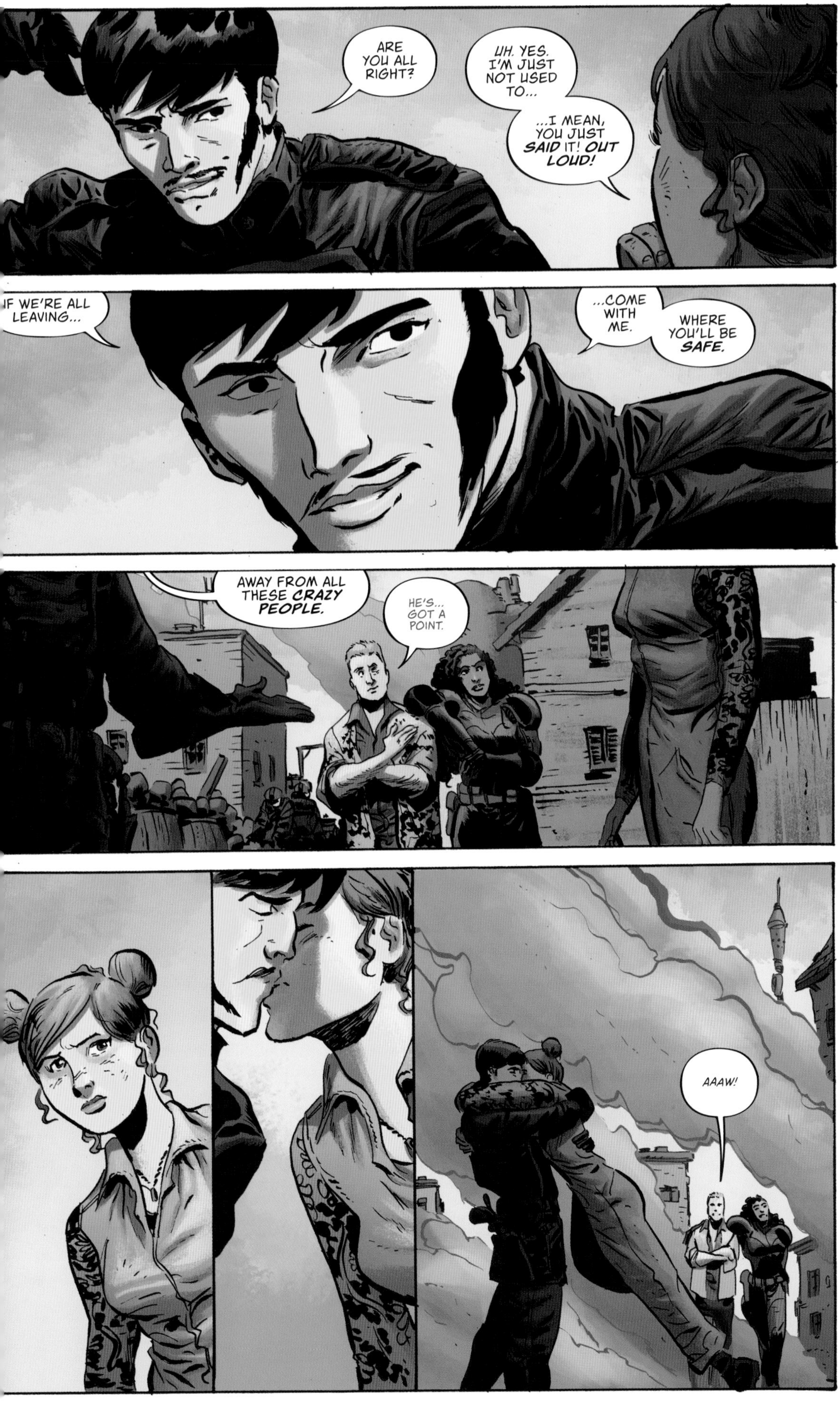
ARE YOU ALL RIGHT?
UH. YES. I'M JUST NOT USED TO...
...I MEAN, YOU JUST **SAID** IT! **OUT LOUD!**
IF WE'RE ALL LEAVING...
...COME WITH ME.
WHERE YOU'LL BE **SAFE.**
AWAY FROM ALL THESE **CRAZY PEOPLE.**
HE'S... GOT A POINT.
AAAW!

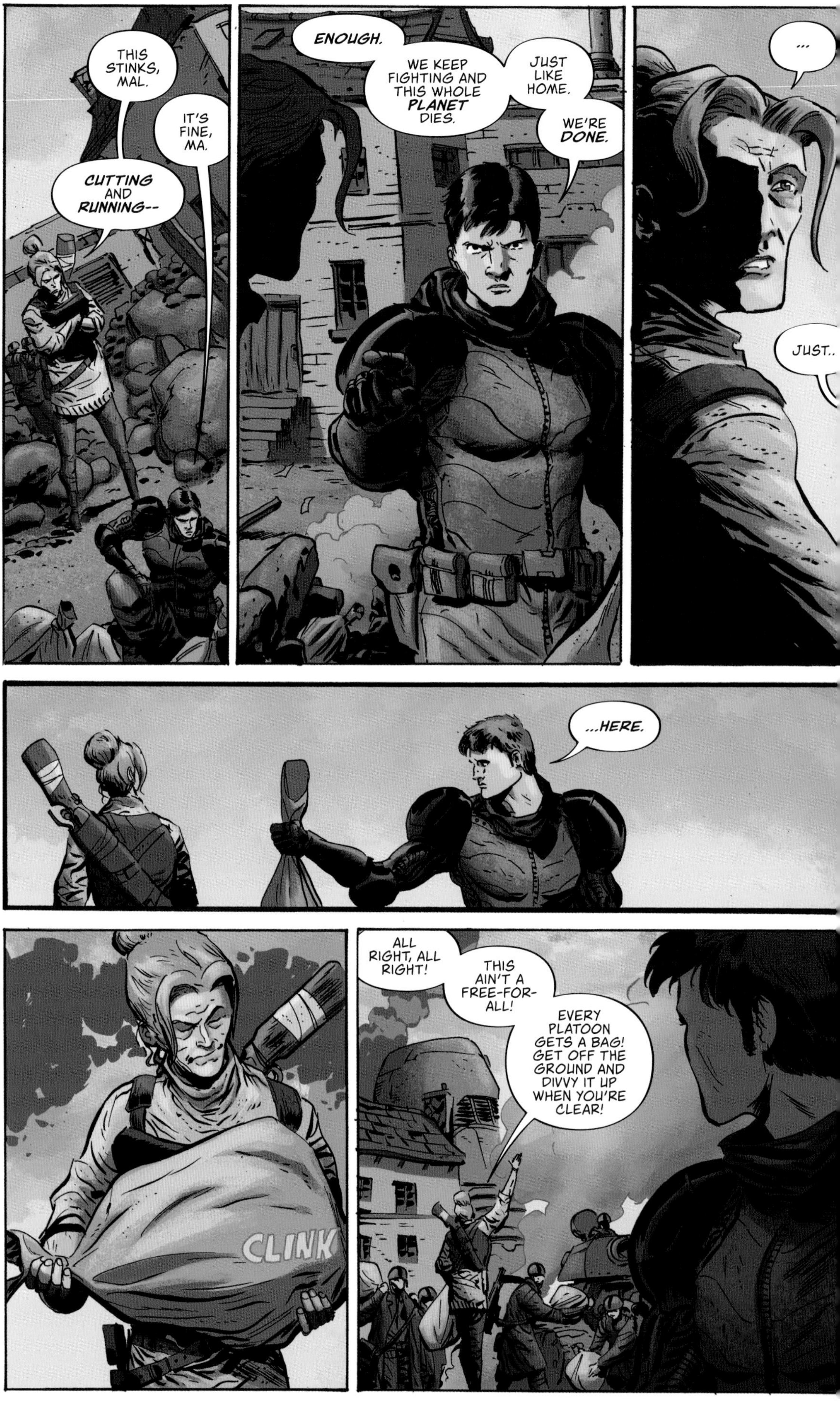
THIS STINKS, MAL.
IT'S FINE, MA.
CUTTING AND RUNNING--
ENOUGH.
WE KEEP FIGHTING AND THIS WHOLE PLANET DIES.
JUST LIKE HOME.
WE'RE DONE.
...
JUST..
...HERE.
CLINK
ALL RIGHT, ALL RIGHT!
THIS AIN'T A FREE-FOR-ALL!
EVERY PLATOON GETS A BAG! GET OFF THE GROUND AND DIVVY IT UP WHEN YOU'RE CLEAR!

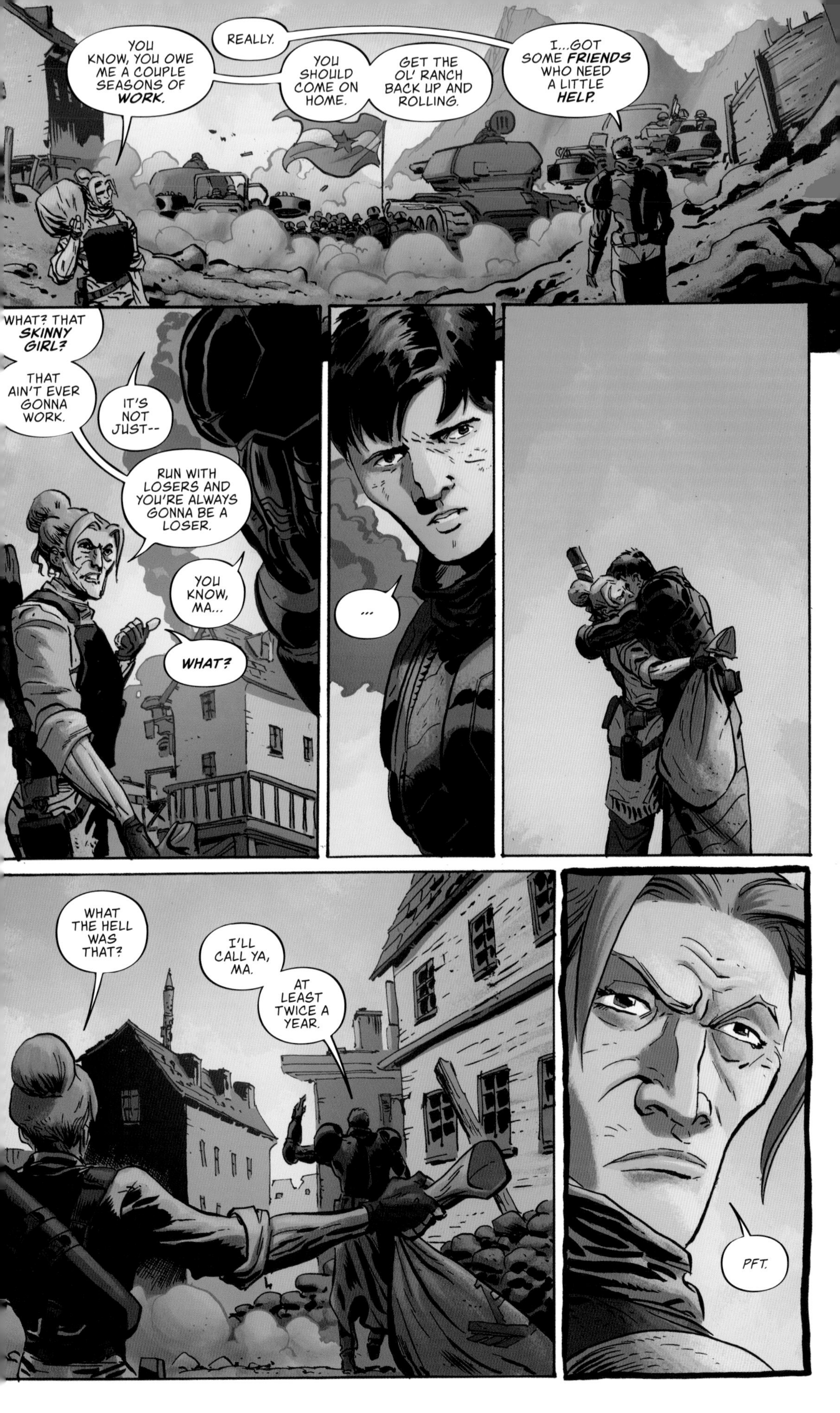
YOU KNOW, YOU OWE ME A COUPLE SEASONS OF **WORK.**
REALLY.
YOU SHOULD COME ON HOME.
GET THE OL' RANCH BACK UP AND ROLLING.
I...GOT SOME **FRIENDS** WHO NEED A LITTLE **HELP.**
WHAT? THAT **SKINNY GIRL?**
THAT AIN'T EVER GONNA WORK.
IT'S NOT JUST--
RUN WITH LOSERS AND YOU'RE ALWAYS GONNA BE A LOSER.
YOU KNOW, MA...
WHAT?
...
WHAT THE HELL WAS THAT?
I'LL CALL YA, MA.
AT LEAST TWICE A YEAR.
PFT.

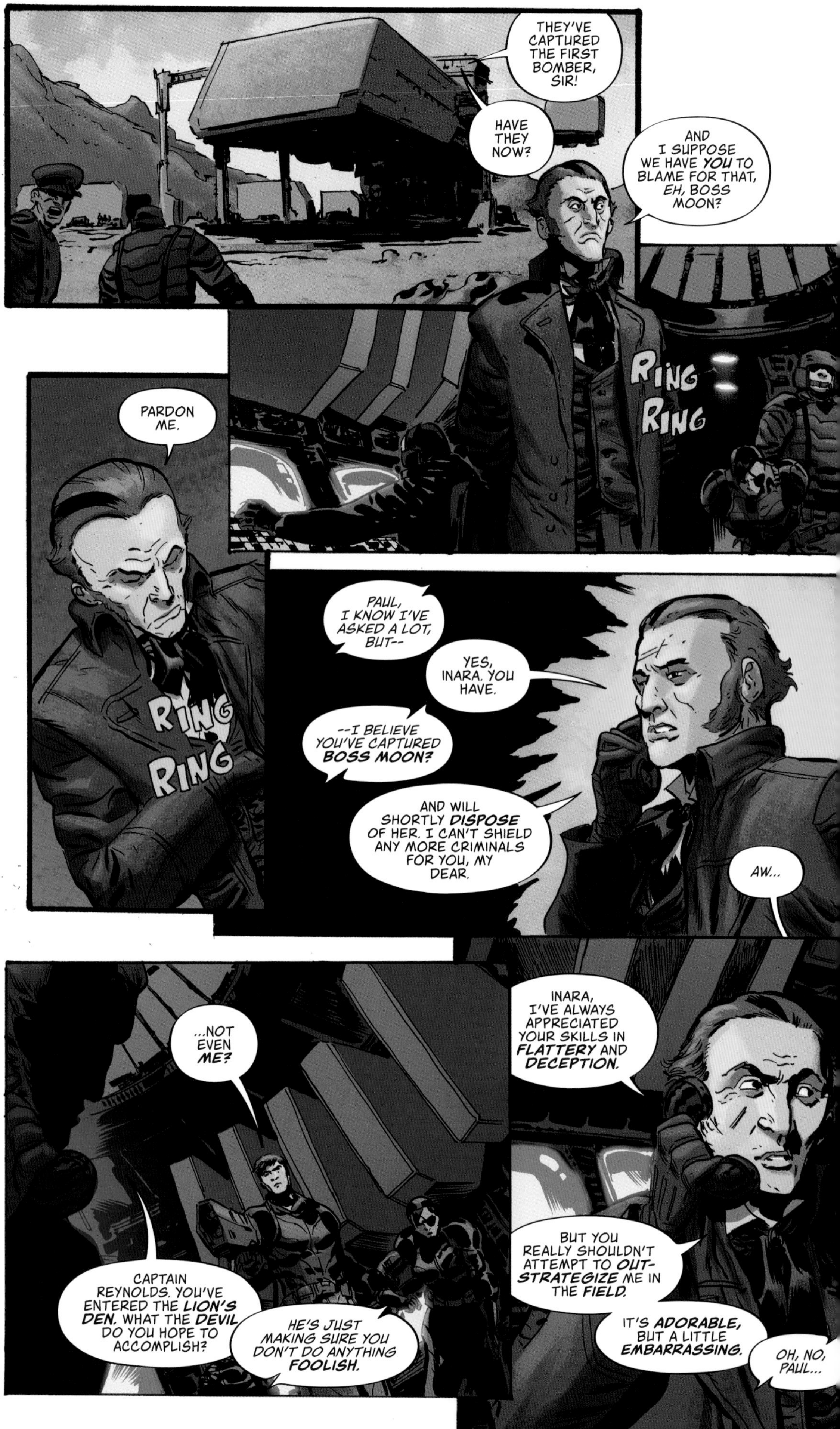
THEY'VE CAPTURED THE FIRST BOMBER, SIR!
HAVE THEY NOW?
AND I SUPPOSE WE HAVE YOU TO BLAME FOR THAT, EH, BOSS MOON?
RING RING
PARDON ME.
RING RING
PAUL, I KNOW I'VE ASKED A LOT, BUT--
YES, INARA. YOU HAVE.
--I BELIEVE YOU'VE CAPTURED BOSS MOON?
AND WILL SHORTLY DISPOSE OF HER. I CAN'T SHIELD ANY MORE CRIMINALS FOR YOU, MY DEAR.
AW...
...NOT EVEN ME?
INARA, I'VE ALWAYS APPRECIATED YOUR SKILLS IN FLATTERY AND DECEPTION.
BUT YOU REALLY SHOULDN'T ATTEMPT TO OUT-STRATEGIZE ME IN THE FIELD.
IT'S ADORABLE, BUT A LITTLE EMBARRASSING.
OH, NO, PAUL...
CAPTAIN REYNOLDS. YOU'VE ENTERED THE LION'S DEN. WHAT THE DEVIL DO YOU HOPE TO ACCOMPLISH?
HE'S JUST MAKING SURE YOU DON'T DO ANYTHING FOOLISH.

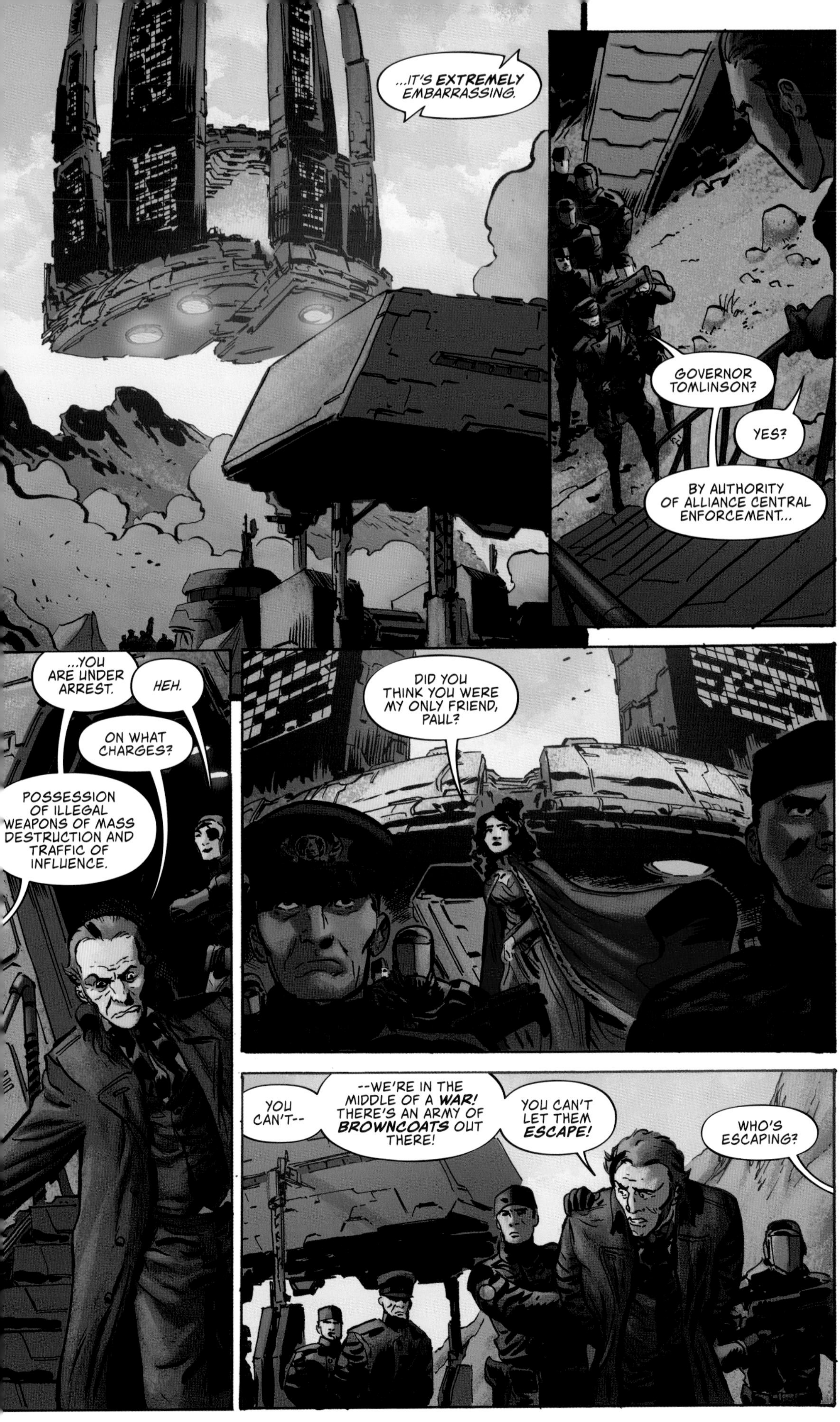

...IT'S EXTREMELY EMBARRASSING.
GOVERNOR TOMLINSON?
YES?
BY AUTHORITY OF ALLIANCE CENTRAL ENFORCEMENT...
...YOU ARE UNDER ARREST.
HEH.
ON WHAT CHARGES?
POSSESSION OF ILLEGAL WEAPONS OF MASS DESTRUCTION AND TRAFFIC OF INFLUENCE.
DID YOU THINK YOU WERE MY ONLY FRIEND, PAUL?
YOU CAN'T--
--WE'RE IN THE MIDDLE OF A WAR! THERE'S AN ARMY OF BROWNCOATS OUT THERE!
YOU CAN'T LET THEM ESCAPE!
WHO'S ESCAPING?

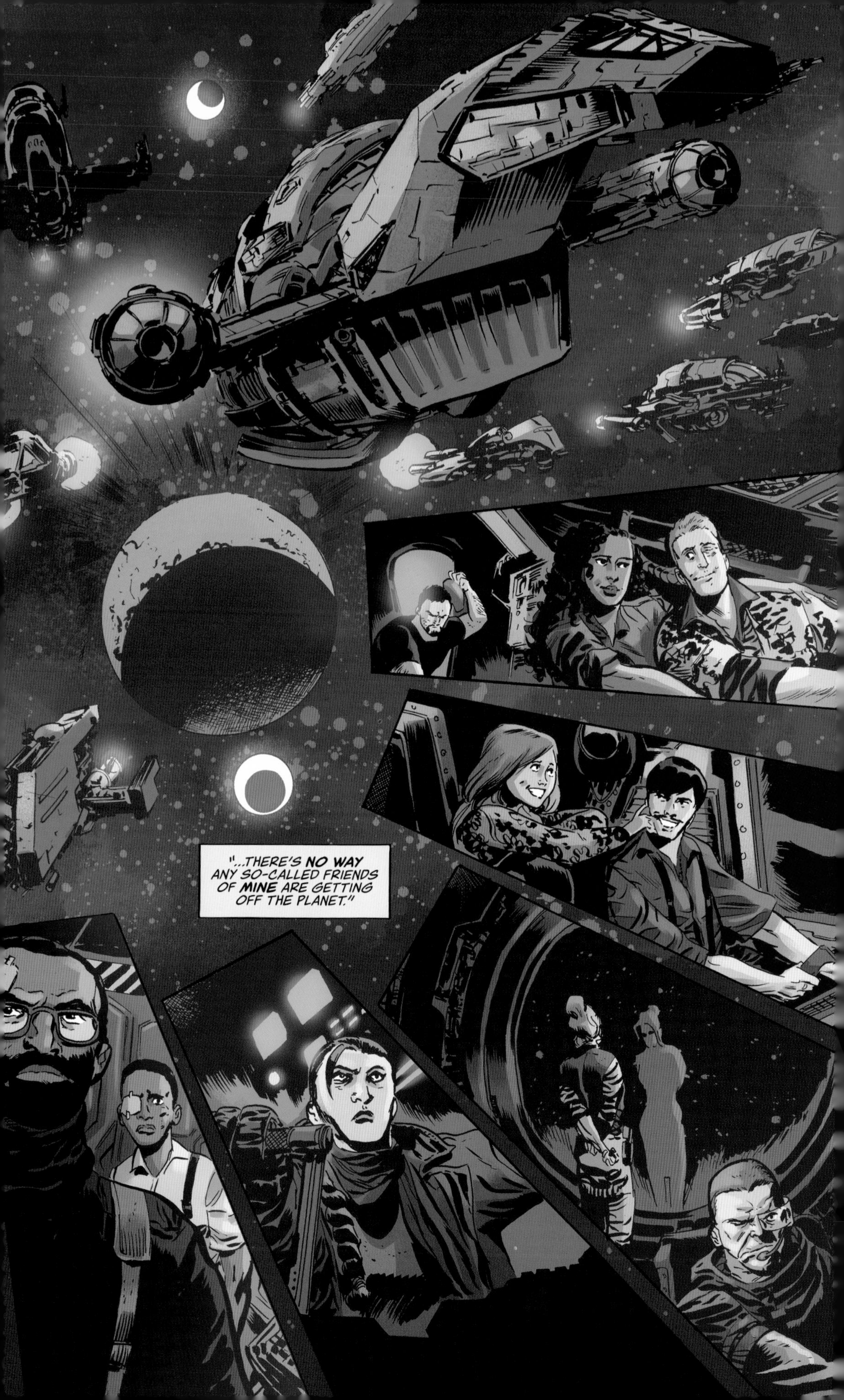
"...THERE'S NO WAY ANY SO-CALLED FRIENDS OF MINE ARE GETTING OFF THE PLANET."

WE'VE GOT US SOME CRIME TO BE DONE.

YOU'RE LO

WE ALL A

喧闹 起来

WHAT MAKES US SPE

This is why
lost, you k
SUP

te me where I cannot stand. I don't care, I'm still free, you can't take the sky from me.

You'd care
AWFUL
ED IN MY SKY.

d spot, sir. She still has the a

I don't care, I'm still free, you can't take the sky from me. Take me out to the black, tell them I ain't co

Burn the land and boil the sea, you can't take the sky from me. There's no place, I can be, since

Ship like this will be with you 'til the day you die. That's 'cause it's a death trap.

Sir, I think you have a problem with your brain being missing.

Put this crew together with the promise of work, which the alliance makes harder every
year. Come a day there won't be room for naughty men like us to slip about at all

SO HERE IS US, ON THE RAGGEDY EDGE

喧闹 起来

SHINY. BE

BAD GUY

LET'S BE

INEVITABLE

BETRAYAL. WE'D BE DEAD.

Curse your sudden but

Can't get paid if you're dead.

If you

CA

H

Ys

It's a real burden
BEING RIGHT

Fruity oaty bar!

Fruity oaty bar!

Fruity oaty bar!

ke us?

What did I say to you about
barging into my shuttle? Tha

I brought you some supper. But
if you'd prefer a lecture I have a
few very catchy ones prepped.

SIN AND
HELLFIRE.
ONE HAS
LEPERS. 旅

MANLY AN
IMPULSIVE

BLUE
SUN

Preacher, don't t
pretty specific tha
Quite specific

said

寿日

COVER GALLERY

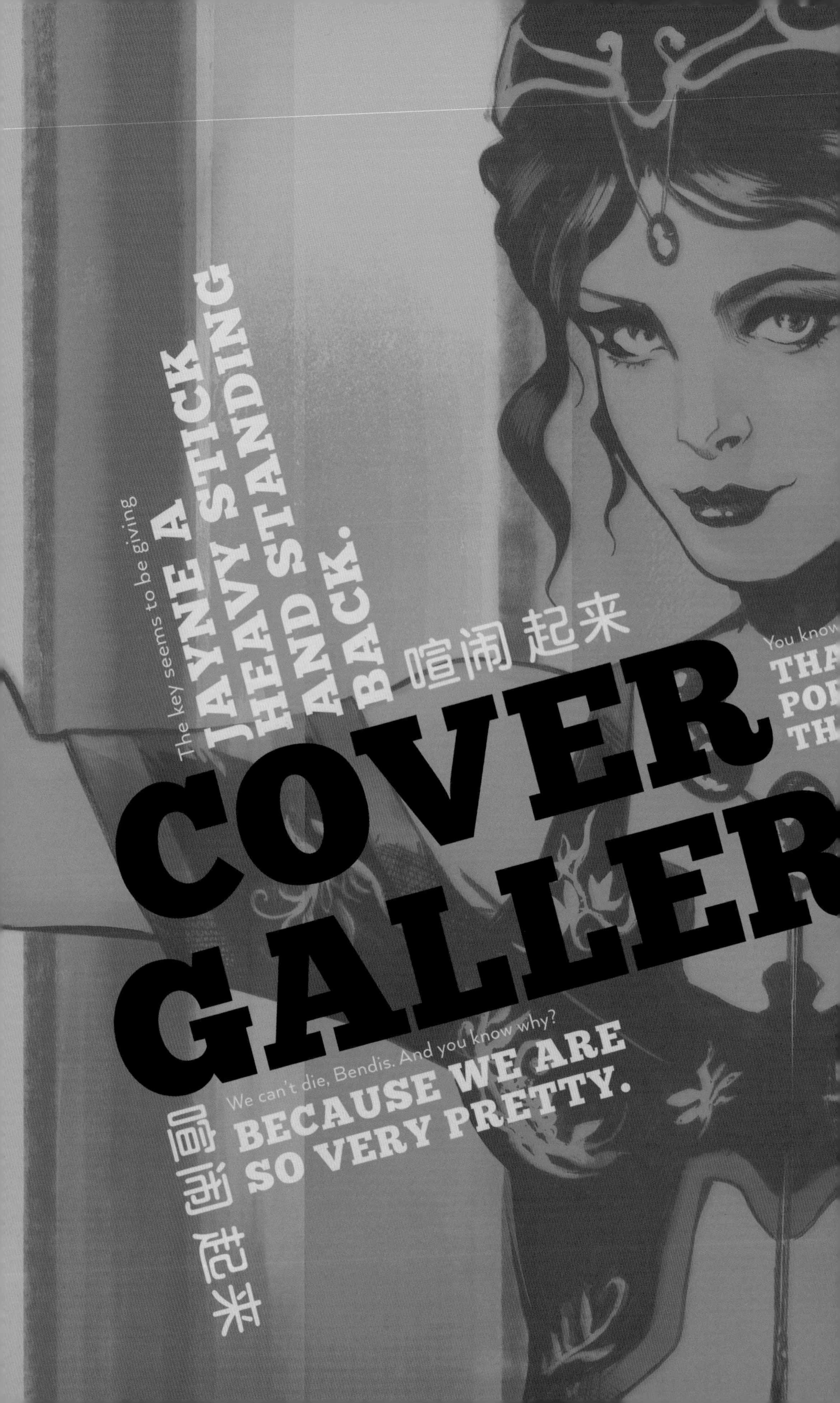
The key seems to be giving
JAYNE A HEAVY STICK AND STANDING BACK.
喧闹起来
We can't die, Bendis. And you know why?
BECAUSE WE ARE SO VERY PRETTY.
喧闹起来
You know

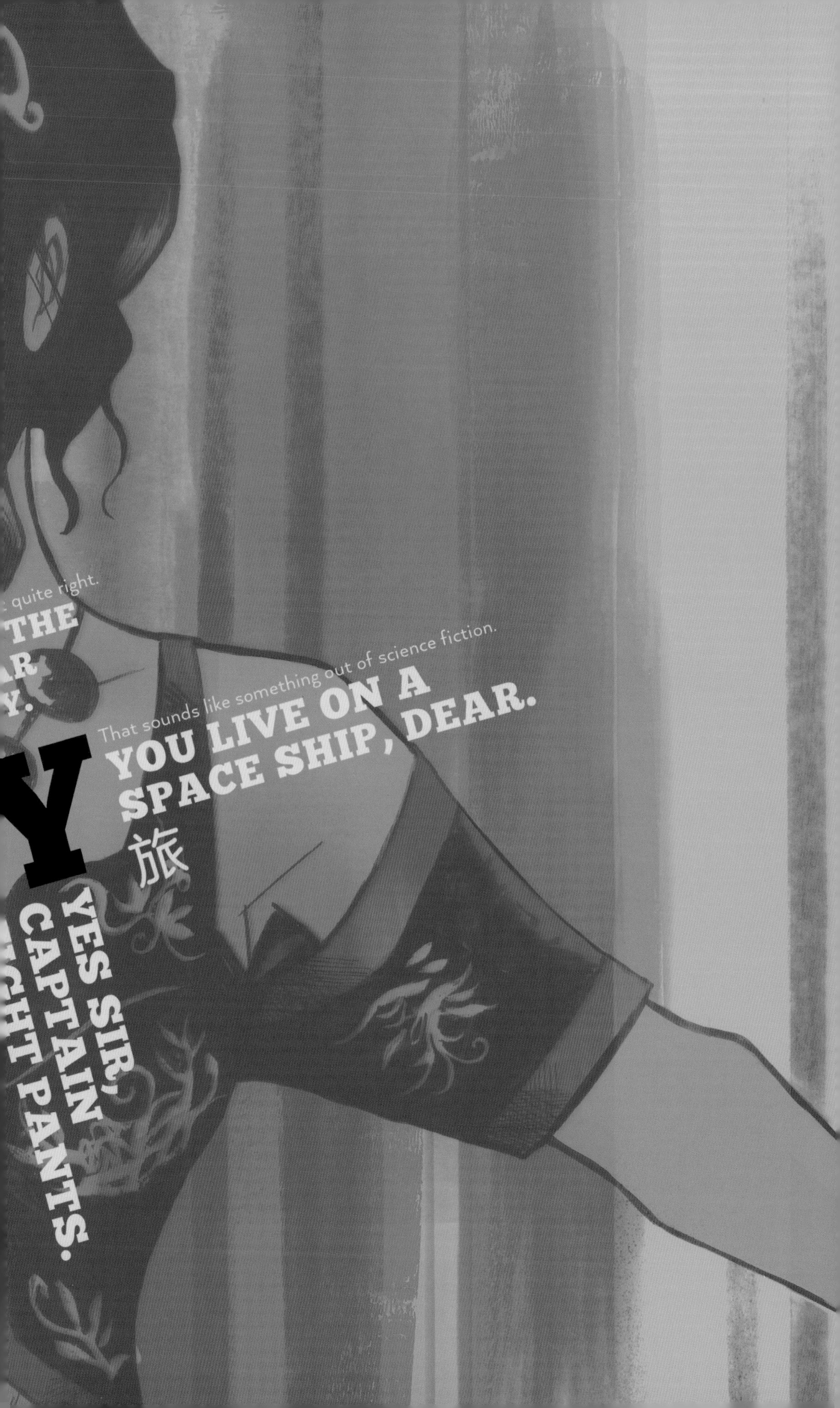
quite right.
THE
That sounds like something out of science fiction.
YOU LIVE ON A
SPACE SHIP, DEAR.
Y
旅
YES SIR,
CAPTAIN
CHT PANTS.

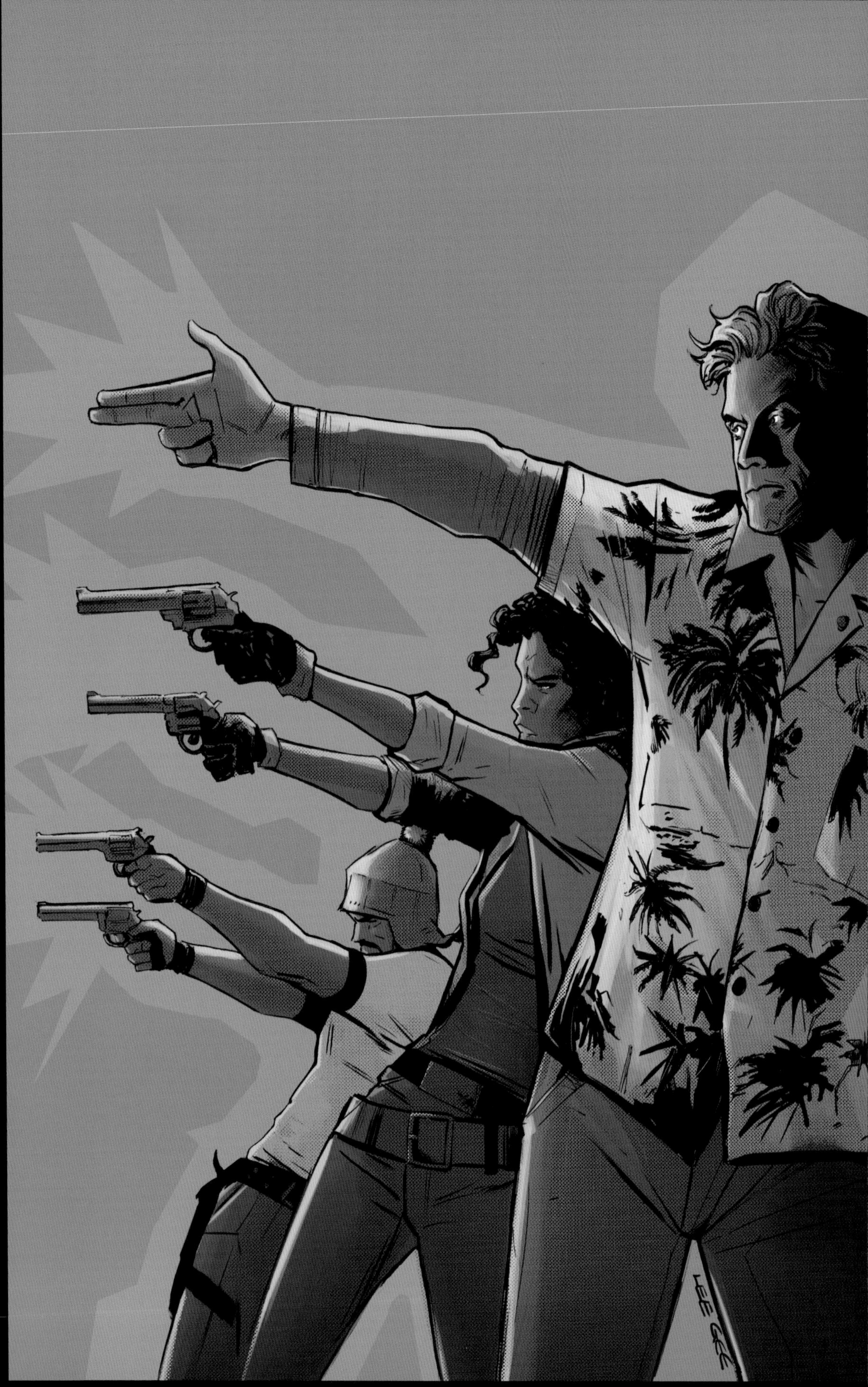

Firefly #9 Cover by **Lee Garbett**

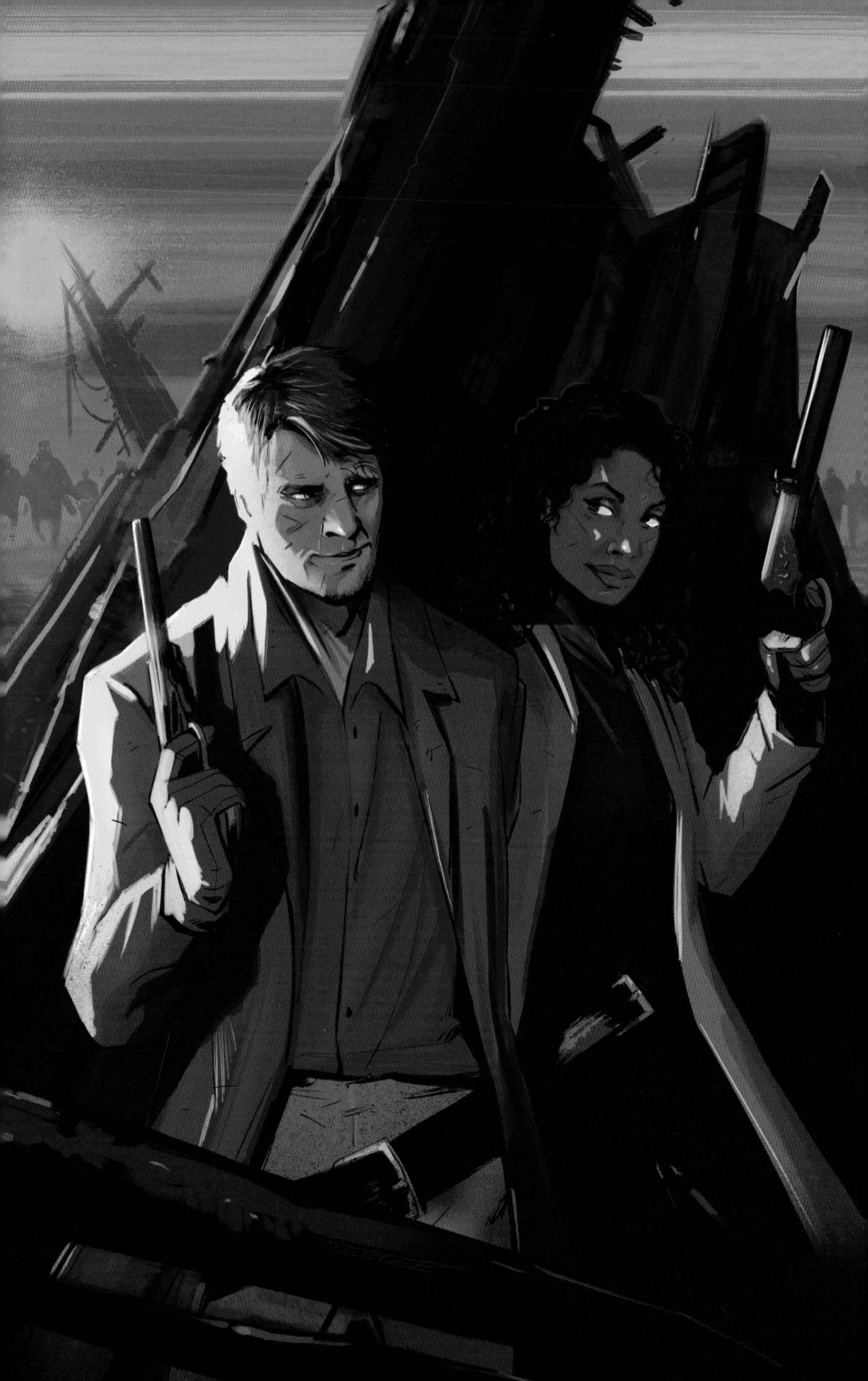

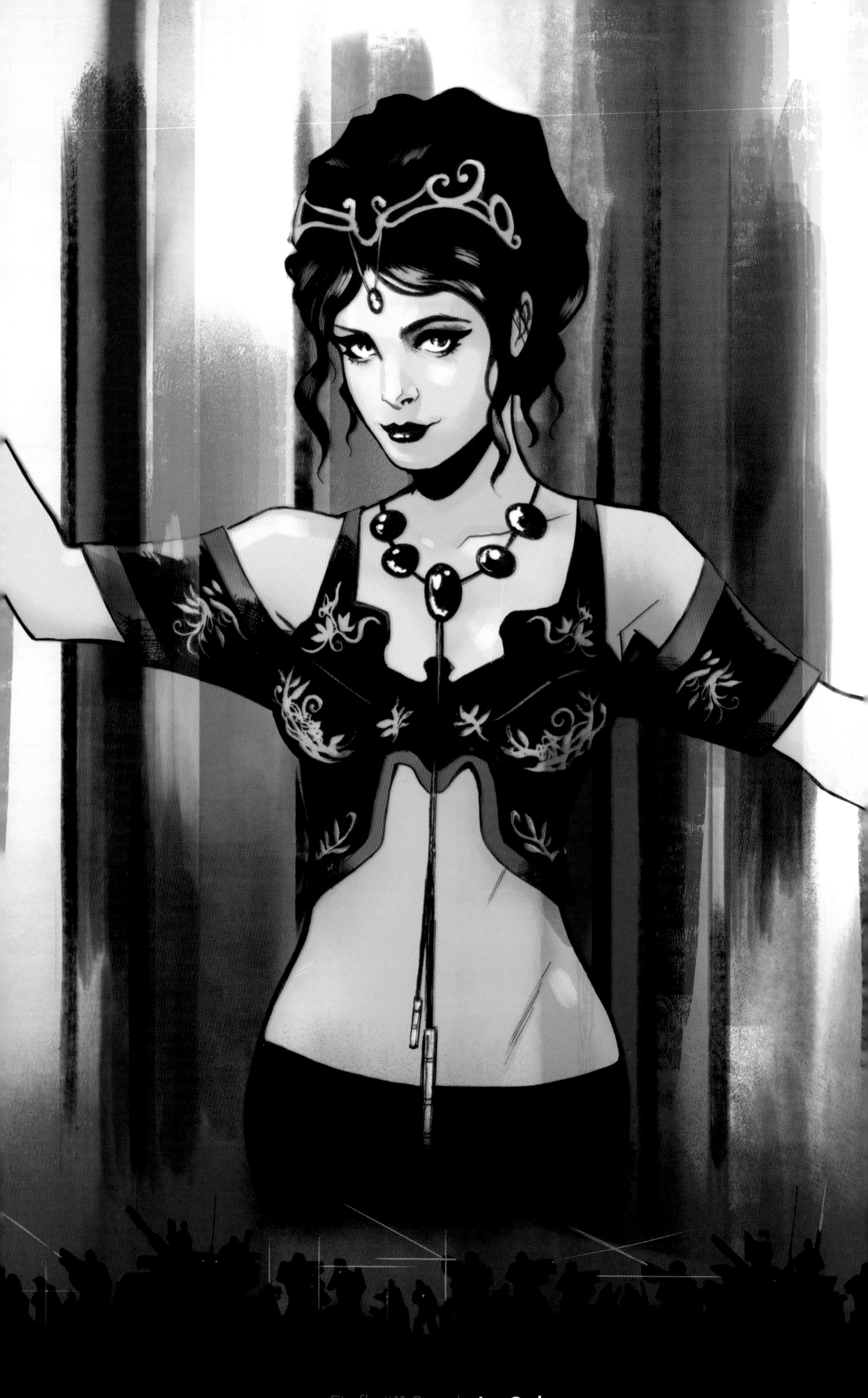

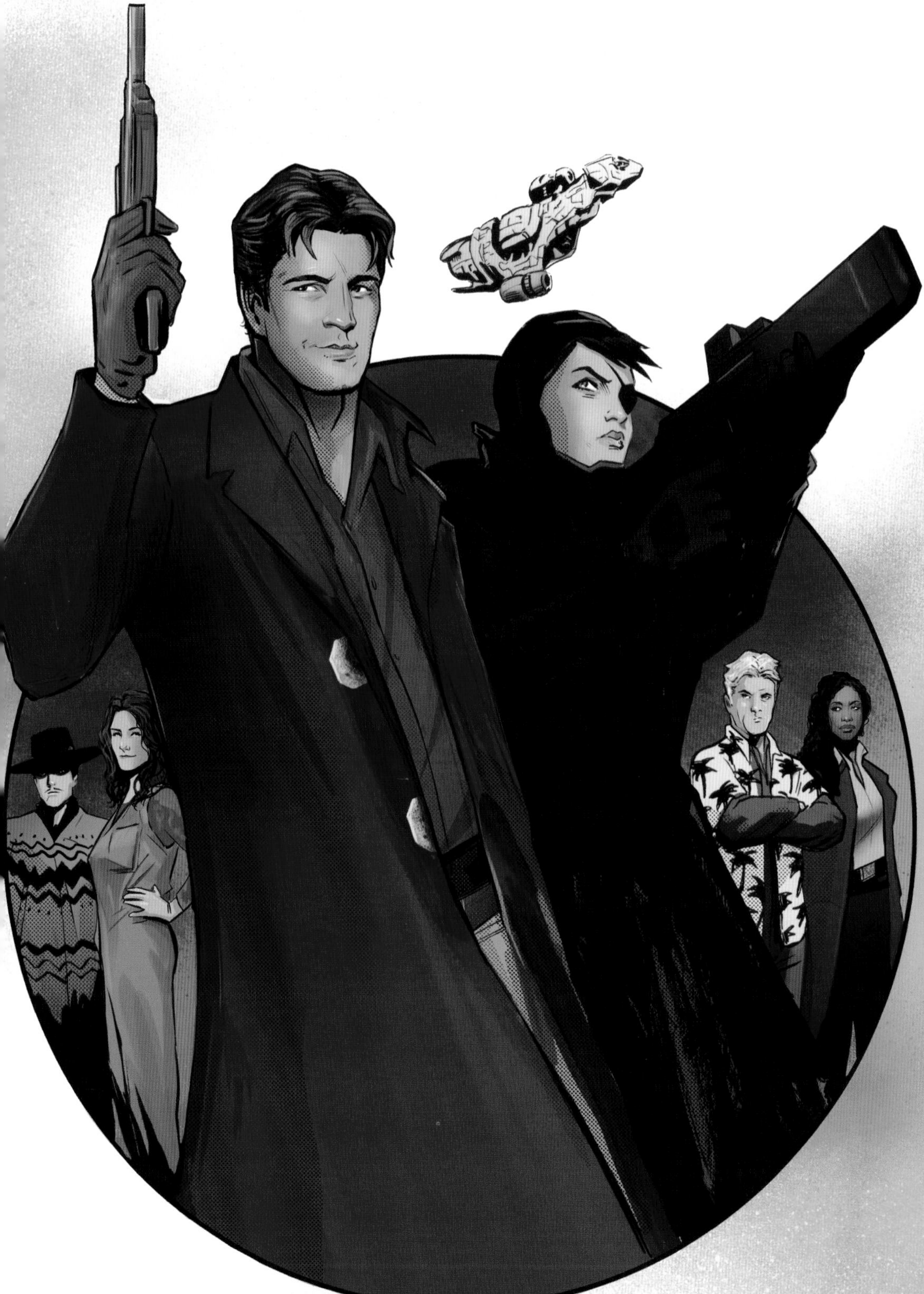

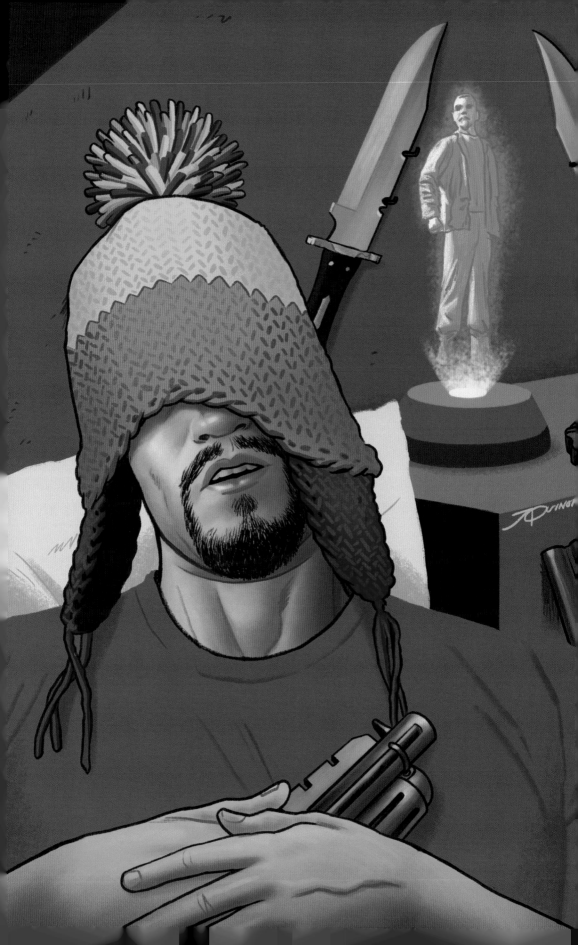

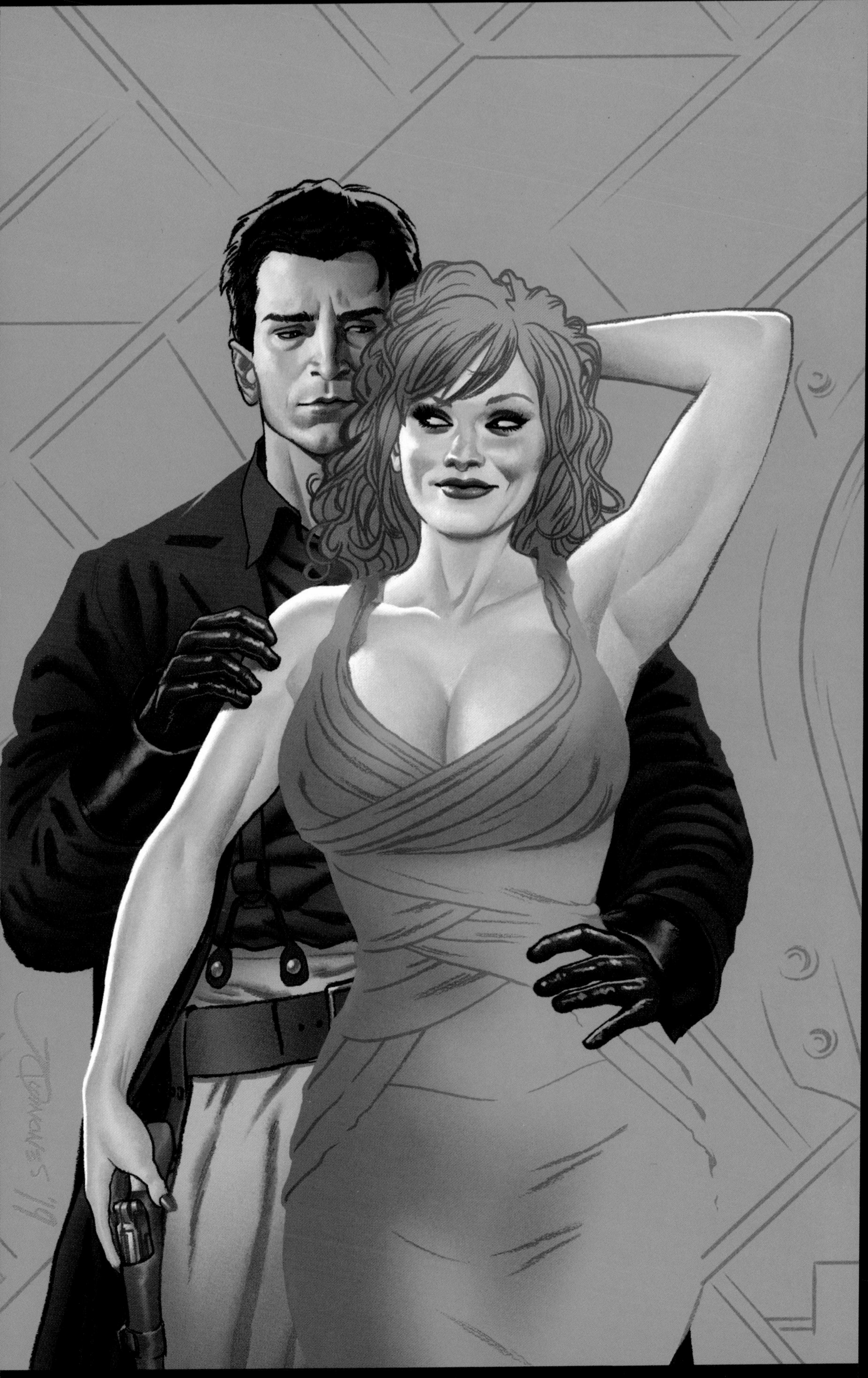

Firefly #10 Preorder Cover by **Joe Quinones**

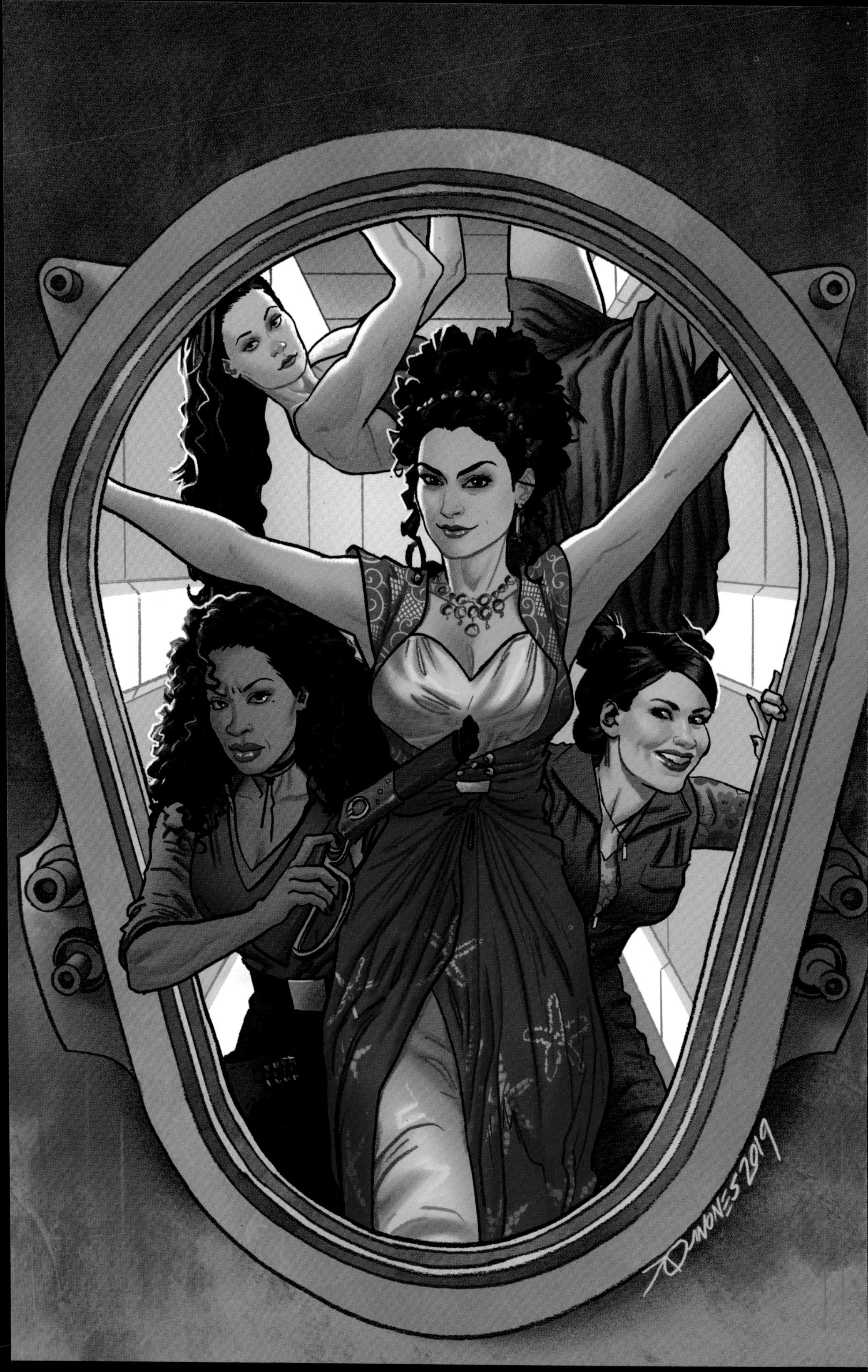
QUINONES 2019

Firefly #11 Preorder Cover by **Joe Quinones**

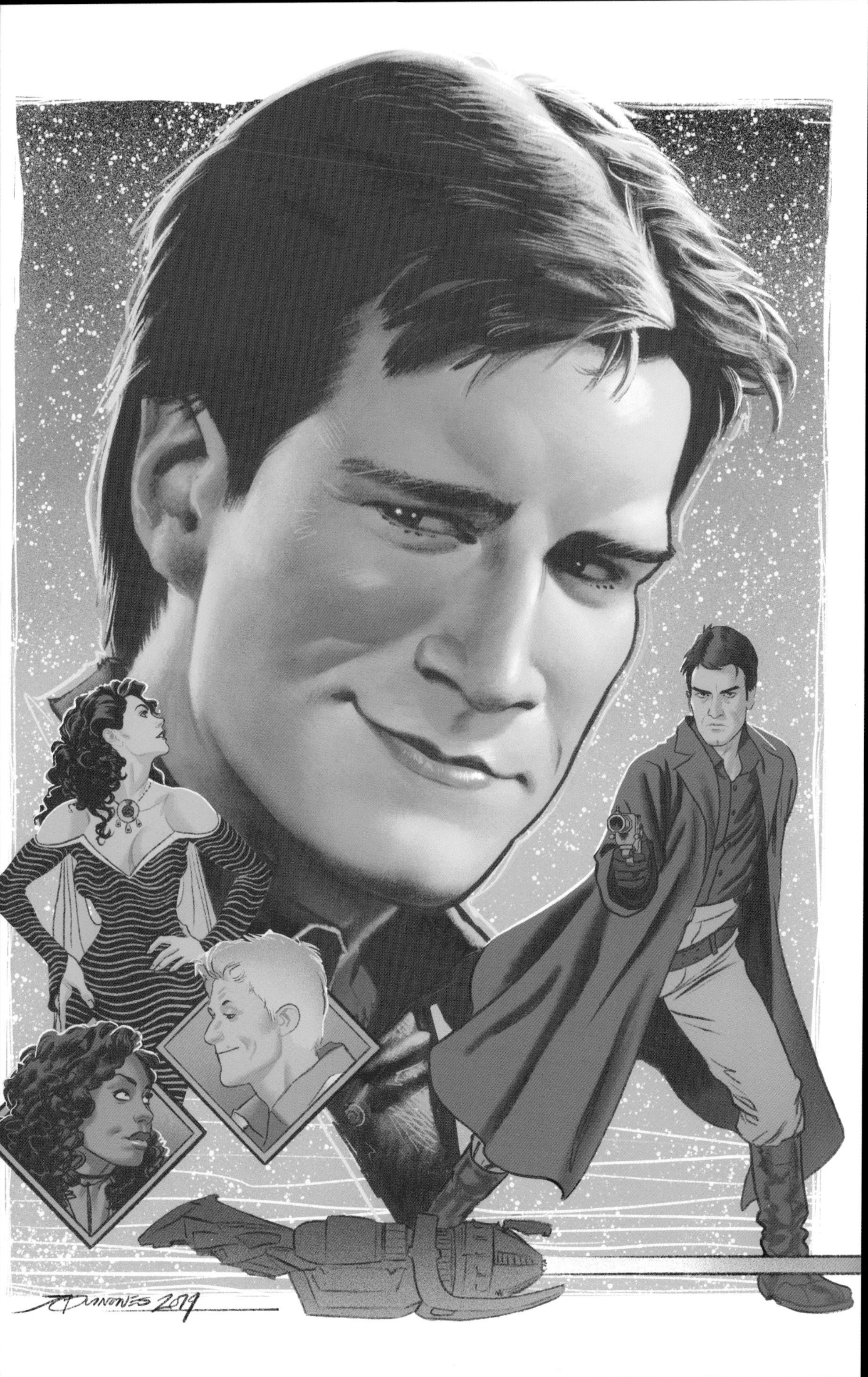

Firefly #12 Preorder Cover by **Joe Quinones**

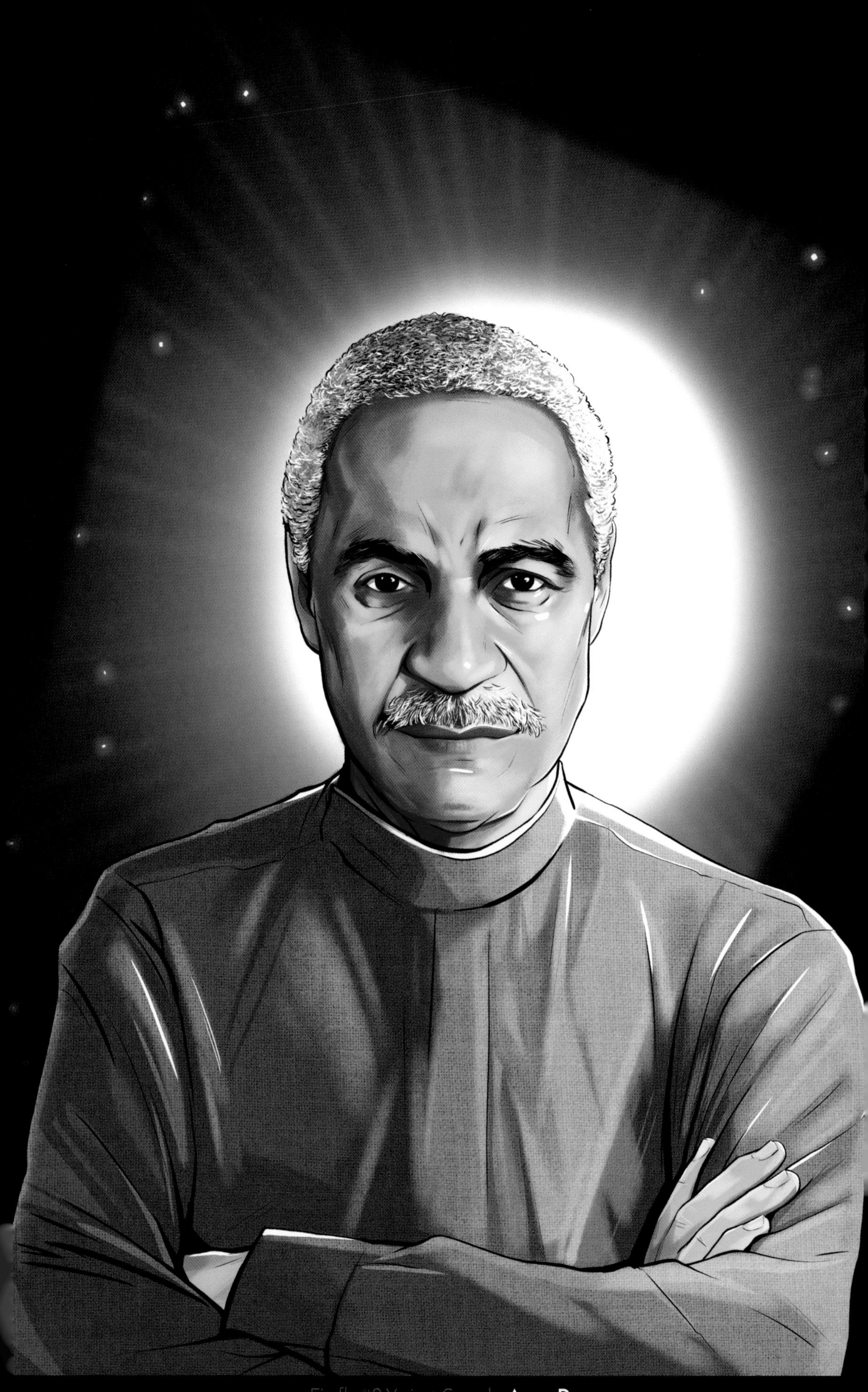

Firefly #9 Variant Cover by **Aaron Dana**

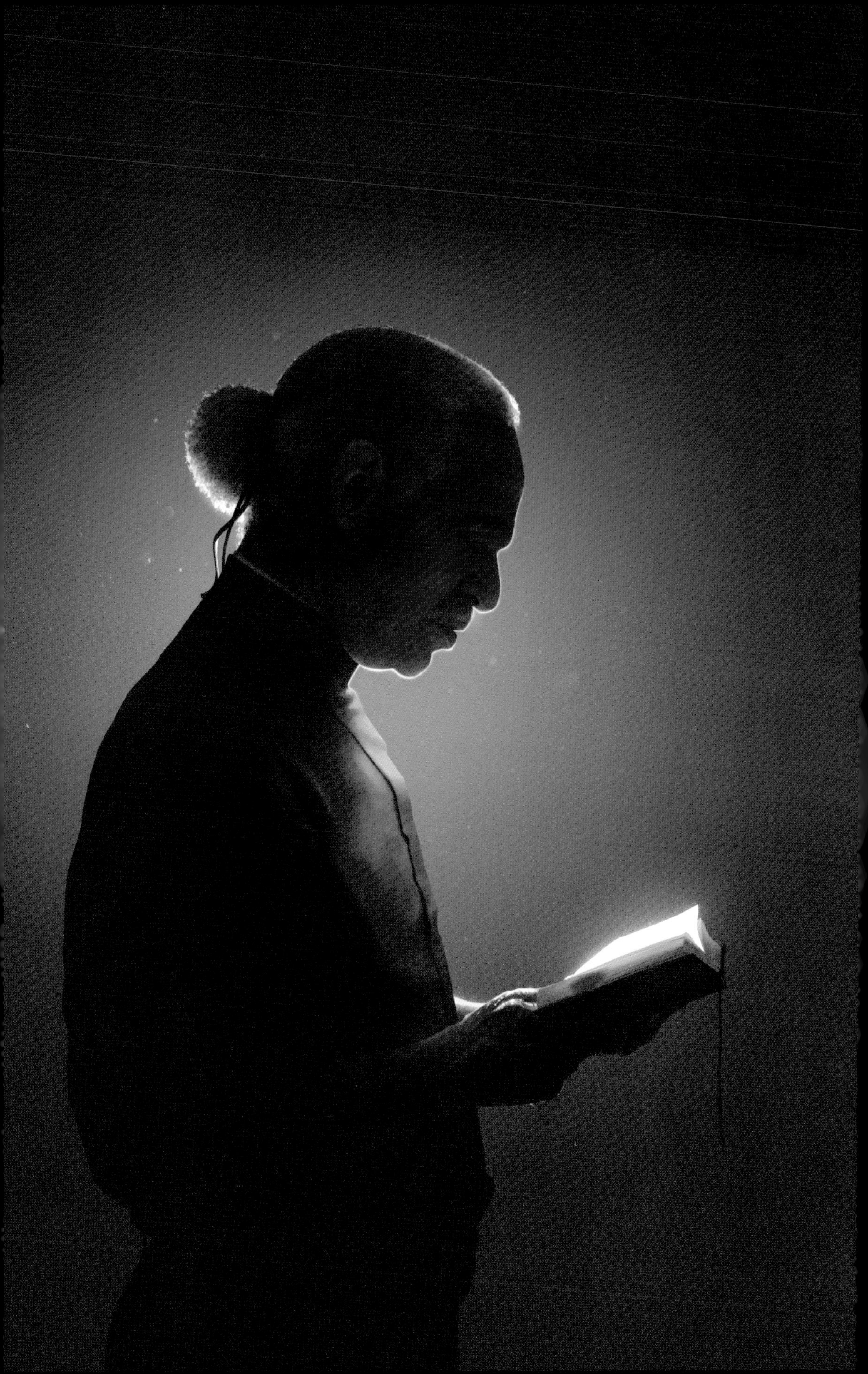

Firefly #10 Variant Cover by **Rahzzah**

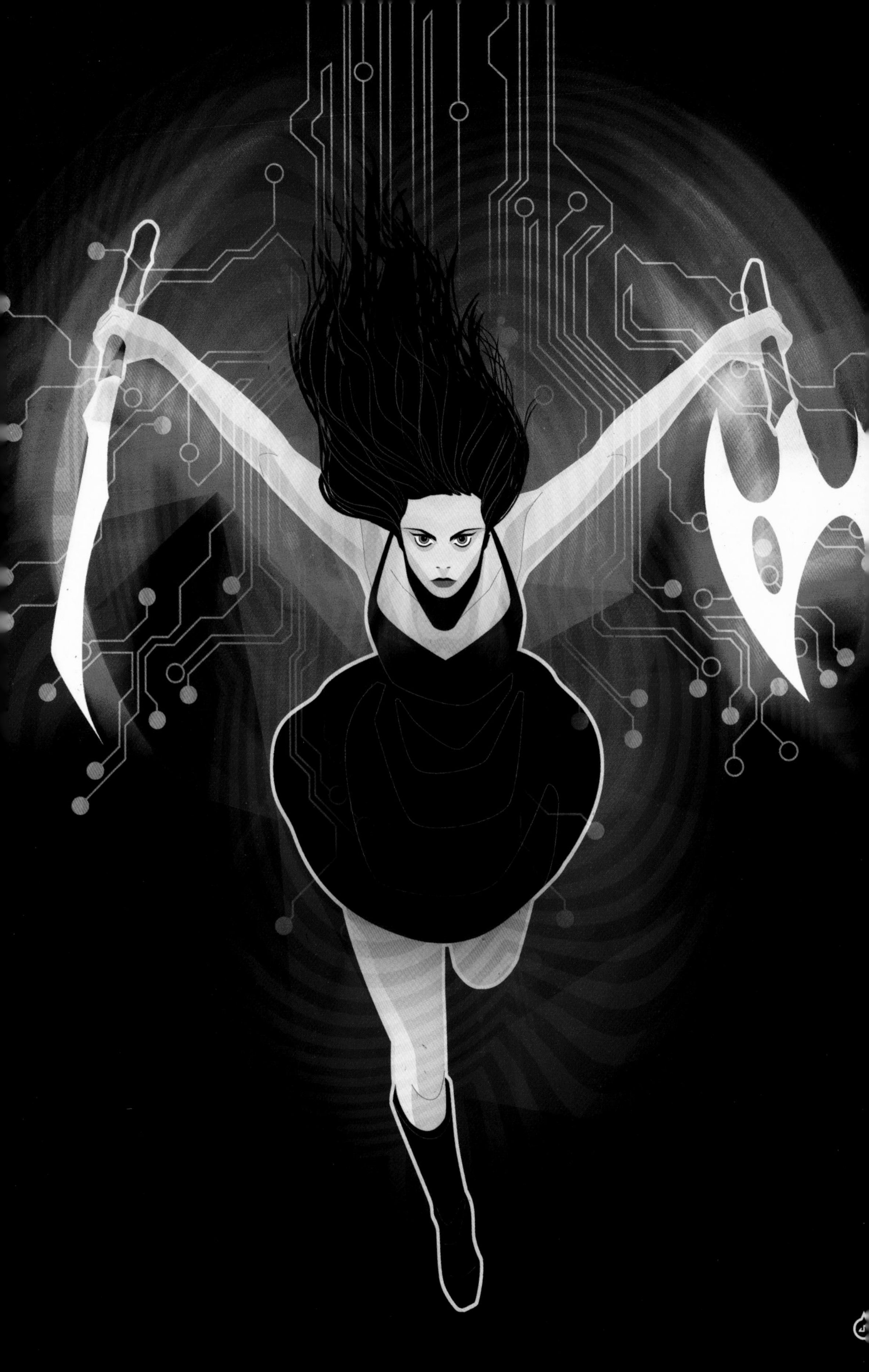

Firefly #11 Variant Cover by **Juan Doe**

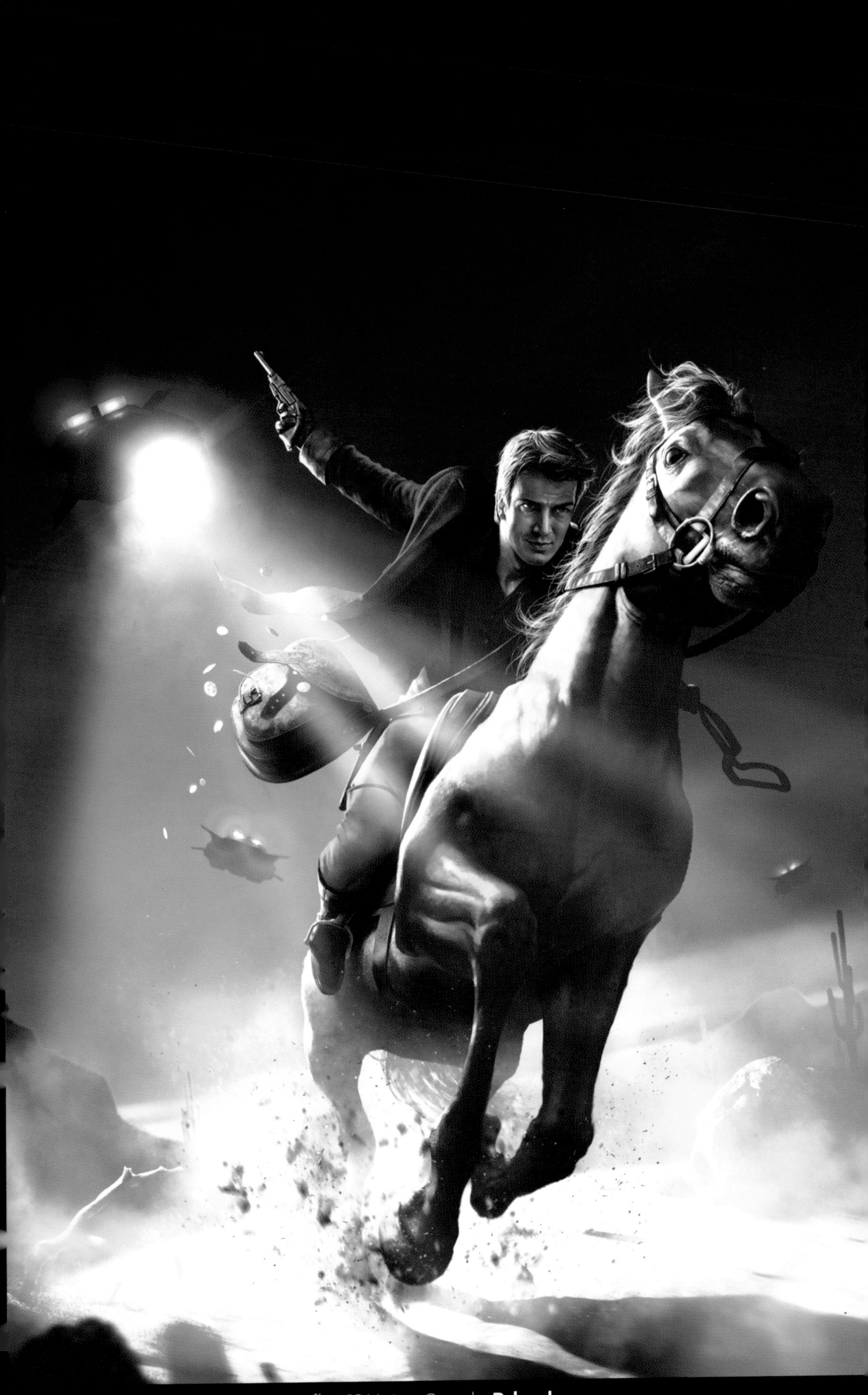

Firefly #12 Variant Cover by **Rahzzah**

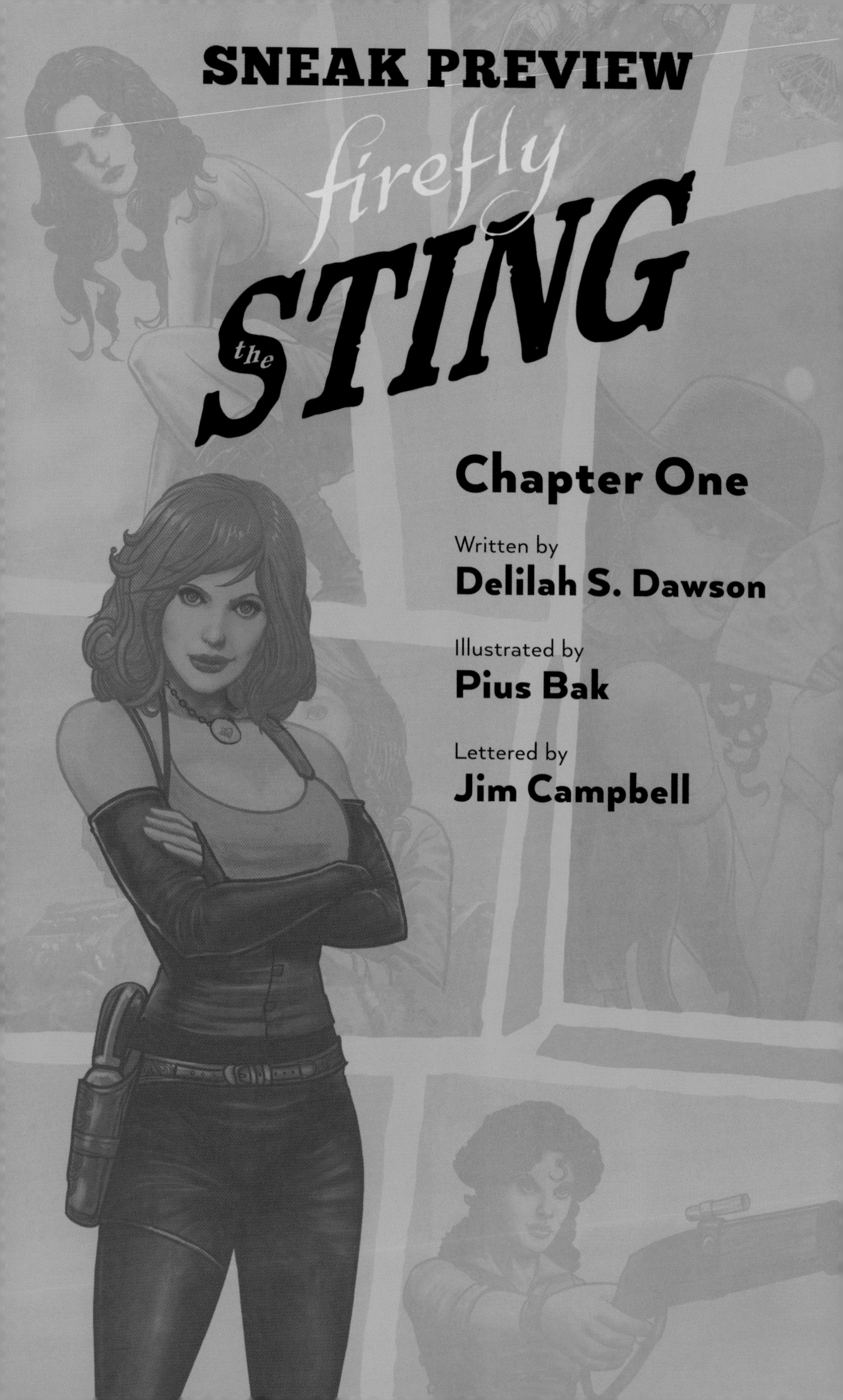

SNEAK PREVIEW

firefly
the STING

Chapter One

Written by
Delilah S. Dawson

Illustrated by
Pius Bak

Lettered by
Jim Campbell

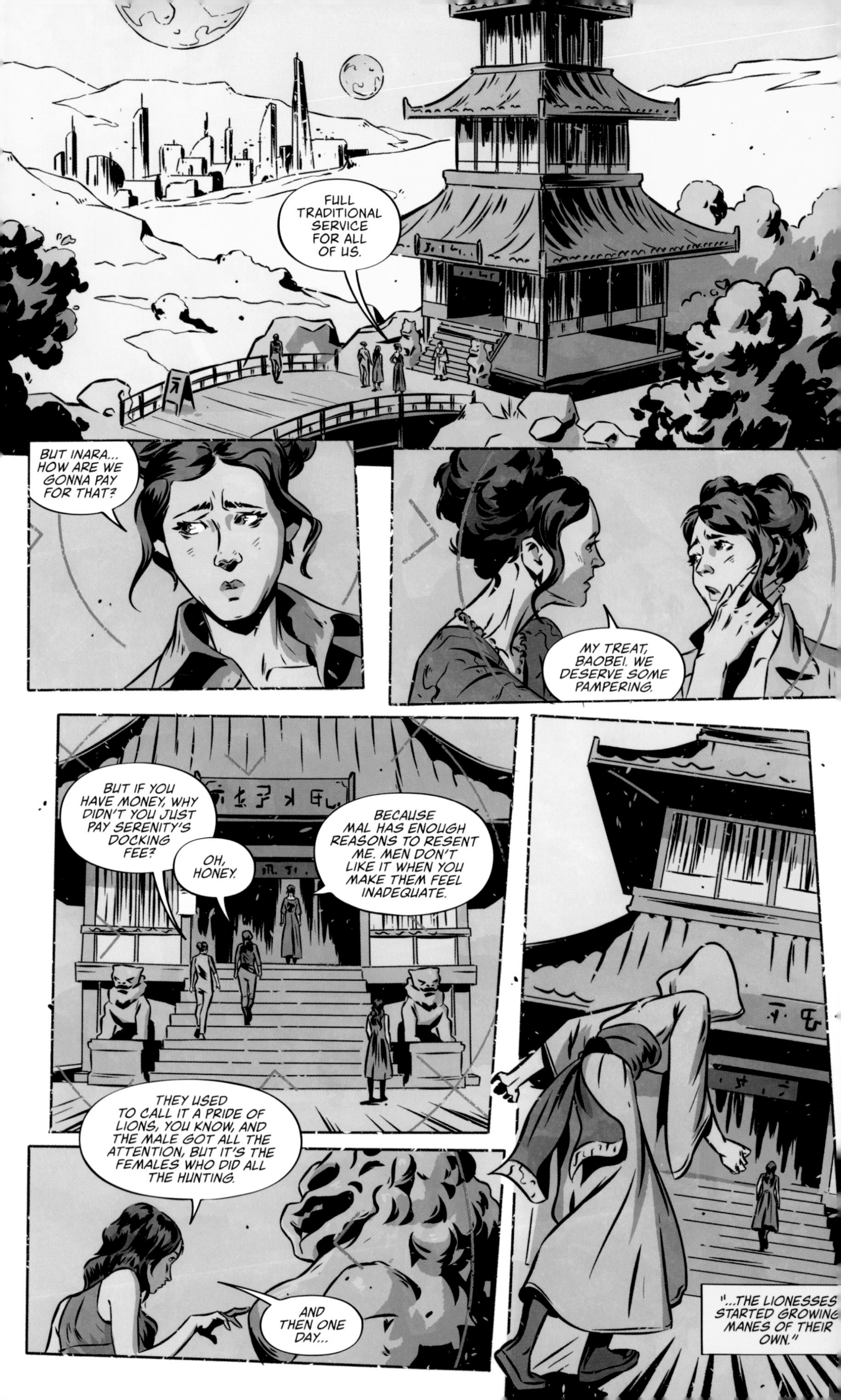
FULL TRADITIONAL SERVICE FOR ALL OF US.
BUT INARA... HOW ARE WE GONNA PAY FOR THAT?
MY TREAT, BAOBEI. WE DESERVE SOME PAMPERING.
BUT IF YOU HAVE MONEY, WHY DIDN'T YOU JUST PAY SERENITY'S DOCKING FEE?
OH, HONEY.
BECAUSE MAL HAS ENOUGH REASONS TO RESENT ME. MEN DON'T LIKE IT WHEN YOU MAKE THEM FEEL INADEQUATE.
THEY USED TO CALL IT A PRIDE OF LIONS, YOU KNOW, AND THE MALE GOT ALL THE ATTENTION, BUT IT'S THE FEMALES WHO DID ALL THE HUNTING.
AND THEN ONE DAY...
"...THE LIONESSES STARTED GROWING MANES OF THEIR OWN."

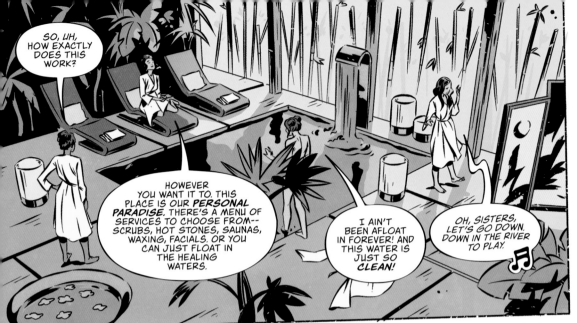

SO, UH, HOW EXACTLY DOES THIS WORK?

HOWEVER YOU WANT IT TO. THIS PLACE IS OUR *PERSONAL PARADISE*. THERE'S A MENU OF SERVICES TO CHOOSE FROM-- SCRUBS, HOT STONES, SAUNAS, WAXING, FACIALS. OR YOU CAN JUST FLOAT IN THE HEALING WATERS.

I AIN'T BEEN AFLOAT IN FOREVER! AND THIS WATER IS JUST SO *CLEAN!*

OH, SISTERS, LET'S GO DOWN. DOWN IN THE RIVER TO PLAY. ♫

SOUNDS LIKE THEY DO AN AWFUL LOT OF...TOUCHING HERE.

I NEVER CONSIDERED YOU SQUEAMISH.

WE NEVER TALKED ABOUT ME BEING NAKED WHILE OTHER PEOPLE PUT LITTLE ROCKS ON MY BUTTOCKS BEFORE.

WELL, I THINK IT SOUNDS REAL NICE. THERE'S EVEN A TREATMENT WHERE THEY BEAT YOU WITH FLOWERS! JUST SMACK YOUR BACK WITH BIG OL' ROSES AND WHATNOT.

SO SHINY!

THINGS ARE GOING TO CHANGE, YOU KNOW. THEY ALWAYS DO. LIKE WAVES CRASHING. CAN'T STOP 'EM.

THEY HAVE A COUPLES' MASSAGE. NOW THAT MAYBE I COULD HANDLE. WASH WOULD--

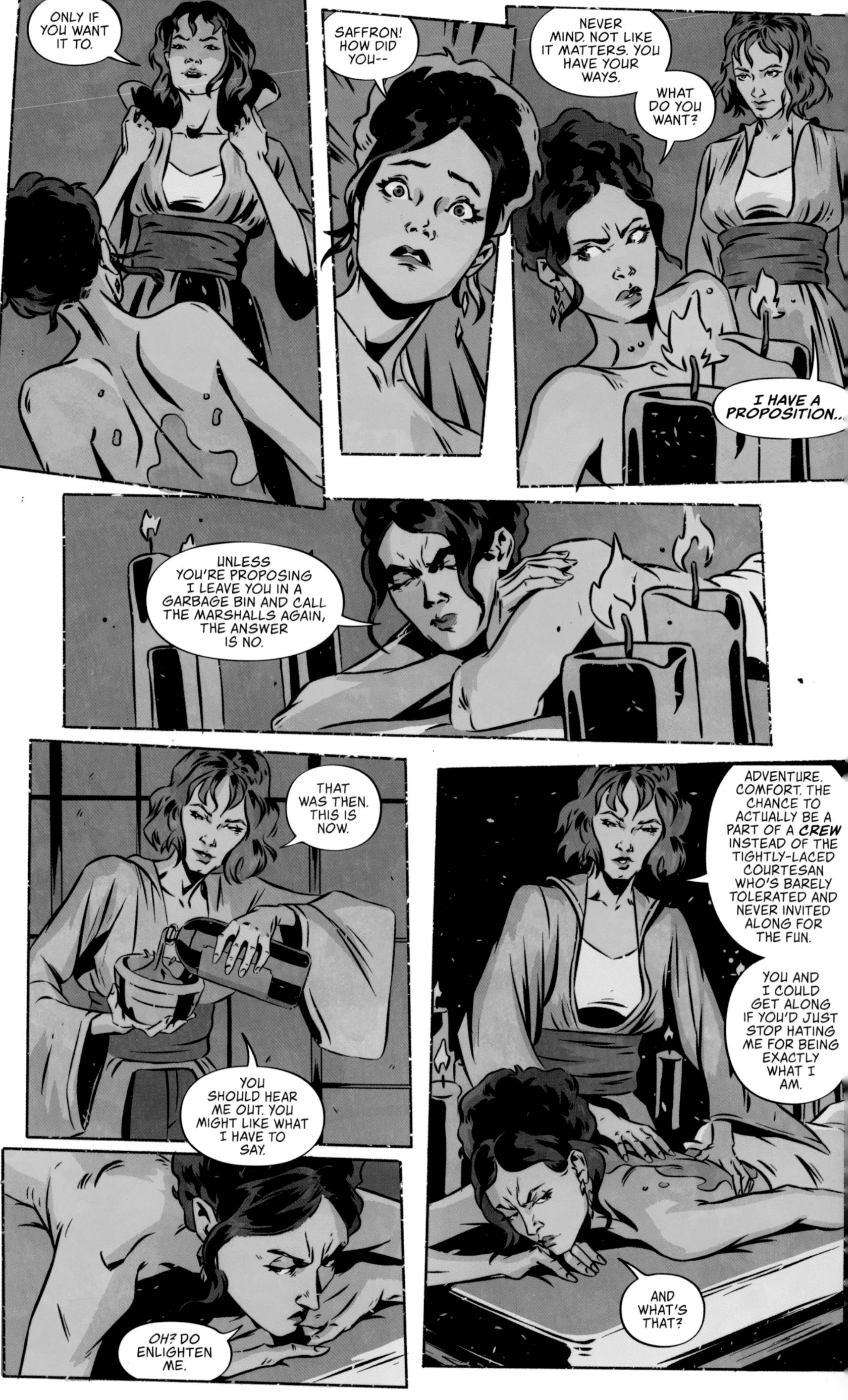
ONLY IF YOU WANT IT TO.
SAFFRON! HOW DID YOU--
NEVER MIND. NOT LIKE IT MATTERS. YOU HAVE YOUR WAYS.
WHAT DO YOU WANT?
I HAVE A PROPOSITION...
UNLESS YOU'RE PROPOSING I LEAVE YOU IN A GARBAGE BIN AND CALL THE MARSHALLS AGAIN, THE ANSWER IS NO.
THAT WAS THEN. THIS IS NOW.
YOU SHOULD HEAR ME OUT. YOU MIGHT LIKE WHAT I HAVE TO SAY.
OH? DO ENLIGHTEN ME.
ADVENTURE. COMFORT. THE CHANCE TO ACTUALLY BE A PART OF A CREW INSTEAD OF THE TIGHTLY-LACED COURTESAN WHO'S BARELY TOLERATED AND NEVER INVITED ALONG FOR THE FUN.
YOU AND I COULD GET ALONG IF YOU'D JUST STOP HATING ME FOR BEING EXACTLY WHAT I AM.
AND WHAT'S THAT?

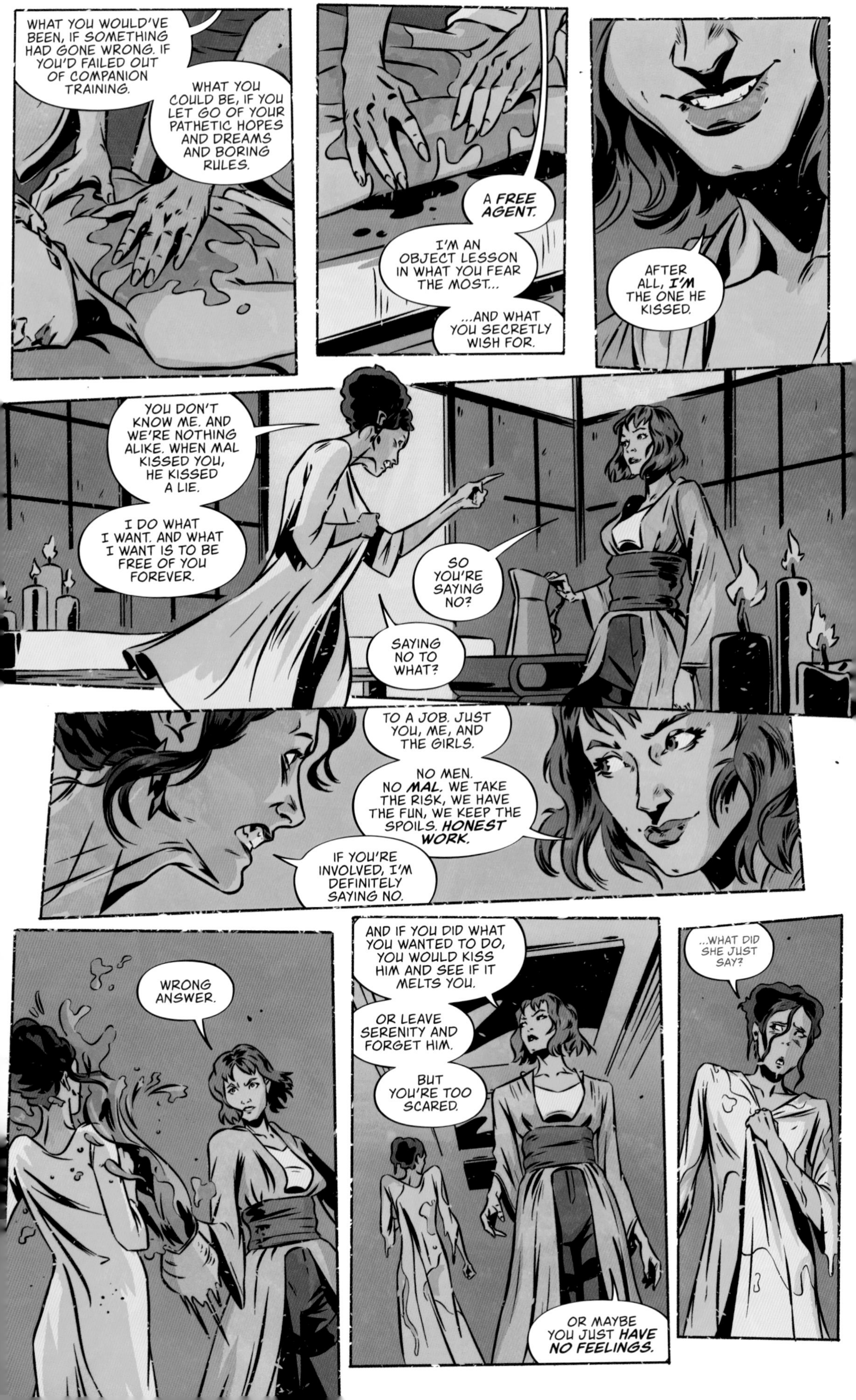

WHAT YOU WOULD'VE BEEN, IF SOMETHING HAD GONE WRONG. IF YOU'D FAILED OUT OF COMPANION TRAINING.
WHAT YOU COULD BE, IF YOU LET GO OF YOUR PATHETIC HOPES AND DREAMS AND BORING RULES.
A ***FREE AGENT.***
I'M AN OBJECT LESSON IN WHAT YOU FEAR THE MOST...
...AND WHAT YOU SECRETLY WISH FOR.
AFTER ALL, ***I'M*** THE ONE HE KISSED.
YOU DON'T KNOW ME. AND WE'RE NOTHING ALIKE. WHEN MAL KISSED YOU, HE KISSED A LIE.
I DO WHAT I WANT. AND WHAT I WANT IS TO BE FREE OF YOU FOREVER.
SO YOU'RE SAYING NO?
SAYING NO TO WHAT?
TO A JOB. JUST YOU, ME, AND THE GIRLS.
NO MEN. NO ***MAL.*** WE TAKE THE RISK, WE HAVE THE FUN, WE KEEP THE SPOILS. ***HONEST WORK.***
IF YOU'RE INVOLVED, I'M DEFINITELY SAYING NO.
WRONG ANSWER.
AND IF YOU DID WHAT YOU WANTED TO DO, YOU WOULD KISS HIM AND SEE IF IT MELTS YOU.
OR LEAVE SERENITY AND FORGET HIM.
BUT YOU'RE TOO SCARED.
OR MAYBE YOU JUST ***HAVE NO FEELINGS.***
...WHAT DID SHE JUST SAY?

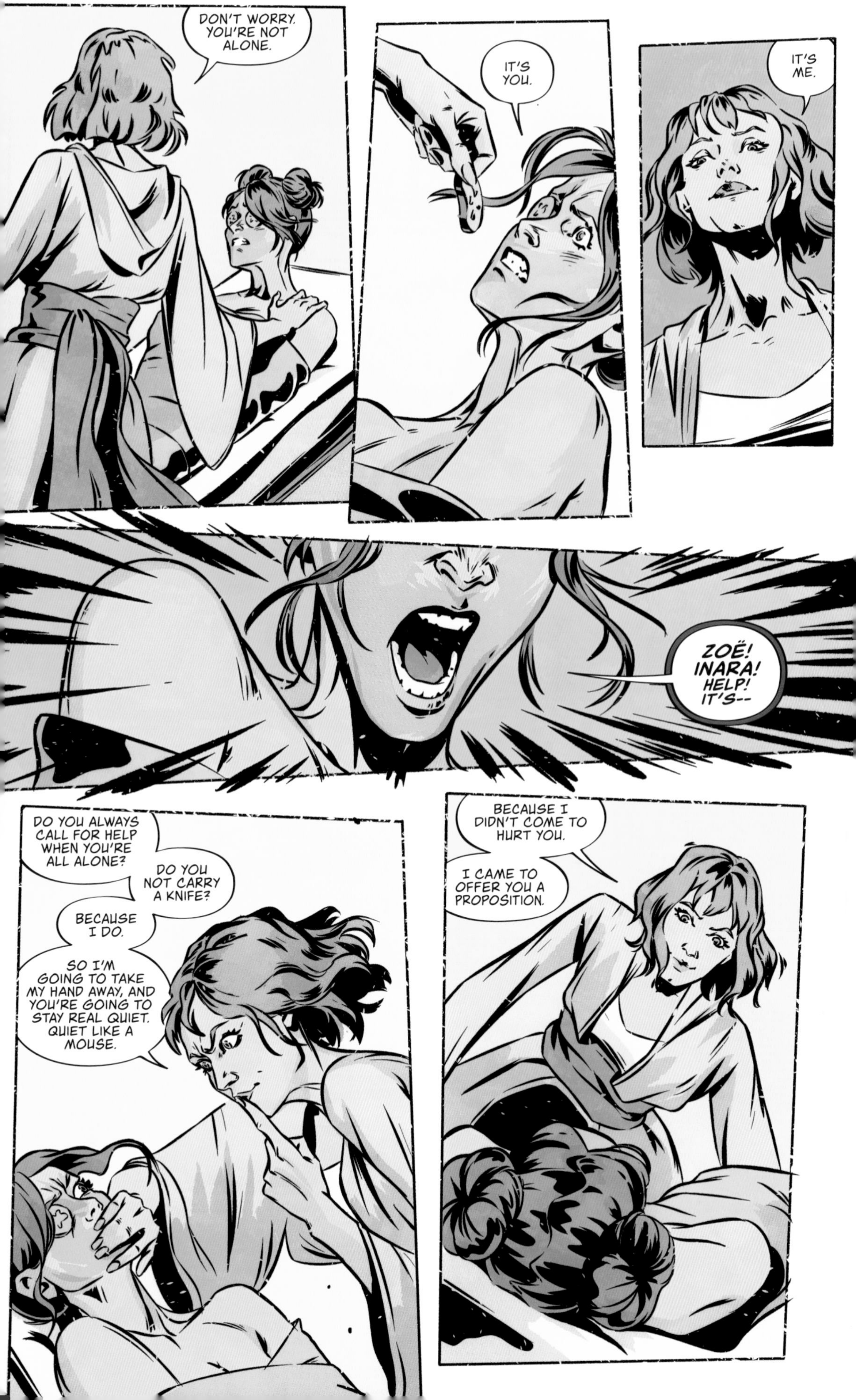

DON'T WORRY. YOU'RE NOT ALONE.
IT'S YOU.
IT'S ME.
ZOË! INARA! HELP! IT'S--
DO YOU ALWAYS CALL FOR HELP WHEN YOU'RE ALL ALONE?
DO YOU NOT CARRY A KNIFE?
BECAUSE I DO.
SO I'M GOING TO TAKE MY HAND AWAY, AND YOU'RE GOING TO STAY REAL QUIET. QUIET LIKE A MOUSE.
BECAUSE I DIDN'T COME TO HURT YOU.
I CAME TO OFFER YOU A PROPOSITION.

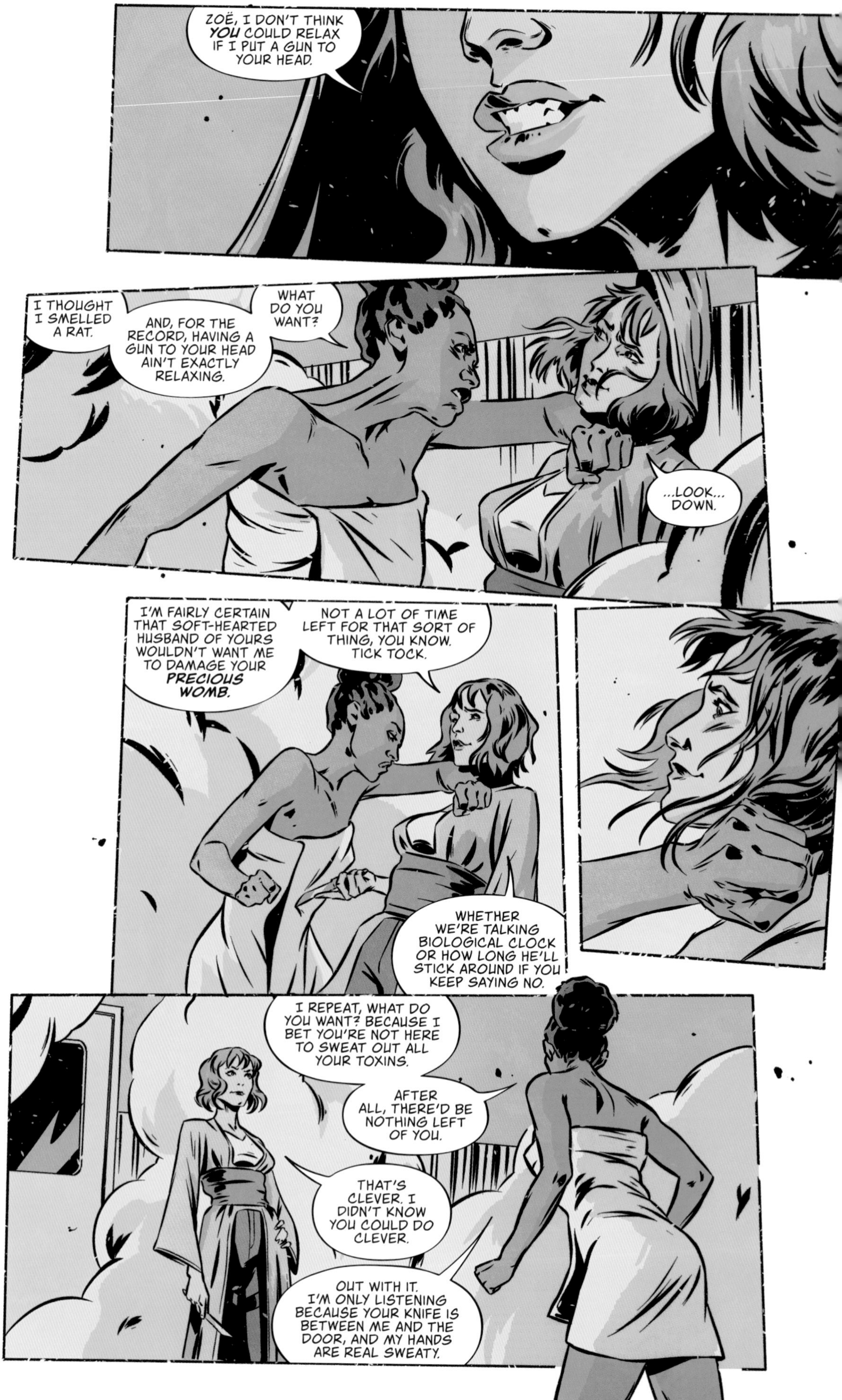
ZOË, I DON'T THINK ***YOU*** COULD RELAX IF I PUT A GUN TO YOUR HEAD.
I THOUGHT I SMELLED A RAT.
AND, FOR THE RECORD, HAVING A GUN TO YOUR HEAD AIN'T EXACTLY RELAXING.
WHAT DO YOU WANT?
...LOOK... DOWN.
I'M FAIRLY CERTAIN THAT SOFT-HEARTED HUSBAND OF YOURS WOULDN'T WANT ME TO DAMAGE YOUR ***PRECIOUS WOMB.***
NOT A LOT OF TIME LEFT FOR THAT SORT OF THING, YOU KNOW. TICK TOCK.
WHETHER WE'RE TALKING BIOLOGICAL CLOCK OR HOW LONG HE'LL STICK AROUND IF YOU KEEP SAYING NO.
I REPEAT, WHAT DO YOU WANT? BECAUSE I BET YOU'RE NOT HERE TO SWEAT OUT ALL YOUR TOXINS.
AFTER ALL, THERE'D BE NOTHING LEFT OF YOU.
THAT'S CLEVER. I DIDN'T KNOW YOU COULD DO CLEVER.
OUT WITH IT. I'M ONLY LISTENING BECAUSE YOUR KNIFE IS BETWEEN ME AND THE DOOR, AND MY HANDS ARE REAL SWEATY.

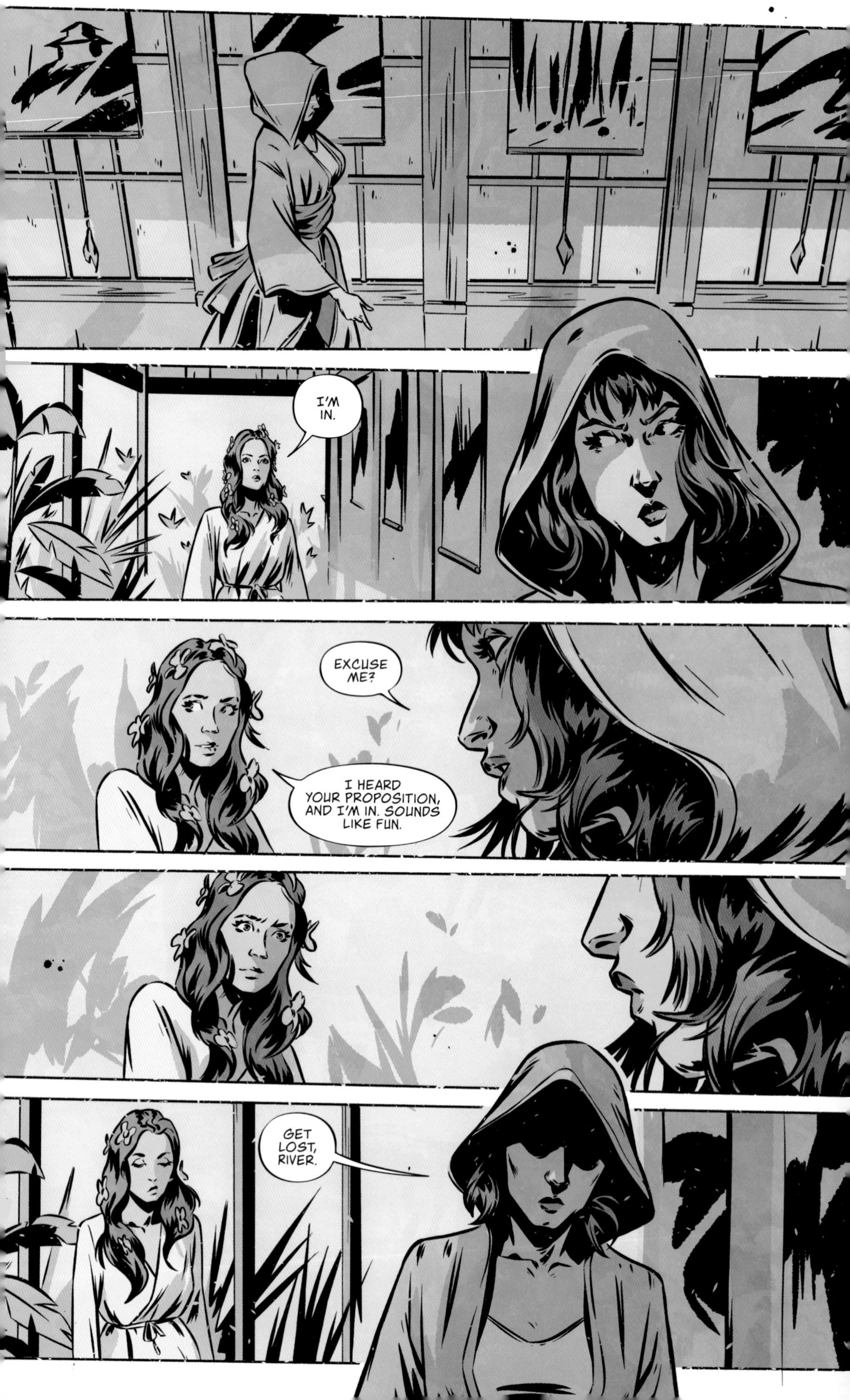
I'M IN.
EXCUSE ME?
I HEARD YOUR PROPOSITION, AND I'M IN. SOUNDS LIKE FUN.
GET LOST, RIVER.

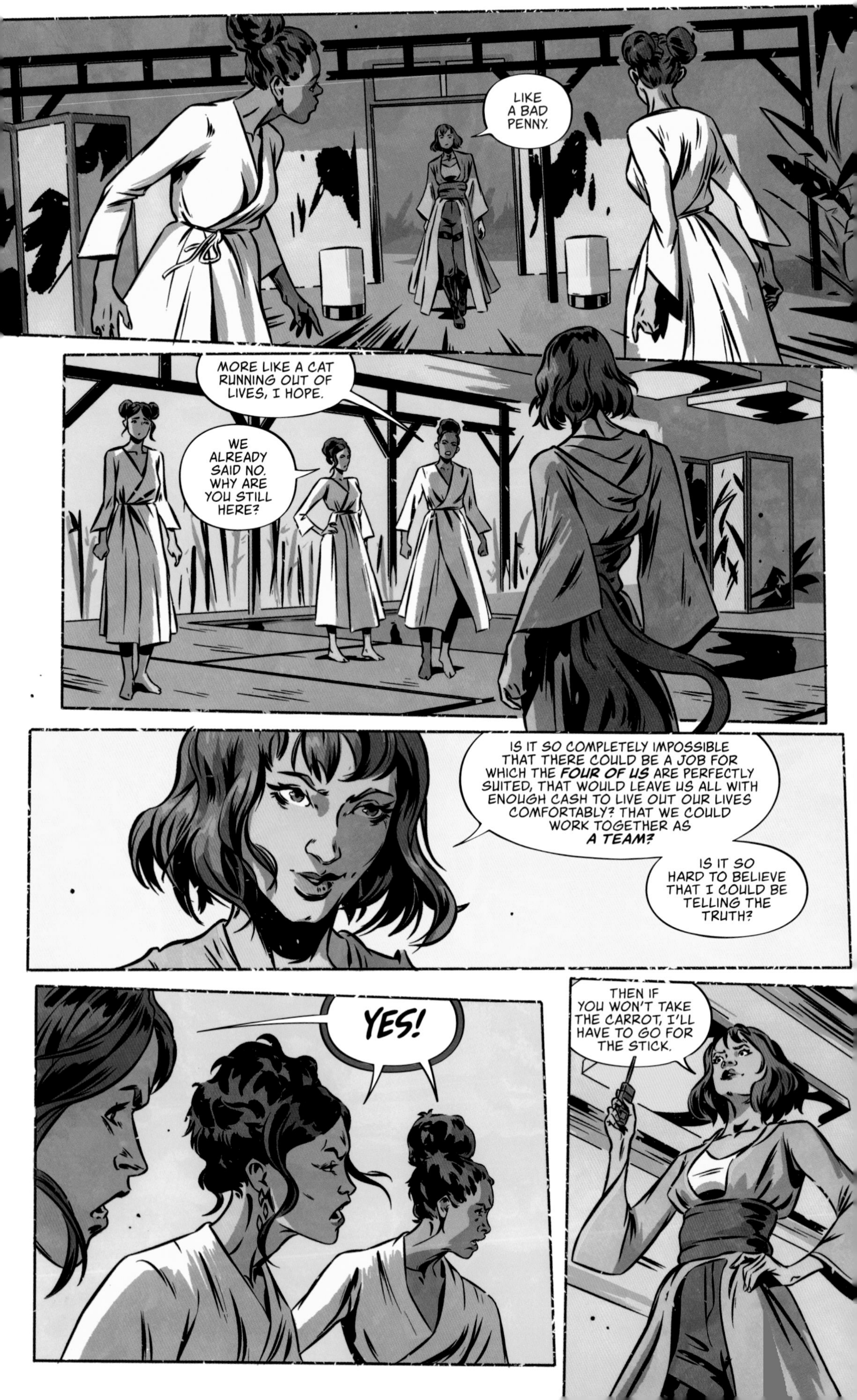
LIKE A BAD PENNY.
MORE LIKE A CAT RUNNING OUT OF LIVES, I HOPE.
WE ALREADY SAID NO. WHY ARE YOU STILL HERE?
IS IT SO COMPLETELY IMPOSSIBLE THAT THERE COULD BE A JOB FOR WHICH THE FOUR OF US ARE PERFECTLY SUITED, THAT WOULD LEAVE US ALL WITH ENOUGH CASH TO LIVE OUT OUR LIVES COMFORTABLY? THAT WE COULD WORK TOGETHER AS A TEAM?
IS IT SO HARD TO BELIEVE THAT I COULD BE TELLING THE TRUTH?
YES!
THEN IF YOU WON'T TAKE THE CARROT, I'LL HAVE TO GO FOR THE STICK.

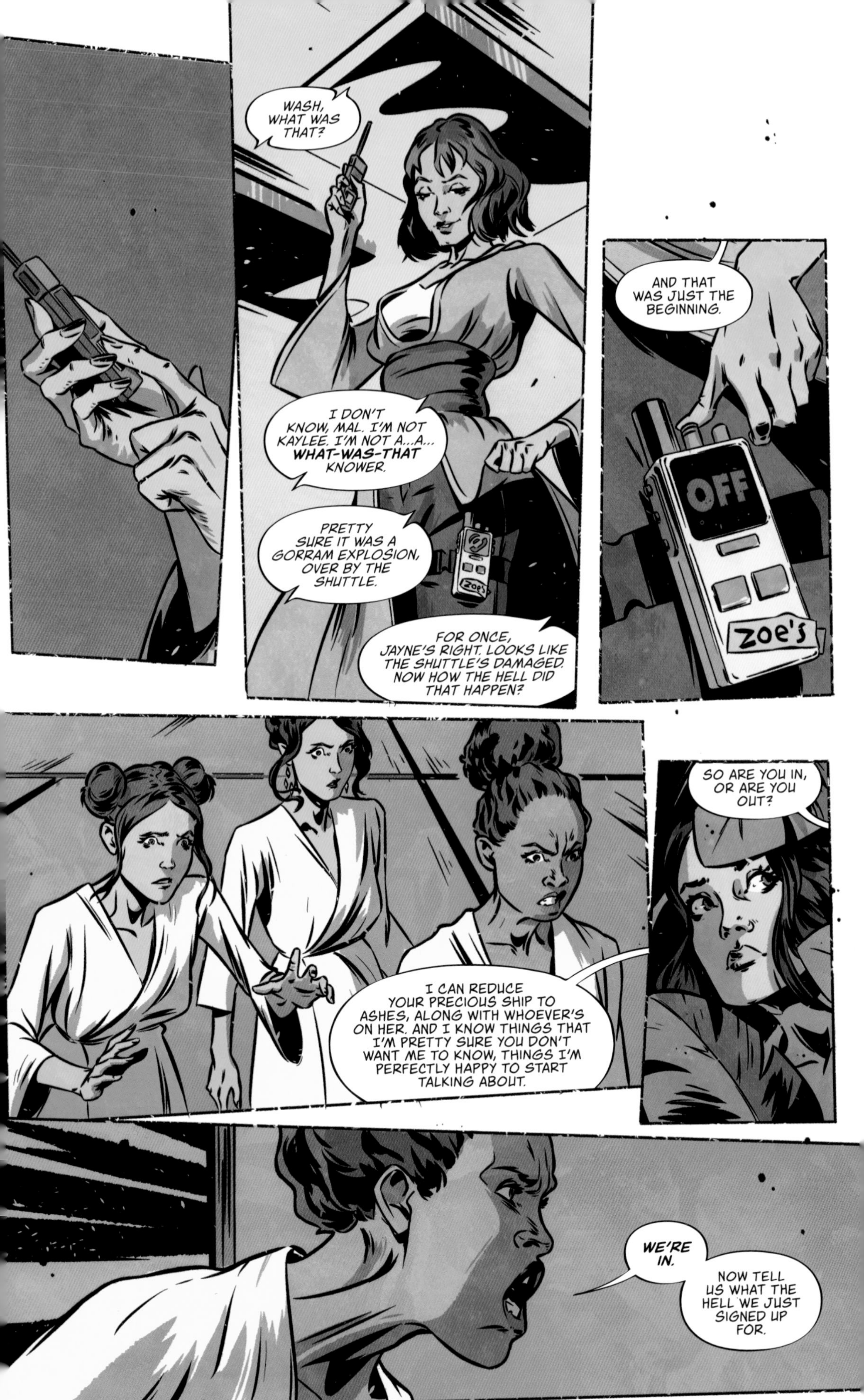
WASH, WHAT WAS THAT?
I DON'T KNOW, MAL. I'M NOT KAYLEE. I'M NOT A...A... WHAT-WAS-THAT KNOWER.
PRETTY SURE IT WAS A GORRAM EXPLOSION, OVER BY THE SHUTTLE.
FOR ONCE, JAYNE'S RIGHT. LOOKS LIKE THE SHUTTLE'S DAMAGED. NOW HOW THE HELL DID THAT HAPPEN?
AND THAT WAS JUST THE BEGINNING.
OFF
ZOE'S
I CAN REDUCE YOUR PRECIOUS SHIP TO ASHES, ALONG WITH WHOEVER'S ON HER. AND I KNOW THINGS THAT I'M PRETTY SURE YOU DON'T WANT ME TO KNOW, THINGS I'M PERFECTLY HAPPY TO START TALKING ABOUT.
SO ARE YOU IN, OR ARE YOU OUT?
WE'RE IN.
NOW TELL US WHAT THE HELL WE JUST SIGNED UP FOR.

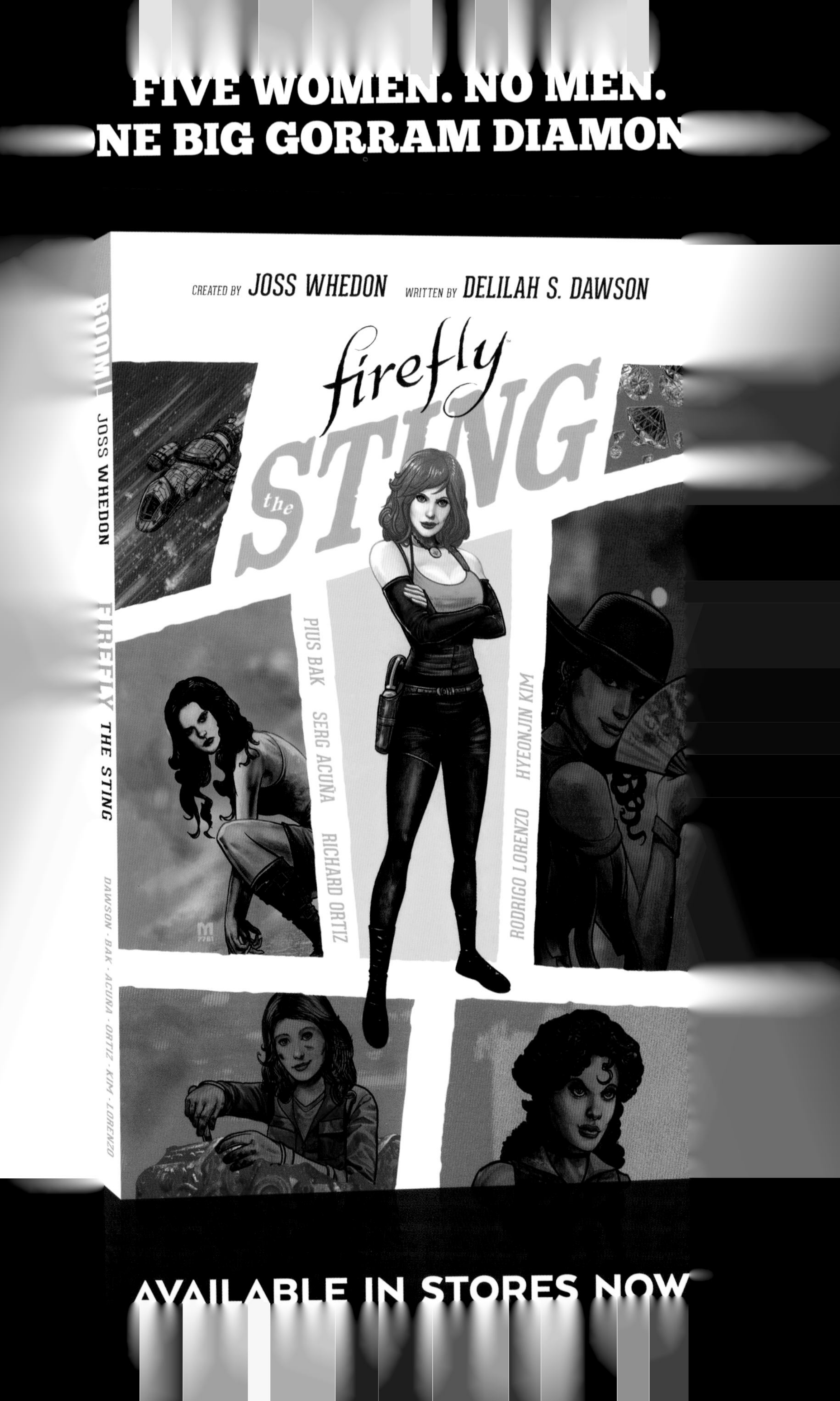

FIVE WOMEN. NO MEN.
NE BIG GORRAM DIAMON
CREATED BY JOSS WHEDON WRITTEN BY DELILAH S. DAWSON
firefly
the STING
PIUS BAK
SERG ACUÑA
RICHARD ORTIZ
HYEONJIN KIM
RODRIGO LORENZO
BOOM! JOSS WHEDON FIREFLY THE STING
DAWSON · BAK · ACUÑA · ORTIZ · KIM · LORENZO
AVAILABLE IN STORES NOW

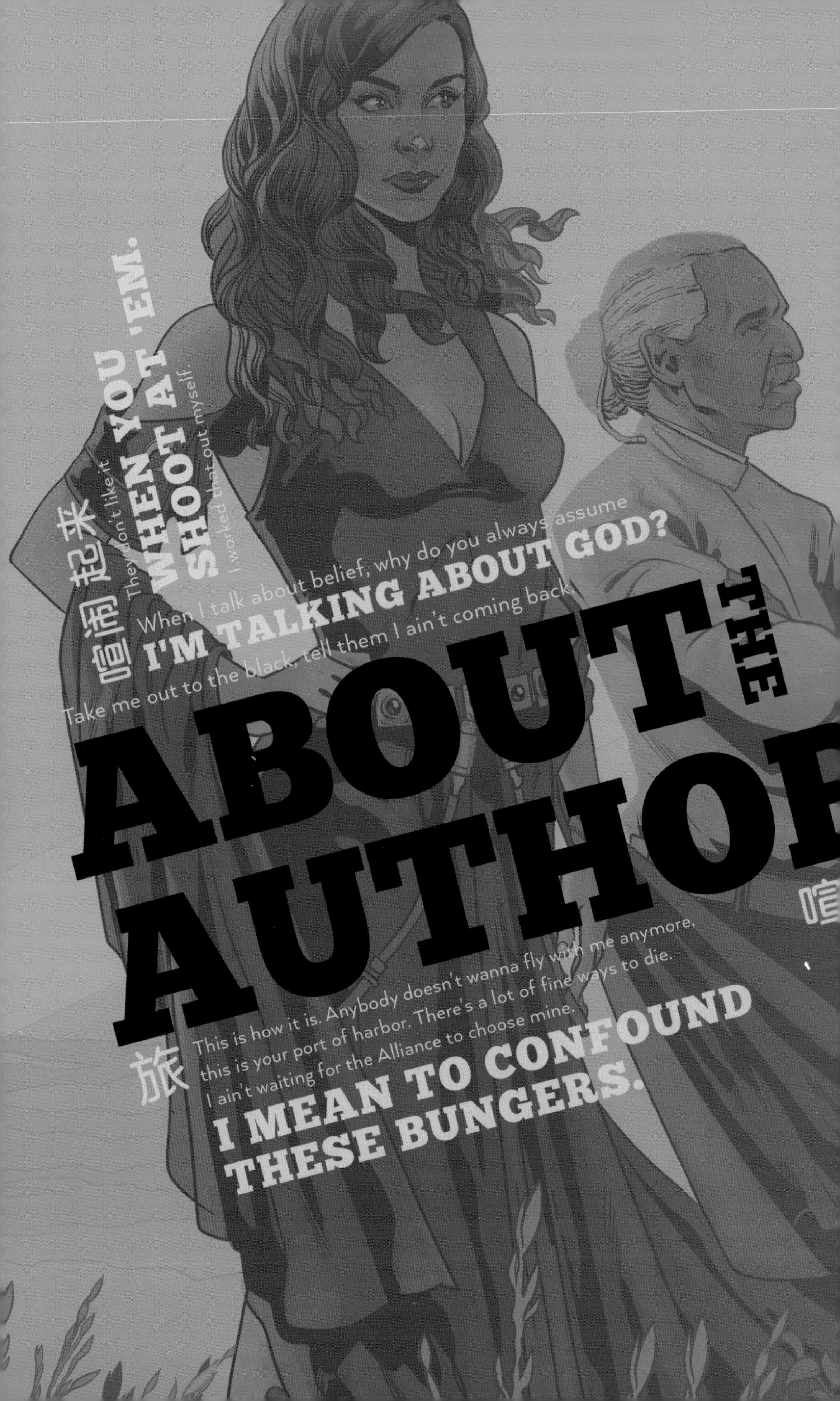
喧闹起来
They don't like it
WHEN YOU SHOOT AT 'EM.
I worked that out myself.
When I talk about belief, why do you always assume
I'M TALKING ABOUT GOD?
Take me out to the black, tell them I ain't coming back.
ABOUT THE AUTHOR
喧
This is how it is. Anybody doesn't wanna fly with me anymore, this is your port of harbor. There's a lot of fine ways to die. I ain't waiting for the Alliance to choose mine.
旅
I MEAN TO CONFOUND THESE BUNGERS.

Joss Whedon is one of Hollywood's top creators, scripting several hit films including Marvel's *The Avengers*, which was a breakout success and became one of the highest grossing films of all time, and its sequel *Avengers: Age of Ultron*, and creating one of television's most critically praised shows, *Buffy the Vampire Slayer*. In 2000, Whedon garnered his first Emmy nomination in the category of Outstanding Writing for a Drama Series for his groundbreaking episode entitled "Hush," and he earned an Academy Award nomination for Best Screenplay with Disney's box-office smash *Toy Story*. Originally hailing from New York, Whedon is a third-generation television writer. His grandfather and father were both successful sitcom writers on shows such as *The Donna Reed Show, Leave It to Beaver* and *The Golden Girls*.

Greg Pak is a Korean American filmmaker and comic book writer best known for his award-winning feature film *Robot Stories*, his blockbuster comic book series like Marvel Comics' *Planet Hulk* and *World War Hulk*, and his record-breaking Kickstarter publishing projects with Jonathan Coulton, *Code Monkey Save World* and *The Princess Who Saved Herself*. His other projects at BOOM! Studios include the award-winning creator-owned *Mech Cadet Yu* and *Ronin Island*.

Dan McDaid is a British comics artist and writer with a lustrous head of black hair and a full, healthy beard. After breaking into comics with the UK's *Doctor Who Magazine*, he went on to co-create *Jersey Gods* for Image Comics and *Time Share* for Oni Press, as well as drawing cult favorites *Big Trouble in Little China* and *Dawn of the Planet of the Apes*. Following a well-regarded run on IDW's *Judge Dredd*, he launched his own webcomic, *DEGA*, and is currently drawing the new adventures of the Serenity crew in BOOM! Studios' *Firefly*. He lives in Scotland with his partner Deborah and a large gray cat whose name means "Dark Stranger".

Vincenzo Federici is an Italian comic book artist from Naples. After his Classical Arts studies, he started to work in comics for French publishers, like Soleil Éditions and on a creator owned project for the Italian publisher Noise Press, called *The Kabuki Fight*. He then moved to American publishers, working with IDW Publishing, Zenescope Entertainment, Dynamite Entertainment, BOOM! Studios and more, on series like *Army of Darkness/Bubba Ho-Tep, M. A. S. K., Star Trek, Firefly, Go Go Power Rangers* and more. He also is a teacher in different Italian Comic Art schools.

Marcelo Costa is a comics artist and colorist. As a colorist, he's best known for his work on *Power Rangers: Shattered Grid* and *Power Rangers: Soul of the Dragon*, and *Planet of the Apes Visionaries*. As an artist, he's worked on Zenoscope's *Grimm Fairy Tales*, Action Lab's *Season 3*, and the episode "Star Trip", from the Society of Virtue YouTube Channel. Currently, Marcelo is also working on *Self/Made* and *Teenage Mutant Ninja Turtles: Shredder in Hell*, in a partnership with Matheus Santolouco.

Joana Lafuente is a self-taught illustrator that has a Master's degree in computer engineering, but gave up on programming to follow her dream as an artist as soon as she could. She has been mostly working in comics, but not exclusively, having also worked for game and advertising companies.

Jim Campbell has been lettering comics professionally for almost a decade, before which he worked in newspaper and magazine publishing for even longer. He knows more about print production than mortal man was meant to know and has also scanned more images than you've had hot dinners. Unless you're ninety years old. If you're very unlucky, he might start talking to you about ligatures.

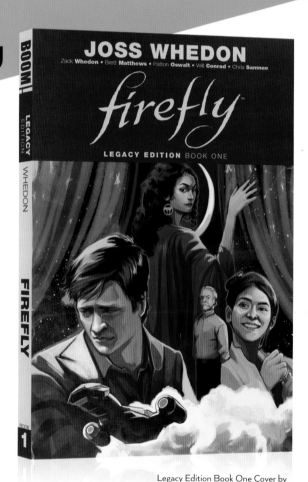

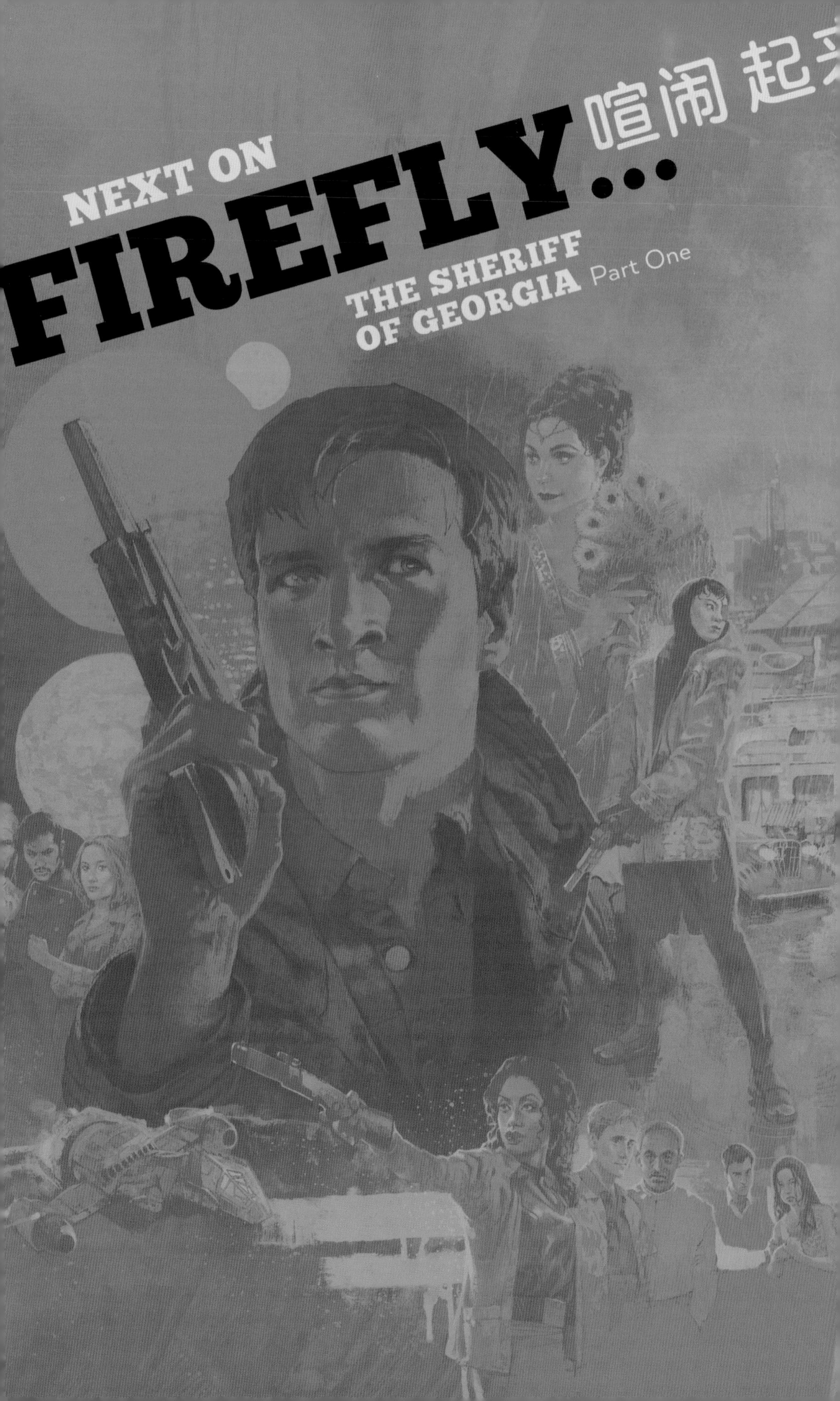

NEXT ON
FIREFLY...
喧闹 起
THE SHERIFF
OF GEORGIA Part One

DISCOVER
VISIONARY CREATORS

THE
WOODS
JAMES TYNION IV • MICHAEL DIALYNAS
"The Woods is creepy, funny, charming, and mysterious. My favorite kind of comic, a deep mythology mixed with equally deep character work. Get in on the ground floor of something great!"
—Jeff Lemire
VOL. 1
THE ARROW

"The Spire is fantastic! My kind of genre free-for-all."
—BRIAN K. VAUGHAN
(Saga)
THE
SPIRE
SIMON SPURRIER
JEFF STOKELY
ANDRÉ MAY

MARK WAID • PETER KRAUSE
IRREDEEMABLE
AFTERWORD BY
GRANT MORRISON

MARK WAID • JEAN DIAZ
INCORRUPTIBLE

MICHAEL ALAN NELSON
DAN MORA
GABRIEL CASSATA
HEXED
THE HARLOT & THE THIEF VOLUME ONE

ABNETT & CULBARD
WILD'S
END
FIRST LIGHT
"IT'S REALLY GREAT!"
JEFF LEMIRE

James Tynion IV

The Woods

Volume 1
ISBN: 978-1-60886-454-6 | $9.99 US
Volume 2
ISBN: 978-1-60886-495-9 | $14.99 US
Volume 3
ISBN: 978-1-60886-773-8 | $14.99 US

The Backstagers

Volume 1
ISBN: 978-1-60886-993-0 | $14.99 US

Simon Spurrier

Six-Gun Gorilla

ISBN: 978-1-60886-390-7 | $19.99 US

The Spire

ISBN: 978-1-60886-913-8 | $29.99 US

Weavers

ISBN: 978-1-60886-963-3 | $19.99 US

Mark Waid

Irredeemable

Volume 1
ISBN: 978-1-93450-690-5 | $16.99 US
Volume 2
ISBN: 978-1-60886-000-5 | $16.99 US

Incorruptible

Volume 1
ISBN: 978-1-60886-015-9 | $16.99 US
Volume 2
ISBN: 978-1-60886-028-9 | $16.99 US

Michael Alan Nelson

Hexed The Harlot & The Thief

Volume 1
ISBN: 978-1-60886-718-9 | $14.99 US
Volume 2
ISBN: 978-1-60886-816-2 | $14.99 US

Day Men

Volume 1
ISBN: 978-1-60886-393-8 | $9.99 US
Volume 2
ISBN: 978-1-60886-852-0 | $9.99 US

Dan Abnett

Wild's End

Volume 1: First Light
ISBN: 978-1-60886-735-6 | $19.99 US
Volume 2: The Enemy Within
ISBN: 978-1-60886-877-3 | $19.99 US

Hypernaturals

Volume 1
ISBN: 978-1-60886-298-6 | $16.99 US
Volume 2
ISBN: 978-1-60886-319-8 | $19.99 US

BOOM! STUDIOS

AVAILABLE AT YOUR LOCAL COMICS SHOP AND BOOKSTORE

To find a comics shop in your area, visit www.comicshoplocator.com

WWW.**BOOM-STUDIOS**.COM

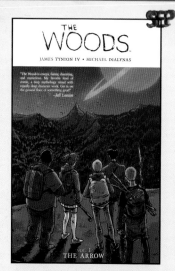

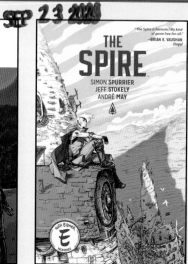

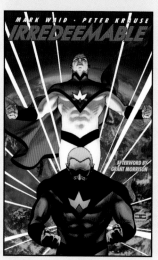

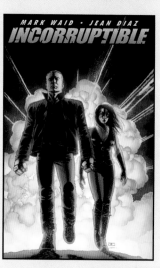

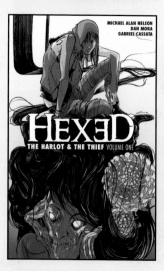

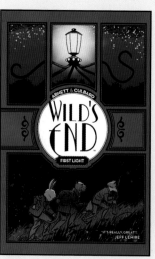

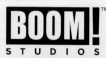